All rights reserved by the author. All contents and corrections are the responsibility of the author.
Kindle direct 2024

Disclaimer

Any resemblance to a person either living or dead to the exclusion of family and friends of the author is purely coincidental.

Any information which is written that could possibly be considered to hold a medical or educational overview is purely fictional. It may bear resemblance to life situations but should be discarded and not taken seriously.

Other work by Beatrice Finn

The value of hindsight	1999
Eileen a Mayo girl.	2014
Erin Go Braugh	2015.
Old Ireland left behind.	2015
Full circle for the Toweys.	2016
The circle of life.	2016
Secrets lies and deceit	2017
Let's be friends	2017
Whispers from Cloontia	2018
Revenge is sweet	2019
Jacintha an Irish Emigrant	2020
Coventry to Indiana. Sequel to Jacintha.	2020
Jacintha part three – The Trilogy.	2021
Simply Moira	2022
The very strange years	2022

Beatrice Finn

Rooney's and the Regan's

Identity and Roots

Acknowledgements

To everyone in my life who has offered encouragement and support, I want to say "Thank you." You all know who you are! Without your much-appreciated help I could not have continued on this journey.
The tribute to my parents, 'Pakie Finn and Mary Ann Forkin' from Derrinabroock, Cloontia, Mayo West Ireland, which was written in my first novel 'Eileen a Mayo Girl,' continues to be a tribute to them today. Without their love, their support and their encouragement throughout my life, I would not have the ability or the confidence to be the person which I am and do what I enjoy doing so very much.
Hope you all enjoy the read as much as I enjoyed the work.
Much love to you all

Introduction

I have a new supporter with my efforts at writing who gives me much encouragement. He has written a chapter for this novel, which I have slotted in where I felt would be most appropriate. He is a man with a great love of Ireland and a great love of Irish music. He is a musician who plays regularly in Irish clubs in Birmingham, England, together with his wife and many other musicians. His name is John Perrins. 'Thank you' John, for your very encouraging messages of support over the years and for the lovely and very interesting piece which you have produced for this novel.

Table of Contents.

Seeking information	p09
Discrimination and racism.	31
Frankie in therapy	42
Goodbye to Alana	54
Other side of Frankie	62
Bring change to the wards	75
Rooney's new baby	81
Enter Charlie Regan.	93
Ever changing plans	102
Life in Portugal	137
Back in England	164
Analysing Joseph	187
Teachings not for everyone.	207
Vulnerable brother	237
Unexpected situations	245
Big changes looming ahead	290
Holiday in Ireland.	313
Decisions to be made	327
A journey of discovery.	333
What to do and how to do it.	355

Character Reference.

Frankie's dad Johnnie
Frankie's mother Isobel
Frankie Chigozie
Mikey Rooney
Catherine Rooney
Joseph Rooney.
Helen Jones.
Charlie Regan
Charlie Regan Junior.
Brendan Regan Twin
Anthony Regan Twin.
Teresa Riley (Joseph's Supermarket manager)
Moira McGuire. (Joseph Rooney's wife).
Mairead Dooney (Brendan Regan's wife)
Alice Nixon. (CJ Regan's partner)

Seeking information.

  A fateful late summers evening for the Chigozie family in Yorkshire England, is an evening which is never to be forgotten by their daughter Frankie. The year was 1967. She was just 5 years of age. The night she climbed into the car together with her parents and her younger sister, no one could ever have told her, that very shortly she would be living in a children's home. The shock was pretty awful. It was too much and especially so for such a young child. Waking up in a strange place Frankie initially appeared quite calm. Taking in her surroundings she looked quietly traumatised one minute. She was screaming the next. The woman standing by her bed had a calm almost angelic type of voice. She spoke with deep compassion.
  "Frankie it's all right- your safe here with us. Police brought you late last night. Try not to be worried."
Frankie sat up in her bed staring at the staff member and looking confused. Looking as though she was still in shock.

  Screaming stopped momentarily and then she started again, this time kicking her heels onto the mattress. Having a typical childs tantrum but for more serious reasons than others might, Frankie was in a tough situation. Wearing clothes which she didn't recognise, she tugged and pulled at them till they were no longer touching her body. Throwing the pyjamas across the room towards the staff member she sobbed as she told her.

"Get that away from me and you get away from me. I want my own clothes where are they? I want my mum. Where's my mum?"

No one suitably qualified on duty at that time to answer that question, staff did all which they could do to help the child by the use of distraction techniques. With hindsight I would question if there was ever a staff member on duty who was qualified to answer that type of question, in that type of situation.

Frankie was given the day clothes which she was wearing when brought in to the home late the previous evening. Grabbing her belongings, she told the woman to get out of the bedroom, slamming the door behind the staff member. More tears and more screaming showed people that this was an angry and an upset child. She appeared to have no memory of events from the accident, or if she did she either didn't want to speak about it, or she had buried them deep at the back of her mind. Encouraged to leave the bedroom she went with staff to see they're small communal area.

"We know you will like the toys Frankie because everyone likes toys, so let's see what there is?"

No words were spoken by Frankie not even a smile, but she did follow staff to the play area. A small musical merry go round was playing in a corner of the room. No attention was given to it or to anything in that area by Frankie. Children in there playing with building blocks just looked at the sad looking girl, who they presumed was joining them in the house. No one said a word. It was as if the kids were aware how troubled they're new companion was. Taken to other parts of the house she slowly followed in silence. Hospital reports after the accident had given Frankie a clean bill of health. Psychologically it wasn't so good. The words "This child is traumatised "were highlighted on the envelope containing the hospital report. Seen by the local doctor too Frankie refused to speak about or acknowledge the accident. Introductions later that day to other kids living at the home had a positive feel. Some older ones including myself, initially took her under their wing whilst others tormented and bullied her. Through the eyes of an adult, she would now say that life in the kids' home wasn't the greatest experience she's ever had in life but was not the worst either.

      Having had our own special chores to do and being involved in our home, gave all of us a degree of belonging, a sense of security and something that slightly resembled a sense of stability. We all know that stability is important. Chores would usually be very age appropriate, depending on which staff member was giving out the instructions. Frankie stared into the air as she recalled.

"Putting away toys and books was my job when I was younger."

Sharing that chore with 2 other kids she often did the lions share. Isn't that the thing with kids- No one supervising them they can do and will do whatever they want. Often taking advantage just because they can, was a regular occurrence in the life of Frankie Chigozie. Her peers' young voices could be especially piercing, when they needed to be sure Frankie would be obedient. Often heard telling each other to be louder they did that.

"She won't like it she doesn't like noise. She'll do the extra jobs just to make us be quiet."
The kids were right and who would have thought they could be that devious. Frankie didn't like loud piercing voices or loud noise and they knew that. She would give in to their demands simply to shut them up.

Little by little on a daily basis we both worked our way through our time in the kids home. Chores changed as we aged but the bullying of Frankie continued to a degree. Some days being more palatable than others the better ones got her through. Eventually it was time for her to leave the home. Together with some other kids, well teenagers, even young adults by that time, they enjoyed a leavers disco party held in the largest room in the building. Music was courtesy of a staff member with finger food provided by the resident chef. Frankie and I had both done very well academically. Having key workers in the home we received lots of encouragement over the years. Despite being tired of hearing many people's advice of.

"C'mon Frankie your smart you can do it."
All they ever got back from her was a polite nod showing acceptance of their comments. Never a rude response back from her like most of the other kids, including myself on some occasions. Frankie was different and no one understood why, nor did they stick labels on her addressing her differences. Hindsight being the most wonderful thing allows her to see that an assessment of some description could have been useful. It would have helped make her life easier.

College behind her she was now 18 and leaving the care home for University. Frankie was secretly proud of the person she had become and furthermore would become, as she gained her degree in Psychology. Time to face what life on your own might feel like, she thought how the world seemed a bit frightening yet she was determined. Often wondering where her sense of determination came from, whilst longing for that knowledge she had no real answers. Perseverance and patience combined with determination, was what she decided would see her through the following years.

That's quite a few years down the road behind her now, but she never forgot and never will forget what put her in that kids home. Frankie is on a mission to find more information. She's been travelling the 4 miles by bus from her house over to Gerry's restaurant, every Tuesday evening like clockwork over a period of several months. Making that journey by herself appeared to come natural to Frankie. Determination always got her there irrespective of the weather. No one could ever have guessed or imagined why she made those weekly trips other than staff at Gerry's. Having some ideas regarding her regular presence, they would share knowledge which they considered she was seeking. This one particular evening she wore a heavy waterproof coat. Its wrap around fur collar kept the chills out. Seeing the coat in a small local shop which sold used goods, had stirred up the urge within her to investigate further.

Frankie was and still is a seeker of all things pre-loved. Seeing something remotely appealing her curiosity would take control. She would have to dig deeper on her journey of discovery. Being very much a regular pre-loved shop customer, gave her the feeling she was contributing to the saving of our planet. Despite her young age, thoughts about the planet and how to best protect it were prevalent in her mind. Determination in every aspect of Frankie's life was a strong quality she possessed.

"We all have to do our bit Helen. The world won't sort itself out."

Hearing those words would always gain my approval of her behaviour. Not that she needed my approval but always appreciated it. I was not at all that way inclined. Would I ever become planet conscious was the burning question? Deciding there's more ways than one to show respect for our very beautiful earth, I was confident to find something which would impress my friend. Being raised mostly with hand me downs I wasn't overly keen on other people's clothes. Deciding I probably wouldn't ever go used shop clothing, I thought it best I kept that decision to myself.

The risk of offending Frankie might have been too great if I was truthful. She wasn't and isn't a person who generally speaking would easily take offence. Where protection of the planet was and is concerned, it becomes a different story. Her passion for preserving it overrides her every other thought. Protecting myself from guilt I decided It was only a white lie and white lies didn't count. Often dictating to me, how recycling belongings could only be good for the environment and definitely good for her wallet, much to her annoyance I wasn't always ready to listen. Her large brown eyes would open wide as she told me.

"I'm never a cheapskate Helen so don't go thinking that about me. My motto is that one man's trash or in my case a woman's trash, is another person's treasure and it's a huge help to the environment too."

What could I say to that? - what could my defence or my argument be? Realistically there wasn't one. My acknowledgement to my friend was little more than a smile, with a short comment of "we'll see." Knowing me as she did she would draw her own conclusion from my response. She would decide that pre-loved would most likely never be for me- She was right; however, I wasn't ready to openly tell her that.

Not being 'quite there with her' as yet in regards to the environment, I was never the less trying to get my brain focused in that direction. Some empty promises were made by myself to myself. Promises that I would investigate the local used goods stores were beginning to come together. Visions of more of the pound notes in my purse could be the catalyst, which I thought would eventually get me into those shops. Smiling to myself at the very thought of what extra money could and would do for me, reinforced my promise. Smiling at the thought of Frankie's expression, when I would eventually be able to tell her how I've made my first pre-loved purchase, was another catalyst for me. And it wouldn't need to be clothing.

Admiring her own reflection in the shop mirror with a degree of confidence, she could be overheard in what was almost a whispering voice.
"Not bad, not bad at all"
Frankie considered how much better the coat looked on her. Way better than it looked on the mannequin in the window. She wasn't the vain type but in terms of competition with a mannequin, the result was simple- she would have to be the clear winner. Her lips tightening up in the corners was her look whenever she felt impressed by herself. That was one of those occasions. She took a chance on the shop assistant as she searched for an opinion. He was an elderly gentleman with greying hair. Being slightly bent forwards around the shoulders she quietly wondered if he suffered pain. She

considered how painful his stature looked. She also thought that maybe he was ever so slightly familiar looking. With feelings of almost self-shame, she then decided that perhaps all elderly gentleman looked similar to each other. In her view this gentleman would have some life experience. Her words came out rather quietly yet holding a slight air of confidence. Telling him instead of asking for his view reminded her of her younger self.

"Suits me doesn't it."

Raising his eyebrows, the assistant who to that point had been reserved was quick with his response.

"Yes, indeed! It certainly does! Looks good against your dark hair and dark complexion and its cheap too."

Frankie could never resist a bargain. She considered the coat to be a great one. Thinking what more could a girl wish for and without further hesitation the deal was done.

"Cheers- no need for a bag I'll wear it."

Smiling as she told the assistant that no packaging or bag required-it went straight onto her body- and then a swap occurred as she passed over her own jacket.

"Here have this one. It's as old as the hills but someone might like it and I'm in a generous mood."

"Thanks Frankie. There's big demand in the 2nd hand clothing business. I'm sure it won't be here for too long."

Smiling at the gentleman her words were said with a sense of surprise and curiosity.

"You know me. You know my name? You know who I am?"

"Yes, I do know you Frankie. I was employed by the council to work in the kitchen at the kids home many years ago. You haven't changed a bit. The same cheeky Frankie. Chigozie that I knew then, just a bit bigger now and more

grown up."
She felt embarrassed.
"Oh, ok see ya." And she was gone.

Head held low she had hastily left the shop whilst quickly pulling the heavy door behind her. Her flippant response was borne out of her embarrassment and not being sure how she felt about this man remembering her. Considering how he must think of her as being so rude she cursed to herself. Being remorseful for her abruptness towards him wasn't helping either. Frankie wouldn't get pleasure from the knowledge of anyone thinking of her as being a rude person. Almost having a complex about the way other people perceived her at that time, wasn't doing my friend any favours in life.

Having bade goodbye to the shop assistant she took the short walk down the high street. Mind racing like a grand prix competitor she knew it couldn't possibly be productive. The mixture and variety of thoughts swirling in her head prevented any clear thinking. Remembering some 'calm you down' sessions from her time in the home, she knew what would be useful and work for her. Deep breaths in and she was calm. Quietly wondering if the man had maybe known her or her family before the children's home, she had options to make that discovery. Being able to redeem herself for her rudeness was a consideration in her decision making. A little unsure how she would feel, should the gentleman have known her and her family outside of the kids home, raised further questions for Frankie. Might he have known about their shameful lifestyle? Yes, she had considered her parents lifestyle as being shameful. She decided that holding onto that thought for another day would be the sensible thing to do.

The Frankie I knew and still know was and still is good at holding onto thoughts. Especially so when she felt they might raise any cause for concern or distress on any level for anyone, unless the distress would be justified for that person. Often thinking and sharing with her how she should have been christened Frankie 'thoughtful' Chigozie would cause us both to have a much-needed giggle. Admiring the vibrancy of the high street wasn't enough to totally distract and calm her mind that evening. Her thoughts were still back there at the pre-loved shop and the gentleman who recognised her. Trying again to dismiss those thoughts she had little success. Her mind was behaving like a roller coaster going around and around. Did she want her childhood from her time in the kids home to be remembered by anyone? She wasn't sure.

Leading into the bus depot which was known to some as the bus station, it was not the most scenic of places. On her approach Frankie cursed quietly to herself.

"Damn it all. Some people are just reckless. No respect for their surroundings or for the environment. It doesn't have to be like this."

Rubbish strewn everywhere on the metal seating areas and on the dark tiled floor. Graffiti all over the beautifully painted bright orange walls. The whole scenario made her heart sink. The stench of half eaten discarded hot dogs and burgers caused her to heave ever so slightly. Its only redemption was the great service which she always received whilst travelling. Smiling in appreciation of her local transport system, she always expressed gratitude to the driver, as she embarked and disembarked from bus number 33, heading into and out of the city. Knowing the bus was always clean was something of a comforting thought for Frankie.

Travelling that journey alone for the previous sixteen weeks, appeared to be the beginnings of what might turn into a long-term event for her. Six o'clock sharp and Frankie Chigozie would push open the restaurant door. Waiters escorted her to the same table on every visit after the first one. In their humble view she would be there with her usual consistency. Considered by the staff at Gerry's to be a very predictable young lady, they're observations were accurate.

"No one's sitting even close to that table. We all know you're going to show up. We saved it for you Frankie as per usual, oh and by the way - nice coat."

Taking compliments wasn't something which she was great at, however, she took it and showed some appreciation. Getting the message, that her presence was comfortable to the staff at Gerry's felt good for her too. She showed her appreciation for that.

"Thanks. It's good to know you're comfortable enough with me to offer compliments."

She gave the waiter one of her broadest smiles. Those eyes would light up a room whenever she smiled. Wondering if he would still compliment her coat had he known it was from the pre-loved store, she gave him benefit of the doubt. Again, expressing her appreciation for his compliment, she swiftly followed the man across the room making small talk as they walked. She had learned over the years. She knew that would be the right thing to do. Knew it would be the expectation if the customer was a sociable person. Frankie wanted to be thought of as being sociable especially in that situation at Gerry's. Having learned how to fake it she used it for her own benefit. Her theory which was a little devious was that the more staff liked her, the more likely they would be to share any knowledge and any information they might hold regarding her family. That being a priority in life for her in those days, she would behave in whatever way she felt was required in order to gain some family information.

Commenting to the waiter on the beautiful view from across the river and how it reminded her of her childhood days, was quite a clever cover up by Frankie for her almost crippling anxiety. That's what she did when attacked by what she considered to be her enemy. That's how she coped with those awful feelings when in a public place. There couldn't be anywhere much more public than a restaurant. Frankie amazed herself by how much she could say, from entering the door to being seated in the far corner of that room. In later life she shared with me how- never having shared that thought with another human being, she had worried they probably knew all about her anxiety and were aware of her ways of covering it all up.

"How could they not know Helen. It's not normal to be like that. I'm not normal. Despite how hard I work to cover up people must see through me."

Reminding me of how she would never be prepared to allow anxiety to totally control her life and the way in which she lived it, gained her my deepest admiration. Sharing how alternative coping strategies for her would not be seen as coping, but more of tantrum throwing or something similar, we agreed she had made the best choice. I had to applaud her for her determination and her resilience.

She had however hoped that perhaps people didn't know. Hoped that her acting skills had been good enough to hide and gloss over the real Frankie. A great debate ensued between us about the meaning of that awful word called 'normal.' Eventually concluding that there's no such thing as normal, or that everyone's 'normal' is a different experience, we had both felt that 'what's right for one person could easily be wrong for another'. The idea felt very comfortable so we left it right there. Back at Gerry's that evening the waiter had pulled out a chair from under the table, pushing it back in again as Frankie sat down. She was being treated with great respect. Treated like the lady which she was and still is.

Being predictable had meant an awful lot to Frankie. Often speaking about that we made attempts to analyse, exactly why predictability and being rigid meant so much to her, yet never had any success in discovering an answer. She was a creature of habit in every aspect of her life in those days. She needed routine and she didn't like or appreciate change very much at all. All round Frankie was a pretty complex lady. Never able to understand why she was so rigid in her ways, she eventually accepted the fact without question. Only acknowledgements ever made by concerning her rigidity, came from a great perspective.

"It's related to routines only Helen. I've been saved from the lack of ability to understand other people's needs and emotions. That's a great escape from so much else that could be wrong in my life."

Having to agree with that statement, reassurance was given to my friend that being rigid about routines wasn't always a bad thing.

"If you can cope with some flexibility then I'm sure you'll fly through life, just as freely and with the same ease as our migrating birds fly around the world."

We laughed as she reminded me how my humour could always be relied on to lighten a situation. Never having considered myself to be especially humorous her comment surprised me ever so slightly but I took it.

Having become quite predictable with her weekly visits to Gerry's, everyone there was always happy to see Frankie. Having been to that restaurant many times with her parents when she was a very young child, she felt as though she was on familiar territory. Head buried in her hands momentarily, she had flash backs of their very last visit to Gerry's as a family.

"I see it almost on every visit there Helen but can't make sense of it. Despite it being painful I'm glad to have the flashbacks. Hoping that one day I'll be able to tie up all the pieces together."

The lump which begun growing at speed in her throat felt as though it was almost suffocating her. It was a harsh reminder of how she had a sense of longing for family life, like she hadn't experienced in a very long time. Wiping her tears away she told me how.

"Having only a few good memories of my parents and my sister, Gerry's restaurant has provided me with some of those ones which have felt very precious to me."

Remembering what a private person she was, she knew and I knew that I would always respect that fact and never push Frankie for any information about her early childhood. Her sharing some thoughts about her past with me was very special. I felt honoured. Flicking back her dark wavy curls from her face Frankie's eyes lit up as she told me.

"It's been a long time since losing the family Helen. I think some memories have been blocked out, maybe for my protection but I need to know and understand more about what happened. What I recall when sitting there in Gerry's is like a dream come true for me. Makes me feel as excited as a kid in a sweet shop or maybe even how they feel on the eve of Christmas day."

Wondering quietly what Frankie's life must feel like, there were no questions asked. My hopes for lifting her mood prompted my compliment of her, on her never dying and always enriching sense of humour. I was left feeling disappointed. One of her great smiles was her only response.

Being something of an optimist and a very deep thinker too, Frankie could often see many better things which lay ahead for her in life. Living in the hopes of many more memories coming back, was what she called her logical reasoning, for making those trips over to Gerry's restaurant with such frequency.

"Can't move on properly Helen without answers to my questions. I'm hoping to find them at Gerry's."
Not sharing her level of enthusiasm and no wish to give her false hope I simply smiled. She was and is as we know a pretender too and very skilled at it. Her face lights up with the smile she always paints on, regardless of how she might be feeling inside. Believing that somehow that painted on smile can in fact become a true smile, has given her the strength and the courage required to keep up that game of pretence.

Oddly for her Frankie took off her red coat that evening at Gerry's. Keeping a coat on in a public place always seemed to help her feel secure, safe and protected. Never understanding her own thoughts, around that which she considered to be very bizzare behaviour, she had promised herself she would break the cycle. Wearing the new coat, it had felt to her like a good time to start with a change in her behaviour. Placing her coat on the large peg on a wall beside the window, her view to the outside world was a little more than slightly hindered. Swiftly running her finger along the window ledge, she grimaced.

Wiping thick dust from her fingertip she raised her hand to get the waiters attention. Frankie was and is a kind woman who would never want to cause trouble for anyone. She had a very quick change of mind. Almost shocking herself with the ease at which she lied, she told the waiter.

"It's nothing Shaun but I'd love a glass of tap water please. Such a thirst going on all day today. I almost wonder if I might have diabetes."

Diabetes? Frankie wondered where that thought had come from? Her mind went on overdrive and on one of its marathons. She had never known anyone with diabetes. Not being able to leave the thought there, the fact she lied to the waiter annoyed her for the whole of the evening.

Shaun was a smart man. She was aware he wouldn't be easily convinced and that was a concern for her. Being a man around twice her age also told her he wouldn't be fooled easily. Life experience had counted for something when it came down to putting Shaun in a Pidgeon hole. She could only hope for his belief in what she had said. Wishing her outdoor view from the window was a better one, she knew the solution for that could be a simple one and so easy to achieve. Calling the waiter over again, she took a deep breath in as she looked up at him with hope in her eyes.

"I'm looking for part time work Shaun. A few hours of an evening or at the weekends or better still maybe both. Any type of work would be good for me. Any ideas?"

The waiter smiled quite a knowing smile.

"I know what you're thinking so tell them Frankie. You're a regular here they would listen to you."

Shaun continued to explain his thoughts.

"Yes, we do need a cleaner. So, this might be a bit of an exaggeration but the place is almost bordering on being

filthy. I'm surprised that we've not been reported to environmental health. All staff including myself have spoken to management but they don't really listen to us. Always saying they will sort it but obviously never have done."
Frankie gave him one of her knowing looks.
"We're 2 of a kind Shaun me and you."

Considering the waiter's statement was something of a huge exaggeration, Frankie nevertheless felt delighted in hearing his view and his suggestion that she speak to management at Gerry's. She wouldn't generally speaking be a devious type yet she felt no regrets for this. Her plan for a good cause had worked. The seeds had been sown with the waiter now she would wait to see if they would germinate. Taking a well-deserved break from his duties Shaun pulled up a chair beside her at the table. As usual he had a soothing tone in his voice. With a degree of compassion, he told Frankie.

"Let me share about your family till dinner arrives then eat in peace and quiet. It's been rather a long time Frankie. Your weekly presence here has brought the story back to all of our minds."
Always loving to hear new information Frankie listened intensely.
"Thanks Shaun all of you here really help me build up a picture. It's not the greatest of pictures but your candid way of telling it means so much to me."

Thinking how maybe the restaurant might employ her as a cleaner if she spoke to management, she again wished that her outdoor view from the window was better. Not being able to see the river from her table Frankie felt was quite a let-down. Remembering how staff from the children's home often made up a picnic and took the kids to a local river, that vision of water running around and over the small rocks was a very soothing thought and memory for her. She wanted that experience at Gerry's. Frankie wondered to herself if perhaps the lack of cleanliness might be the reason for that particular table always being available. Struggling to see through the greyish looking net curtain hanging to the window, she gave out a deep sigh. She again considered that perhaps not everyone's standards for cleanliness, might be the same or as particular as hers. This however was a food establishment so surely there would be levels of expectation, even if your ideas did fall slightly below what might be considered to be standard. She braced herself. She was ready and wasn't prepared to let this opportunity pass her by. Prepared to bite the bullet she proceeded with a stride in her step, to what Shaun had told her was the restaurant office.

Scarcely able to hide her surprise at the environment in which she had been invited into, Frankie practised some deep breathing in the most discrete manner possible. Lack of space being the problem, she described it as no more than a glorified walk in cupboard. Shaun's words were echoing in her ears. Knowing this would be the best chance to bring about change she took in a deep breath ahead of letting the following roll off of her tongue.

"Mrs Jackson, Rosaline, you probably know that I'm a regular here on Tuesdays nights."
She was interrupted mid-stream before she could continue.
"Yes, I've seen you in here quite a few times. Never understand why you keep coming back week upon week, but glad that you do for the sake of our income. How can I help you tonight?"
Frankie's first thoughts for a response were how very rude the woman was for interrupting her like that and how very

detached she was from her customers. Waiting staff at Gerry's all knew why Frankie went there week upon week. Shaun had shared how staff speak about the Chigozie family on a pretty regular basis.

Mrs Jackson in the absence of that knowledge was clearly also very detached from her staff. Whilst the inner Frankie, the real Frankie, wanted to say, clean your place up before you get shut down, she didn't. She used a great deal of self-restraint in hiding her true feelings.

"Could I suggest to you that perhaps business might improve somewhat, if the restaurant looked a little more appealing."

Frankie then thought about how very discrete she had been. Mrs Jackson showed her some degree of interest but again almost in a rude manner.

"Tell me more of what you have in mind."

Frankie had many things in mind which might meet her need and the needs of others, but unsure Mrs Jackson would approve of a complete overhaul of Gerry's, she left the idea right there in her own thoughts. Focusing on the lack of cleanliness for the time being seemed the safest option. She appeared to be listened to.

Having completed that conversation with the restaurant manager, Frankie found herself with a part time job. Cleaning for them one evening per week, at the rate of four hours per evening over the next three months, would provide what she considered to be a badly needed boost to her income. It would hopefully help to bring a bright new image to the restaurant too. Struggling to contain her excitement she needed to share her news.

"We did it Shaun. You prompted me to speak to them. I've got the job so that means more money for me and

a cleaner more hygienic environment for all of you to work in. We should consider ourselves to be the genius team."
Shaun punched the air. Delighted, he shared how he would prepare for a joint celebration on her next visit to the restaurant. Reminding him she would be there the following evening in the capacity of a staff member, she accepted his invitation for a drink once both finished their duties.

    Sharing a giggle Frankie and Shaun parted company for that night. Saying goodbye till the next time on that occasion had a different meaning for them both. Taking the short walk back to the bus station she thought how the road and its pot holes, looked a bit like a war zone. Deciding her attitude was perhaps over the top, she needed to stop being so dramatic. She filled her head with thoughts about her great achievement at Gerry's. Thinking about like for like cost wise and menu wise, of restaurant competition in the same area as Gerry's, she raised her eyebrows just a little. That was Frankie's reaction to what many would consider to be a non-understandable situation. Throughout the period she had been going to Gerry's, it appeared to be on an equal footing from a customer head count perspective, with all others in the surrounding area. On previous visits to the restaurant she had shared her thoughts with Shaun. Assurance given by him that he had been to visit at other restaurants and how there were no issues with cleanliness at any of them.

    "Then it's your charm Shaun which brings people here. It has to be."
Again, they had a giggle. Frankie's secret thoughts were how she managed to be so outgoing when inside she was almost crumbling. She couldn't help but wonder how her time at Gerry's would go, had she been unable to project that confident image.

Flashbacks from her younger childhood years, Frankie remembered just how particular her mum had always been with hygiene and cleanliness. She told me the story in a very eloquent manner.

"Thursdays regular as clockwork was clean the house day. Mum never missed. The smell of furniture polish would aggravate your nose soon as you walked through the door from school."

Having nasal allergies back in those days was always at the least a nuisance. So many products on the shelves to control what would often be Frankie's incessant sneezing, yet nothing seemed to do the job as per the product description. She chuckled to herself at the thought of her mother's view, on how she was managing her home in those days. Frankie had standards and yes, they were pretty high, however they were not bordering on obsession as were her mums. Concluding that mother would not be impressed by her daughters' standards, she left her thoughts there.

Tucked away in that quiet corner of the restaurant Frankie always felt that her privacy would not be invaded. She had memories of coming to this place with her parents prior to that awful accident occurring. All staff at Gerry's remembered her and her parents too, so yes, she was on first name terms with everyone. Now quite a petite looking young woman aged just turned 21 years, she was attempting to make some sense of her past and decide how her future might possibly look. The vision for her going forward wasn't always looking the best. Tugging at what she considered to be her lucky charm bracelet Frankie's mindset would suddenly change.

Reminding herself just how far she had already come

in life and what she had achieved, there would now be no stopping her. Life would be upwards and onwards for Frankie Chigozie. She would not allow her past to define her or to define her future. Perching herself upwards on what she considered to be her thinking chair at Gerry's, the woman felt quite a great sense of relief. Mind finally made up for Frankie she would only engage with positive thoughts from here onwards. She would address the problems from her past in order to gain a peaceful mind- then the whole scenario would finally be put to sleep never to be woken up again. Her plan appeared to be a good one or so she thought. However, no one could be too certain it would be successful That being a road which she would need to travel and now was well prepared to do so, she held the wish that it would be everything which she hoped for it to be.

Discrimination and racism

Years had gone by; A whole lot of them since Frankie had last seen her parents alive. Some memories were there in abundance, whilst others were removed from her mind for what appeared to be forever more. That was how she had felt about the situation. At times being delighted by having what she considered to be a goldfish like memory, she considered it to be a negative too. Taking in a deep breath followed by one of her heavy sighs she told me.

"Sometimes Helen I need to forget. I'm glad to have forgotten then other times it's the flip side of the coin. I just want to remember and very often I can't. To say the whole situation frustrates me is a huge understatement."

Knowing how there was little else I could do for my friend or could offer to her in terms of understanding of her situation, I gave her one of my warm embraces. You know the sort. The one you hope will have said.

"Everything will be all right in the end."

But you're never too sure of your own conviction.

Being raised and having lived in a large children's home in Yorkshire, from the age of 5 years, was an experience that no child should ever have to endure in an ideal world. It was an experience that no decent parent would ever want for their child. Frankie's life experiences have been somewhat up and down and, on some occasions, they've been quite traumatic. She was born into what many would consider to be, a large and very dysfunctional English family with heritage from Ghania too. The family being so dysfunctional were of no help at the point of her parents' sudden death.

Intensive searches and interviews conducted by the local authority, concluded there was no one considered suitable by social services to care for children. That decision resulted in Frankie going through the care of the local authority. She has very little memory of her extended family. Despite her young age at the time when it occurred, she has some good recall from the terrible accident which took the lives of both of her parents and her sister. She can now speak about it with limitations. She has collected some other memories through her regular visits to Gerry's restaurant.

Another full evening spent together found Frankie and I reminiscing again. Taking that trip down memory lane we spoke a little about her parents' accident. Emotional pain was etched across her face as she made attempts to share aspects of it with me. Knowing she was being sparse with the truth I figured that more would probably come to light as time went on. Deciding it was not my place to probe or to ask questions, I continued to listen and show compassion. Placing my hand over hers occasionally I was aware that Frankie would appreciate the gesture and she did. Eventually hearing how she recalled seeing both of her parents lying there at the roadside she grimaced as she told me they were Dead. Having had a great surge of empathy and compassion for my friend and with care oozing from my voice I quickly told her what I considered she needed to hear.

"That had to be the most awful vision for a 5-year-old child Frankie. It's something I'm sure most adults wouldn't wish to have seen or to have in their memory recall. You're an amazing woman don't ever forget that."

Pushing her long curly brown hair behind her ears Frankie slowly glanced in my direction then looked away again. Knowing her as well as I did, from that look I knew she was going to share something else. I knew it would be deeply important and perhaps very painful for her too.

"Don't be shocked Helen when I tell you that my father was a big-time villain. He was a drug dealer and a user too, an alcohol abuser, a rogue and a thief. He had friends who were drug dealers, drug users and who carried guns. Can you imagine us living like that? Imagine our way of life and how it impacted on our mother?"

Without a struggle- no I could not imagine their way of life.

Trying to hide my sense of shock at what I just heard was never going to be my best move. She knew mw as well as I knew her. My response could be considered to be a little pathetic. It was however all I could think to say.

"You were just a kid Frankie. Could you be wrong about the guns and maybe about the alcohol and the drugs too?"

She was adamant and quite stern in her tone by now.

"I know there were drugs and guns Helen because I saw them. I saw mum hiding them on more than one occasion when police called at our house. Searching for evidence of someone who would be somehow connected to Johnnie, on that occasion there was no evidence found. Mum had reached right to the back of the tallboy. I saw it wobble in front of her. I thought she would knock the top section off but she didn't. That's where she hid the drugs and guns all wrapped up in small blankets. Thinking back the cops (Law enforcers) weren't all that great at doing their job. I was hiding under the bed. They didn't look there either. She was too stressed out to even know or think about where I was. I'm now in therapy because of it all."

Tears slowly fell from Frankie's eyes as she searched my face for reaction. It was one of relief. Knowing each other as well as we did, words were often not required in order to express our innermost thoughts to each other. Frankie acknowledged that.

"Glad you're not taking the moral high stand passing judgement and that you approve of my decision for therapy. Your opinion matters a lot to me. Would you join me for the next meeting with the therapist?"

Whilst a bit surprised by her request, my expression showed what my feelings to her comments and question were. Side by side with those feelings of how I would support her in whichever way she deemed to be appropriate, was a continued degree of surprise by her request. Thinking how this wasn't like Frankie at all, I was also struggling a little to understand, how my presence could be, or would be, even remotely acceptable to the therapist.

Knowing how much therapy had helped me in my own middle teenage years, I held the same hope and desire for my friend. Thinking how her mountain to climb was still much bigger than mine had ever been, I could only hope for success for her in doing that. She appeared to have the determination to make it work. I gave assurance that I would be happy to accompany her on her next visit, providing the therapist was receptive to the idea of me being present. The week went by very quickly. I soon found myself back in Frankie's company again. Spending an hour or so at the local coffee shop that morning, we ate cake with our coffee and put the world to rights. We made that trip to the office together keeping the mood light. Frankie shared some jokes about University life. Having a laugh ahead of entering through that doorway was important to her.

Introducing me to her therapist named Alana with clear explanation of why I was there, we were assured that my presence would be fine. Having been invited into one of their sessions, I knew would give me me some further insight into what Frankie's early years looked like and perhaps how she was really coping and trying to deal with that awful situation. Alana seemed nice enough. She was pleasant!

"C'mon in Helen. You'll have to sit over there. Hope it's comfortable for you."

I was offered a chair in a corner of the small room. Despite being small the room and its occupant were both very welcoming. Alana was a middle-aged good-looking woman with long dark hair tied up in a bun. Perhaps a bit clinical looking too I thought and then quietly chastising myself for being so judgemental.

Giving my approval that yes it was perfect, Alana smiled. She had a nice smile. It made her look caring and compassionate. Thinking how Frankie had made a good choice I hoped to be right. The room had a sense of calmness to it. Oozing of peace and tranquillity I instantly felt relaxed. But then I was not the client. I'm guessing its always more difficult for the client to relax in their therapy situation. Simple perfection for a therapy room was how I considered it. Aroma from lavender plants came in through an open window backing onto a tiny garden. A small herb garden sat neatly on the window ledge unwittingly giving me ideas for my own window ledges. This was supported by lavender scented incense sticks burning slowly inside the room. I was thinking how it was all about the lavender and how well that could work for me in my home. I was impressed by my own levels of observation and felt it was a knock-on effect from my job in mental health.

    Keeping my thoughts where they belonged was something which I was not well practiced with, when outside of my employment. That situation in Alana's therapy room was no different. Times in the work situation would often find me expressing almost every thought in my head, which was relevant to my employment. Being aware that this was not one of those work situations, I had promised myself I would remain silent ahead of entering the room. Quietly praising myself for that level of restraint which presented me with something of a challenge, I couldn't help but wonder what Frankie would make of my thoughts.

    Everyone being comfortably seated the therapist began by using the words 'Namaste Frankie.' My perception of the word Namaste was one of it being associated with spiritualism. That it might be used to greet people who were or are very spiritual. I was quite surprised by what I had heard. Left wondering if perhaps Alana was a spiritualist, in addition to being a therapist and how that would be a wonderful thing if she were, gave me the desire to ask the question, however once again I demonstrated self-restraint. A sense of pride in myself for using that restraint gave me some feel-good vibes. Having always been interested in spiritualism with a promise to myself to investigate it further one day, I wondered if this was the day I would have my first introduction, to what I considered to be that very interesting topic. Frankie was comfortable with the greeting and returned the same back to her therapist. Again, keeping my thoughts tightly tucked under my hat I simply smiled. Waiting patiently to see how the meeting would progress I had some other thoughts too.

Seeing the many frowns and deep lines on Alana's face, I assumed that she too perhaps had endured something of a troubled life. She was a lady whose face maybe told the world, that she was looking older than the calendar defined her to be. Knowing just how presumptuous I was being and how it was never good to assume about people, I couldn't help but wonder if Alana was making presumptions about me too. Having established once again that we were all comfortable Alana encouraged her client to begin. Through a very sad and serious looking face Frankie recalled how.

"Mum just sat there screaming at our dad Johnnie. She told him over and over not to do it but he did it anyway."

Almost going into shock from hearing that painful and revealing statement, I wanted to reach out to my friend. Painful as it was for her I knew I couldn't do that. I had to remain quiet. Tears began filling up in Frankie's eyes. She wouldn't and didn't want to be seen to be emotional. Pulling herself further back onto the chair whilst breathing in deeply, she then swiftly wiped her tears away. Her strong sense of determination and resilience, were the facts which she knew would get her through that meeting without too much emotion on display. She bravely continued to share how the Chigozie families last day as a family had begun.

"Mixture of cocaine and alcohol was more than enough, to render Johnnie quite incapable of driving with due care and attention that night. Yes, I refer to my father as Johnnie. Is that bad? Don't especially care if it is. Johnnie is what he deserves. His selfish and reckless behaviour has put me and my family in this situation. He has taken their lives away and has made me an orphan. My forgiveness for that will be a long time coming if ever. It most certainly does not come ready made."

Listening to the extent of anger coming from Frankie towards her father was distressing to hear. I'm not sure that even she realised just how angry she was. Did she realise what pent up feelings she had held inside of her for the past 15 years or so? Did she not understand that forgiveness is required, in order to gain some peace for oneself?

Despite having met Alana for the first time, I could see from her facial expression and body language that she was eager to hear more. I was pretty good on picking up on a person's body language even back then. Making no response to her client's statement she sat in silence. There must have been a reason, must have been a point in her silence. Not being able as I should have been to be self-disciplined, I found myself acting on a strong impulsive gut reaction. Automatically getting up from my chair, reaching out and extending my arms to Frankie felt like the right thing to do.

My best friend forever fell into them momentarily. There were no words exchanged between us. Just a warm caring embrace between friends. Knowing her how I did, helped me to understand that her pain was deep. Much deeper than she would like people in general to be aware of. She was vulnerable. She didn't like her vulnerability to be on display or to be recognised. Allowing me to see and hear that vulnerability confirmed to me just how strong our friendship was and still is. For that I was and continue to be eternally grateful. One of Frankie's very pretentious smiles spread across her face. Only person in that room to be fooled would have been and was Alana.

F rankie and I as we know had met in the local kids home back in 1970. We were 8 years of age. She had been there for almost 3 years on my admission. Something had drawn me to her almost immediately upon my arrival there. Hearing some of the other kids expressing and then acting upon their prejudices towards her, was one of my most poignant feelings whilst we lived together in that home. Referring to her as the darkie, or the one with brown skin was so awfully painful to hear. I'm recalling one child in particular who would have outbursts aimed at Frankie when not getting his own way. It was an older boy by about 3 years so he was around 11 and it was adult speech.

"Why don't you just go back to wherever it is you've come from Frankie. Just go home. Your sort are not wanted here. Never have been and never will be."
As kids we were not so aware that it was adult speech. That realisation came much later in life with our own maturity.

I was young but still understood right from wrong. I had great awareness how that was so very wrong. How the colour of a person's skin was irrelevant and how it would never define them. Seeing that situation as an adult, I do wonder how such a young child ever got to be so venomous. My answer is that most likely it was a learned behaviour from adult care givers, ahead of his admission to the children's home. Some staff members at the home were not the greatest at stomping out those remarks either, often not even acknowledging they had occurred. Those particular staff members had been known to make racist comments themselves too. Negative life experiences from our childhood in the kids home, has remained with me and with

Frankie too. Flashbacks of those who were allegedly professional people in charge of vulnerable children, making racist comments to and about children, whose skin had a different colour to theirs at times makes my stomach heave with the need to reach for the tissue box.

Frankie had appeared to be resilient and not allow herself to be distressed by the racist comments. Not all children had that high level of resilience. I have memories of her demonstrating empathy with some other children in those situations. She had awareness that racism was not acceptable. She despite her young age, would find ways to distract others from hurtful comments made to them and on occasion about them. To say she was a caring and sensitive soul even as a young child, would be a perfect description of my friend.

Frankie's tough view of the world was what was going to get her through some difficult and hard life situations. Being of mixed-race heritage, she had discovered this left her open to a degree of racism. Her father originating from Ghania and her mother coming from India, she at times wasn't too sure what she considered her own heritage and nationality to be, or what she best related to. What she was sure about was the fact that racism and discrimination towards anyone would never be acceptable. She shared with me how the race relations act of 1965 in England, which was introduced by the government and enforced in December of that year, would make any racist comments or actions an offence. However, it failed to address discrimination in employment and in areas of housing. Frankie attempted to hide her deep disappointment from me. Knowing her as I did, I was aware that clearly from her perspective and from mine too, how that situation would never be good enough. It felt like such a let down from our government.

Frankie told me how that failure had led to our government introducing a further race relations act in 1968. This time it would be unlawful to discriminate against anyone on the grounds of race or nationality within employment, housing and various other types of advertising. She was forthcoming with her view.

"It's better than the act passed by government in '63 but I'm not sure it's great Helen. Working as a clinical psychologist I've even had racist comments from colleagues, with them often expressing how their comments are acceptable even humorous and that I should be engaging in laughter with them at those comments. Can you imagine?"

She continued to share how ignorance combined with lack of education of some of the human race, had left an awful lot to be desired. Frankie went on to share how there's lots more to be done in the journey of stamping out racism and discrimination. She would be doing her part in that challenge. Having to acknowledge to my friend that I had witnessed behaviour of a racist nature, throughout my time at University and working in the community, that I always had and would continue to be correcting, supporting and attempting to educate racist people whenever opportunity availed itself. Our town was to a large extent multi-cultural. Working in the public sector and meeting a variety of people from those different cultures, would surely provide me with opportunity to address, support and help me do my part, in the stamping out of issues of a discriminatory or racist manner. The challenge was laying ahead of me. I would embrace it with enthusiasm and all of my might.

Frankie in Therapy

Having rarely spoken about our past, other than to say that both of her parents were killed in a car crash, left lots to the imagination. Hearing about her father and his lifestyle had put my brain in overdrive. I couldn't help but wonder if Frankie's mother Isobel had secretly been a drug user too? Had she been backed into a corner by her husband Johnnie? Back in the therapy room Frankie wiped away her tears once more, ahead of sharing some further painful information. Remembering with clarity, she shared how it was a Friday evening just after school had finished for the day. On arrival home after school the children had felt a great sense of relief. Mostly going home to hear their parents, at the best bickering with each other and at the very worst psychically fighting, the family's days were never easy. Their peaceful home life was never taken for granted.

Both parents were in the house that evening. Unusual for them, they were being incredibly pleasant to each other. Frankie's face showed some more unbearable pain. She was very vivid with the description of her father. Alana listened carefully as she heard how.

"Johnnie was a rough looking man with greasy black hair and a short scruffy looking beard. Cracks in his big hands

seemed to go on forever. Mam was always telling him to grease them offering him the pack of lard from the pantry. Johnnie would take lumps from the lard with his dirty fingers, spending 10 minutes rubbing it into the cracks. It never made a difference. I can still feel the roughness from them on my face after he slapped me many times."
She turned to me with such sadness in her eyes as she told me.

"You look confused Helen. Looks like you're thinking that's hard to believe. Let me tell you it's the truth. Yes, he slapped me many times and very hard too, across the face and my little sister he slapped her hard too. As usual mam would then put lard from that pack into the frying pan, usually to fry up some liver and onions or anything she had in the house which could be fried to make a dinner for all of us."
Being unable to respond or have any answer for what she had just said- left me feeling somewhat coward like. Wanting to share my thoughts of that dirty lard being used to cook their dinner or whatever gave me a strong desire to heave.

Expressing a need to use the bathroom Frankie left the room momentarily. Did she need the toilet or did she just need to have a mini emotional explosion in private? On return with a smiling face she continued to share how.

"Johnnie always wore heavy boots with steel toecaps. He could be heard far away as he came running down stairs to meet his druggie friends. Braces holding up his tweed trousers sometimes fell off his shoulder. As a kid you didn't care. As an adult you'd never be proud of the way he looked. That more or less sums up Johnnie Chigozie and our very short life together."

Alana expressing some compassion for that

situation she also enquired if Frankie would maybe like another short interval? Perhaps to use the bathroom again or get some water? Thinking how she needed to take a beak I was willing her to do so. She didn't. Having a strong desire to bring the session to its end, her nod was the clue to the woman that she needed to continue. Going on to share how their tea was going to be quick that awfully fateful evening and would be very basic, brought a few more unwanted tears from Frankie.

"Chips which would be eaten from a rolled and crumpled up old newspaper was what mum had said. See how some of those very painful memories are still there crystal clear in my head."

Frankie had thought about how tea was almost always very basic but she didn't care about that. Through a few more tightly held back tears this time, she continued to share her story. Her lips quivered as she mumbled out the following words. Telling us how Johnnie was often a very angry man her childhood memory of those occasions was also crystal clear. How he was always to some degree angry about something. It was as though there was never any peace in his mind. She stood up from her chair walking towards the window.

"Thinking I can't go on Alana but know I have to."
She turned and sat back down. My heart was breaking for Frankie. I could only silently compliment her for her vivid knowledge of how badly her father had behaved. We heard how on that awfully fateful evening he had fetched their car from the next street and how he hated having to do that. How living in the middle of a terraced row made things very difficult for car owners in those days.

There were no opportunities to purchase council

parking permits, or put money into a machine to buy yourself some parking time like we have these days. It was as the saying goes everyman for himself. A particular expression she recalled hearing from both parents, was that in some parking situations in their area, it was like dog eat dog. Never understanding that expression as a child, combined with lack of explanation from her parents, Frankie told us how she had believed it to be the truth. Believed the idea that dogs were eating each other alive. Those thoughts had created many sleepless nights at the best and awful nightmares at the worst. Staff at the kids home scarcely showed a level of understanding. She had to deal with it herself and perhaps never did so properly.

She shared again how Johnnie was usually angry because he could rarely find a parking space close to home. How he would often be heard cursing about that fact. Cursing about what he considered to be his rightful place outside of their front door and then shouting out with some profanities that it wasn't even their own front door. That was one way in which Johnnie would release his frustration, from the fact that they were living in a rented house, in which they just lived on borrowed time. He had refused to accept the fact the road was a public highway, to which he had no more rights than any other car driver. Frankie surely and sadly did not appear to have any joyful memories of her father. If she did they appeared to be well buried at that time.

Tears began to drip slowly down her face again as she continued. Wanting to paint the full picture she shared how on his return back home with the car that evening, Johnnie was screeching loudly. She turned to me in the therapy room. Her voice was almost at breaking point.

"He was yelling at us like a banshee Helen. We didn't know how to feel. Thoughts about should we be nervous, be sad or be frightened of Johnnie were racing round in my head."

Reaching out to my friend I gave her another embrace. She continued to share how attempts made by her to comfort her younger sister seemed to work. Their mother had suggested he calmed down and give her the car keys. Frankie got up from the chair again. She began to pace round the room- telling us how their mum was often the instigator of bringing peace to the chaos of his mind. She could see potential problems which hadn't yet arisen and would try to divert him away from them. She was always very calm when she spoke to our father in those situations.

"You're under the influence Johnnie. I'm not sure you should be driving."

Johnnie as was often the case with him wasn't listening to a word our mother said. Being non-compliant to her request he again screamed at us kids.

"Get in the car."

He then told our mum to get in too.

"We did and she did. I'm quite shocked by how compliant to his wishes she was. Despite her being uncertain of his driving capabilities that evening, she went along with his wish perhaps borne out of fear. His drinking and drug habits had become increasingly worse over the previous months before he died. I was just a kid. I didn't understand about all that at the time. Looking back through the eyes of an adult, it's as plain to be seen as the day is long that's what had been happening."

We smiled at her analogy. Continuing to share her story Frankie told us again how.

"As a child I didn't understand any of it, but looking back it was obvious he was consistently using alcohol and drugs and guns. Once again, that fateful evening we were on our way to visit one of Johnnies drug addict friends. If you didn't know better, you could be forgiven for thinking we were a stable happy family, having a nice evening out somewhere. That's it. That's the basis of the story of what led up to me becoming an orphan. Forgiveness for all of that is not within me. I'm not sure that it ever will be."
Sitting back down again she turned to me with a smile. A fake smile but nevertheless a smile.

Alana's response to what she had just heard was to express how hard that must have been for her and for the whole family. With her infectious fake smile Frankie's reply was clear and honest. She shared how they had adjusted themselves to the awful situation which they had found themselves in. Alana expressed her thoughts of how the natural thing for them to have done, would have been to follow in their mother's lead as they did. Frankie again acknowledged that was exactly what they both did.

Knowing and being able to read her body language so well was the cause for my grave concern for my friend. Watching Frankie shuffling around on her chair confirmed to me just how difficult this counselling was for her. Wanting to reach out to her again, keeping still and quiet proved itself to be something of a challenge for me. That was perhaps evident in my body language and in my facial reaction too. Secretly praising myself for the self-discipline which I exerted in not reaching out, I did wonder if I was being judged by Alana. Frankie would fiercely disapprove of my fear of being judged by others. She had by this time in her life developed an enviable motto of.

"In this life you take a person for what they are or you leave them. They don't approve of you- that's not to be worried about as someone else will."

Having shared a psychical description of her mother in that meeting, it was plain to be seen how the woman would be challenged in any real attempts to stand up to Johnnie.

"No understanding at the time due to my young age but looking back now, I have the vision of a very thin looking woman. She would not have had the strength to go against him. That thought brings a little comfort. You know how it is. The expectation always being that the mother would defend her child when that's a possibility."

Continuing to share how everyone was singing one second, the next they were screaming, she wondered what our thoughts were about that scenario. To remain silent and non-responsive was the choice made by Alana. Unsure how to respond for the best, I reminded my friend that I understood how painful that must have been for her. She then got a smile and encouragement to continue from me if that's what she wished to do. Hearing in great detail what had occurred on that fateful evening was pretty harrowing for me. 3 weeks of very hot weather followed by an unexpected downpour of rain had caused hazardous driving conditions. Skid marks were seen shimmering across the road. Trauma etched across Frankie's face as she appeared to relive those moments of her life. She froze momentarily as she recalled how the car had somersaulted back on itself.

Memories of police attendance at the crash scene that evening were still very vivid to her.

"Can't get the picture out of my head. 2 guns found in the car boot by police. Watching them open the boot and pull them out made me scream with fear. It's an image I'll most likely never forget."

Taking a moment to breathe and gather her composure, she shared with us how knowing that her father was amongst other things, a gangster, was so very hard for her to deal with. Frankie relived the scenario of how her parents and her sister were all sadly pronounced dead at the accident scene. Clarity of details of that accident for her was as though it was still happening in real time. Suddenly turning her gaze away from Alana and towards me, her face gave me quite a strong and unspoken message. I was hearing from her expression that she needed my support at that moment. Then in almost a whisper she exclaimed how.

"It's almost too much to bear Helen. It's as though it's happening right now in my head."

Extending my arms for her decision on an embrace Frankie got up from her chair. Meeting half way across the room we shared a warm embrace. She returned to her seat.

Alana at that point and much to our surprise brought her session to its abrupt end. Hearing from Alana that her time was up at that very crucial moment after those painful revelations, felt very wrong to me. Talk about working by the clock to the detriment of a person's well-being felt at the least very harsh almost callous. My initial assessment of Alana as being a caring lady, was now clouded by her behaviour and by my own thoughts regarding her behaviour. Saying goodbye to her therapist I took Frankie for a coffee in the town centre. Her wish was that we didn't discuss her past or anything said in her therapy session.

"I'm not unpicking it now Helen. Let the dust settle and see how I feel next time we meet up."

My advice was- that it might be best to never

unpick it. Just let what was said in that room stay in that room and see how it all might work out. Requesting I also attend her next session the following week, she was delighted that I would make myself available to do that.

Therapy being Frankie's route to hopefully change direction in emotional aspects of her life, I was not convinced that was happening for her. Having worked with some patients in the community who had endured childhood trauma- despite adult therapy their outcomes were not the greatest. My secret thoughts for her were that therapy would most likely not be successful.

Frankie in further therapy sessions shared how she had no understanding of how she walked away from that wreckage without a psychical mark on her body. Alana and I shared that view too. From a spiritual or religious perspective which neither of us shared, there's many who would say it was simply her god given life plan. Psychological marks however were there in abundance. They were buried deep within her mind, her heart and her soul. Frankie had a good mind which she addressed on many occasions. Her attempts to remove her painful thoughts however had always been futile. Memories of seeing her family dead at the roadside were still clearly there in her head. More tears ahead of her sharing how.

"Social workers took me to the funeral home. It wasn't a great picture for a child as young as I was. It left me feeling traumatised for many years after the event."

Images of her deceased parents and perhaps especially that of her younger sister laying in their caskets, was something which Frankie struggled to remove from her mind. Determination preventing her from becoming visibly emotional again, she went on to express her thoughts of how that scenario would never occur in these times. How children would be better protected by all professional services involved in their lives. Being equally quick to defend the social workers involved when she was a child, she spoke well of them for their part in every other area of her care plans.

"Regular visits from social workers at the children's home were always appreciated. Staff within the home as you know Helen changed with great frequency. I had the same social worker all through the years I was placed there. Not that I ever spoke to her very much about anything at all, but still it helped me in seeing the same face on every visit from social services."

Sharing her view about consistency with social workers kind of helped both of us in our own chosen careers. Helped us to appreciate and reinforced the idea, that we should make solid attempts to be consistent with our patients and with our clients.

Frankie was aware that she had spoken much more on this therapy visit, than she had done on any of the previous ones. Having consulted with my friend once weekly for the past 6 months, Alana too was aware of the increased input from her client on this particular visit. It was then surprising to hear that Alana wondered if Frankie wished to continue. Not wanting to persuade the woman either way she asked the question.

"What next Frankie. What do you want to do?"

A look of shock must have swept across my face. The very idea of that question challenged my thinking. What did she mean by what do you want to do? What sort of a question was that to the woman who had disclosed so much? Did Alana think her client could expose her vulnerability as she had done and then walk away and leave it there? I found myself secretly questioning the compassion and the professionalism of the therapist. That was yet another thought I needed to keep snugly sitting under my hat. I was sure that Frankie wouldn't appreciate any interference from me in that direction let alone Alana.

With little to no hesitation Frankie stood up from the chair. Watching her push it across the room with some force, to the corner from where it had been collected from, I knew something had stirred within her. Having done that in a manner which could only be considered to be almost bordering on rudeness, I could sense her annoyance towards her therapist. She slowly turned to face Alana who would also be surprised by Frankie's reaction to the question. With an enviable degree of what appeared to be great self-confidence, she enquired with her therapist.

"Same place, same time, same day next week?"

Alana upon checking her diary confirmed the appointment. Having a strong sense of envy for the confident manner in which Frankie had just expressed her thoughts, I hoped that my feelings were not on display. Knowing myself how much I lacked confidence was one matter, I had no desire for others to be privy to that information too. Knowing that for Frankie despite the trauma she had experienced in earlier life, her presentation of herself to the world which was generally to be confident, gentle, calm and collected was a presentation which I had aspired to. The latter 3 I had in abundance, somehow confidence in myself seemed to have escaped me.

Taking something very useful from that therapy session I reminded myself, that if this is how a therapist needs to behave around their client, then I should remember never to become a therapist. I was fine with that thought. Despite it perhaps sounding a bit judgemental it sat very comfortable with me in relation to Alana. Once outside sharing my thoughts with Frankie felt very comfortable for me too.

"Glad I wasn't in your shoes in there Frankie. Alana would have had both barrels from me. Your patience and tolerance amaze me."

She laughed. She aptly reminded me not to mistake her self-control for weakness. That her inner beast was just sleeping and not dead. We laughed we hugged and moved on home after her request to me.

Goodbye to Alana

Leaving her therapists room my friend had extended an invitation. Requesting that I might take dinner with her later that evening, came as something of a surprise for me. Wanting to get to know the adult Frankie better, because we can always get to know people somewhat better than we do, I graciously accepted. Meeting up later at the local pub we enjoyed some good food with a few drinks. The use of alcohol always helped me to unwind. I wasn't too sure how to feel about Frankie using alcohol due to her father's addiction and maybe her mothers too. It was as though she was reading my mind.

"It's all right Helen I'm sensible. I only use alcohol very occasionally and always just socially. I'm not an over the top or sit at home alone type of drinker like my parents were. Ooops, there I've given my mams secret away now too."

Offering my reassurance that she had done nothing wrong brought a look of relief to her face. Frankie smiled and thanked me for being such a good friend. Having a great sense of humour, she tried out one of her jokes on me. Not getting the desired response, she reminded me how that after having once met my mother, it's her view that the apple didn't fall far from the tree. Not understanding her analogy showed on my face. Frankie explained that it means

I'm like my mother as she didn't get Frankie's jokes either. That was one of the great things about our relationship. We could and would be forever honest with each other, to the point where others might say we were being brutal.

Our response to that would and always will be, that in the absence of honesty a person has nothing. Having a burning sense of curiosity regarding Frankie's ancestors, a way forward for the discovery of answers was not obvious to me. I couldn't help but wonder what may have happened in her parent's life's, way back in their childhood days. Life experience has taught me, that unwanted behaviours and addictions, do not just appear without reason in a person's make up. Johnnie and Isobel would most likely have endured some very inappropriate situations themselves in their childhood years.

Having completed her degree in Psychology would hopefully open many doors for her. Frankie felt that the time was right for some serious job seeking. Working part time in a shoe factory had served its purpose. Having given her the provision of money, it was time to say goodbye to the huge variety of shoes she had discovered. Being a person with a modest nature, Frankie was grateful for all which she had learned and experienced on the factory floor. Not meeting her academic needs or challenging her intellectually in any way she shared with her supervisor.

"Time for me to go but thank you for how everyone here has enriched my life in so many ways. I'll never forget my days, weeks and months clocking in and out."

Interviews always appeared to be easy for her. Having that laid-back attitude which we know she has, her view concerning employment was one which was the envy of many her age, myself included in that equation. In her sometimes almost flippant and quite enviable manner Frankie would express how.

"Either people like me, see my value and my worth or they don't Helen. If they don't then perhaps the next one will."

The surprised yet happy look on my face would have shown her my reaction to that statement. Being truly confident that this attitude would see her through life's obstacles and hurdles, I decided I would be leaving nothing to chance. I was compelled to express my thoughts and my sense of pride of her. Frankie laughed ahead of telling me.

"You're not so bad yourself Helen. You and I are 2 of a kind."

Evening having come to its end we walked to the bus station together. We embraced ahead of saying goodbye till the next time.

My walk from where Frankie would board her bus, to arriving at my own bus stop, found my head swimming with thoughts about how the future might look for us both. Feeling in sheer awe of her outlook on life, I craved for some of that resilience and that confidence which she exuded. The fact it was often fake felt quite irrelevant to me. Should I somehow find it, could I then pull it off as she does was the question. Considering the heart wrenching trauma which she had endured as a very young child, everything about the adult version of her was simply amazing.

Having a sense of humour which was always top notch, I sometimes felt envious of the way she would bring humour to many of her sad life situations. Frankie didn't want to be a victim. She had clearly made that decision. She had no time for the self-pity train. She had a way of ensuring that no one would ever see her as the victim, but rather as the survivor. Her desire was to be seen as the one who had learned some valuable life lessons from her childhood experiences. Frankie would often tell me how fortunate we were in life, as I struggled to see light at the end of the tunnel. Smiling broadly with that fake smile or maybe it was for real on those occasions, she would take hold of my hand as she expressed her wisdom.

"Think of the positives Helen and the many great times we've already shared. Don't ever forget how the best is yet to come."

Recalling how she had reminded me about any potential boyfriends for her she had giggled effortlessly as she shared with me, how any potential marriage partner would be alleviated of a large financial cost of any said marriage.

"It's really very simple Helen. I have no family to speak of. Some of them might be and probably are still residing here on this planet in some sort of fashion, but as useless to me as they were back then when I was a kid."
Trying to discuss that further with her my attempt to discuss any potential family contact was not appreciated. She would shut me down quickly. Feeling especially vulnerable and very sad on this occasion she once again told me.

"Any existing family are as useless to me as it would be if you tried selling ice to an Eskimo."
Being the sensitive one I reached out to my friend with arms open wide. Appreciating my embrace, she continued.

"You are my only friend on this earth Helen in fact you are my family. There I've said it now. Sharing that with you and having said it out loud, helps me understand just how very alone I am in this rubbish world and how very special you are to me."

My thoughts reciprocated this time it was Frankie offering me an embrace.

Back then in the years before England went on the downward spiral of gangsters, murderers, paedophiles and many other crazy people doing crazy stuff everywhere, we had both considered this to be something of a rubbish world. By comparison with today's standards, it put a new definition on the meaning of our then description, of what we thought was a crazy world. Reminding my friend that she was so very special to me too brought a beautiful smile from Frankie. Having to agree that any potential weddings for either of us would surely be small, we laughed at our thoughts, as a wedding for either of us could perhaps be several years away if ever. Two weeks having gone by very quickly and there we were again back in the therapy office.

Alana was once again welcoming of my presence. Time having proven that Frankie was more about the sharing of information when I was in attendance, was the primary reason for the therapist allowing me into their sessions. That knowledge being a surprise to both Alana and myself, we duly reached the conclusion that despite her outward show of confidence, my friend had some insecurities just like the rest of us. Having disclosed more painful information about her childhood days, Frankie on this occasion appeared to lack showing any display of emotion. Her disclosures once again brought that very recognisable lump to my throat. I knew I had to remain calm and silent and offer support only if she requested that from me. She didn't. Frankie made yet another appointment to see Alana.

Leaving the office, she shared how there would be a surprise for me that evening. I was intrigued. My eyes glistened at the very thought of what it might be and couldn't begin to imagine. I was eager for more information. I informed Frankie of that fact. Having always gone to Gerry's alone in order to keep her full focus, she was eventually breaking that rule.

"We're going to Gerry's restaurant and hope you like it."

That was my surprise and a very welcome one too. Never having been there I was curious to see the place my friend had almost declared undying love for. She was taking me to the restaurant, which she had told me that through her familiarity there, that almost at times in her dreams she had considered it to be hers. We laughed.

Often having felt intrigued about her Tuesday nights at Gerry's my curiosity would now be fed. I was seeing first hand just what was so special for her about this place. Staff
expressed an element of surprise mingled with approval at my presence.

"Not alone tonight Frankie. It's good though to see you with a friend."

Nodding her approval to his comments, we followed Shaun to the usual corner table. Gerry's to me appeared to be just a run of the mill type of place with no special qualities. It had nothing special to offer through the eyes of the customer it meant little to, other than the purpose for which it was intended. Frankie had the knowledge I would view it that way. However, she wanted to share her special place with me.

"See it from my perspective Helen. It's much more than just a restaurant to me. As you know it provides me with way more than food and fluids. Memories I get from coming here cannot have a price on them."

Having no argument for that statement from Frankie we wrapped up the evening. Both having enjoyed a succulent meal my friend enjoyed little else about our time there. No opportunity for her rekindling memories on this occasion had availed itself to her. She was quick with her comments of, till the next time, be sure to call me and then she was gone. Knowing her as I did, my understanding of her almost abrupt manner towards me at that point, told me she was struggling emotionally. My heart wanted to follow her offering that which a good friend might offer. My head told me that she knew I was available for her, yet she had chosen to be alone. I followed my head and left it there. Knowing Frankie had brought me to her special and private place felt like an honour to me. Secretly wondering how I could ever repay the compliment, how I could ever do something that special for her my mind was left empty without answers.

Many therapy sessions later of which I too attended most of, Frankie decided that she'd had enough. Having explored her early childhood in a thorough fashion she was ready to perhaps put all of that behind her and try to move on with her life. She was sensible enough to understand, that memory of certain aspects of her life such as the car crash and all which that created would never go away. That they would simply become more manageable and somewhat easier to live with. She stopped attending at Gerry's restaurant on a weekly basis too. I wasn't overly sure how that decision might impact her going forward.

"I can always revisit if I need to Helen. For now, I'm drawing the line and have told Shaun I won't be seeing them for a while."

His smile turned to a joke about how devious we had both behaved in the past. How putting our heads together to get the place cleaned up had paid off in our favour. Shaun again expressed his appreciation of me for making that happen. Reminding him that my bank account appreciated it too he laughed.

"It'll be strange here on Tuesday night's Frankie. Come back and see us from time to time if you wish."

Having had some interviews with the local health service Frankie landed herself a freelance contract for a year. Working in different areas of Yorkshire was time consuming for us both. Never forgetting each other we did seem to drift apart from the psychical perspective but never from each other's thoughts.

Other side of Frankie

Sounds from the phone ringing brought me out from the shower almost at the speed of light. Hair dripping and wrapped in a towel I went hastily to the bedroom. Hoping to get there before whoever it was ran out of patience and hung up on me, I was fortunate to make it on time. Times like that one were the times I found myself wishing I could be more decisive in life. Had I gone for the short bob hair style which I had been considering for months, imagine how much easier it would have been to dry off quickly in situations like that one.

Picking up the receiver whilst being slightly out of breath at the same time, was not very conducive to a professional start to the phone call. Having some intruding thoughts concerning how I should maybe address my level of fitness, I dismissed them for that time. Fortunately for me it was Frankie on the phone. I knew she would understand my almost panting voice. It had to be nearly a whole year since the last time we met up or even spoke to each other. Our friendship however was as solid as a brick wall. Both knowing It would always withstand the passage of time regardless of how long it's been since our previous contact, was what allowed us never to be concerned.

"Hi Helen it's been way too long. Your sounding a little out of breath. How are you? "

No changes there then. Frankie projected herself as being as confident as honest and as assertive as she had ever been.

Continuing with the conversation I responded to her question with some honesty too. It was agreed that yes, a trip to the gym or some form of exercise could only be in my better interest. She wondered if we could meet up and the sooner the better from her perspective. It almost felt like there was an urgency in her voice. Like she needed to get this done. I was intrigued.

"That would be great Frankie. When and where? What would work best for you?"

Planning a venue wasn't the easiest to achieve as we worked different hours. My suggestion then was that perhaps Frankie could come to my home. Being happy with that idea I could hear some excitement in her voice as she told me.

"Yep I can do that. See you Saturday around 2ish and loads to tell. I'm sure you have too."

Ending that call and hastily returning back to the bathroom I continued rinsing off the new colour from my hair. Having always wanted red hair, yet never daring enough to change from light brown, eventually I had taken the plunge. Checking it out in the bathroom mirror I could see the actress Maureen O'Hara looking straight back at me. Just the hair sadly without the stunning good looks. Gasping from shock I was left wondering if maybe it was a little or perhaps even a lot too red. Being very little I could do about it at that point my mind was made up. Knowing that I would need to try to embrace my new look and maybe even be proud of it, I changed my mindset to having a spring in my step as I took a venture outdoors. Deciding I might even get a compliment or two I would also try not to think too much of what Frankie might say. Either way I knew that as what was usual for both of us, Frankie would be brutally honest. I braced myself for her comments which I expected might be a little harsh.

Planning for and then enjoying my friends visit was an experience which I could never have been sufficiently prepared for. Frankie looked radiant. Perhaps the best I had ever seen her look. She had some news for me too. Compliments from her regarding my new red head look, raised my confidence considerably. My worries about her potential comments were unfounded.

"You're looking great Helen. Something in life is doing you good. The red head suits you a lot."

"Same goes for yourself Frankie. Your looking great too."

Spending the evening together she and I took another long trip down memory lane. Reminiscing about our time spent in the children's home, rekindled some lovely memories for us both and perhaps some not so great ones too. The journey we were now travelling back to our childhood was proving itself to be somewhat beneficial.

Reminiscing about how despite liking the routine and the boundaries at the kids home, we did not always adhere to them. Looking back, it was clear to be seen how all of that had prepared us well for life. Frankie recalled how some kids had often considered us to be odd, based on our levels of compliance and perhaps they weren't wrong. In many ways our levels of compliance almost seemed weird to ourselves at the time. So much rebellion from other kids had made us look like little angels and we truly were not. She giggled the way Frankie does as she reminded me.

"Remember our many midnight antics which on occasion went unnoticed."

We experienced so much teasing too from other children. That was something which occurred mostly in our teenage years. Kids would be heard loud and clear as they berated us.

"There they go again. Yes sir, no sir, three bags full sir. Proper little goody two shoes aren't they."

Those were regular comments coming in our direction from the more mischievous amongst us and they're were plenty of them. Remembering how some of the teenage girls were often hanging on street corners in the early hours, surely would have given a bad reputation to the home, not to mention the dangers that behaviour posed to the girls. Frankie remembered her thoughts of how no one seemed to really care and how unlucky the girls were with their safety being jeopardised. We giggled as we pondered over those days and wondered what might have become of many of the children with whom we had grown up.

Yorkshire always appeared to have lots on offer for and to its young people. We both recalled how the Leeds international Baths in Westgate, were built in the 1960s causing some great excitement within the children's home. Everyone wanting to go swimming, when lots of us had never even seen water any deeper than perhaps a household bath, with some not ever having that experience before coming to the home. Frankie recalled how you could at times smell the newbie before seeing them.

"Wasn't it funny Helen when you look at that and then how suddenly there were so many great swimmers amongst us."

Sharing her view, I recalled how schedules and rotas

were put in place in order to give all the kids an opportunity. Frankie reminisced how the home staff had taken us both there on many occasions for official swimming lessons. She spoke about heightened levels of excitement within the home, on the day of Neil Armstrong's adventure of walking on the moon in 1969. Despite being just 7 years of age at that time she remembered the event with great clarity. She had memories of walking round the market at weekends and browsing in shops in the Victorian arcade. Sliding down hills in the snow on homemade makeshift toboggans, was a great memory which we both shared. I was left feeling very perplexed in the knowledge that she had so many clear memories of our childhood when I had so few. She knew so much about me and my life. It felt almost as though Frankie knew me better than I knew myself in my younger days.

Deciding she would have been focusing on what was happening around her perhaps more than I was, the idea made sense to me. Wanting to block out memories of the car crash would have created the desire in Frankie to focus on what she should focus on. Remembering how it was the crash which had made her an orphan, was a pretty painful memory and one which anyone would want to forget. It felt like a reasonable way to explain our difference in recalling events. Speaking lots and sharing lots regarding those days in the children's home, our minds were once again taken back to some of the children whom we had grown up with. Reminding me of Mikey, the very cheeky red-haired boy from the kids home and how he considered himself to perhaps be Irish. Basing that assumption on the colour of his hair combined with the name Rooney, we all considered how he could well be correct. Visions of the young Mikey came flooding back to me.

"Wasn't he the one who was constantly running away, climbing onto garage roofs, stealing from local shops and forever in trouble with the local police. Regularly branded as the troublemaker?"

"Yes, that's the one Helen. You have good recall there but then his antics would be hard not to have been noticed and remembered too."

Visions of him in so many different scenarios and how he was regularly known as the resident troublemaker began to flood my mind. Sharing those thoughts with Frankie, she didn't receive them all that well.

Perching herself back some more on the chair in almost a defensive manner she asked if I remembered how staff would constantly tell other children to ignore his antics then leave the conversation there.

"Where was the input in terms of guiding the kids about the wrong doings of Mikey? That combined with him always thinking how his behaviour was so funny, has to be extremely questionable"

Frankie was upholding the view that had staff been more pro-active, then Mikey's behaviours may well have settled down a lot sooner than they did. Not getting much of a response from me to her comments, she continued to share some further memories about Mikey.

"You remember the night he was threatening to jump from a 2nd storey window onto a concrete slab 10 metres beneath him. Staff entering the room caused him to lose concentration. Him falling from that ledge got everyone's adrenalin going. It's nothing short of a miracle that he didn't die."

No hesitation on my part for a response to that.

"Definitely remember that night Frankie it would be almost impossible not to."

Blue light services were fairly common place at the home due to someone doing a misdemeanour of sorts. Theory was that giving the kids an official talking to, would hopefully prevent more serious issues in their future. We recalled how ambulance sirens and flashing lights woke up the whole of the kids home the night that Mikey fell from the window ledge. Taken to the local hospital accident and emergency department he was treated for a broken leg and 2 broken ribs. Complications of infection with a requirement for intravenous antibiotics, seriously impaired what could have been a faster hospital discharge for Mikey. 3 weeks from the accident date he returned back to the home with the use of crutches.

Attempts made by Mikey to continue his antic's but now with the use of crutches, he was quickly segregated from other children.

"You remember Helen when he was almost put into isolation"

"Yep his screams of protest can still pierce my ears" We chatted about him being placed in an area within the home, which was regularly used for therapy sessions or for social worker meetings and how life then suddenly changed dramatically for Mikey Rooney.

"Remember how we could hear him protesting about the unfairness of what had happened for him and how he wouldn't mess with his crutches if allowed back into the communal area."

"Yes, but everyone who knew Mikey knew how that wasn't the truth. How he would need to experience the loneliness of isolation from other kids, in order to bring about any changes in his behaviours."

We laughed as we recalled how the tiger within Mikey eventually learned to a degree how to calm itself down.

Isolation from other kids was the catalyst for that learning, as opposed to it initially being through Mikey's own choice. Gradually he was reintegrated back into the main communal area with great caution. Demonstrating a good degree of respect, the upwards hill was climbed by him without any further menacing with the crutches. Frankie had always been good at reading faces. The raised eyebrows on mine surely told her I was maybe being a little judgemental in my thoughts. She was right I was being very judgemental and did not feel especially proud of myself for having had those thoughts.

Becoming somewhat on the defensive regards Mikey, I had to wonder where her thoughts were coming from. She was quick to remind me how people can and at times do change their behaviours for the better. She was almost snappy as she informed me.

"I know the adult Mikey Rooney. He's a mature gentleman these days nothing like his younger self."

Seeing the look of surprise on my face she waited for a response but not patiently.

"Well say something then Helen."

My response of "okay" felt pretty anaemic to her and she was quick to tell me that.

"That's the best you can do? It's a bit of a watered-down response."

Not being sure what else I could say I invited Frankie to carry on her story.

She continued to share how Mikey came under that category of people who have changed their ways. She had a special glow on her face as she mentioned his name and how those immature and childish days were left behind him. My concentration hung on her every word. This was a woman taking pride and delight in what she had to say, what she had to share with me her oldest of friends. I had to offer the respect her conversation deserved, for her sake more than there being any interest in hearing about Mikey Rooney on my part. Going on to finish her story which shocked me to the core, she took a deep breath in ahead of telling me.

"Mikey is my boyfriend and its very serious between us. We met at my office and been dating now for 6 months."

I could feel an expression of that shock being visible on my face so no doubt Frankie observed it well. In the absence of giving me time to respond she continued to tell me how.

"Mikey is working as a sales rep for a well-known software company. He's changed an awful lot and there's more."

Encouraging her to continue I wondered how much more I could comprehend and deal with it. Her next sentence absolutely floored me. With a look of sheer delight on her face she told me.

I'm pregnant Helen I'm having Mikey's baby."

Ahead of my response and almost choking on my own saliva my thoughts were racing. Knowing Frankie as I did I could see many issues for her. The least not being how she would be made to feel like a kid again, with everyone telling her what to do and what to expect. Then she would have to endure my input which she would find hurtful and not like very much at all. Momentarily I was speechless.

To say I was not surprised by my own thoughts would be a huge understatement. Frankie's a psychologist and very good at reading people. Attempting to hide that from her would not have worked out well. Knowing I had to reveal my honest thoughts was a very uncomfortable feeling for me. Shifting about on the chair I stood up in my attempt to leave the room for coffee. She knew me too well. I was quickly brought to heel. In her usual assertive manner, she told me.

"Forget the coffee Helen. It's just an escape route for You. I know you have worries about Mikey so just spit them out. C'mon let's hear them."

Accepting that my friend was sounding almost challenging in what she had just said to me, made my situation feel a little more uncomfortable. Knowing how I would have to be honest and wondering how she would react to that honesty, wasn't the greatest feeling I had ever experienced. Sitting back down I continued.

"Frankie a leopard never changes its spots."

The knowledge of how judgemental I was being in saying that, was etched across Frankie's face and swirling round in my mind too. Thinking how I could have said it differently, perhaps said it in a better way, but now was too late the words had fallen off my tongue. Her response was snappy and almost at the speed of grease lightning and I guess probably well-deserved by me.

"Short memory or what Helen. Remember the two of us with our many midnight antics in the children's home. Yes, we were mostly compliant but not always. Good job no one was judging us when we applied to University or applied for our jobs. Me being a psychologist and you being a Mental

Health nurse, I'd kind of say we have changed quite a bit, wouldn't you?"

What was there left for me to say in my defence to that. There was no defence worth speaking about. The facts had been put on the table right there in front of my eyes or perhaps rather my ears. She gave me that questioning almost challenging look, which said.

"Well come on then Helen what do you have to say to that?"

I was put on the spot and didn't especially like or enjoy being in that position.

"All right all right. You've got my submission. I take your point and yes I agree that we were never saintly yet never judged."

Knowing how I was defeated I knew there was only one thing left for me to do. I'd have to come down from my judgemental pedestal and lose my awful attitude towards Mikey Rooney. I struggled badly with my own thoughts in wondering how I would achieve doing that. Knowing that for that particular time, I would have to whole heartedly embrace my friend's situation, I was quite proud of myself for being able to do that in the moment - I told her.

"You're so sensible Frankie. I'm guessing the pregnancy was most likely planned. When do I get to meet Mikey the man?"

Her face broadened widely with her beautiful smile, yet she offered no response to the pregnancy assumption which I had just made. That lovely smile I was remembering from her childhood beamed from ear to ear across Frankie's face. I just knew she was happy which in turn raised my happy hormones too. Plans put in place for me to meet up very soon with her boyfriend, we embraced ahead of her preparing to set off for the journey home.

Having said goodbye and shut that door behind Frankie, I was left with my own selfish thoughts. Considering how well she appeared to be doing in life, stirred up thoughts of my own life and how very lonely it had felt and still did feel at times. Having taken stock of my own situation, I wondered if perhaps the time was right for me to disembark from the self-pity train. Thinking how everyone knows the pity train is not a good look, I swiftly acted on those thoughts. Moving forward in life my philosophy would certainly change. Gratitude for all and everything whichever and whatever touched my life would be my motto from that point going forward.

My job working as a community psychiatric nurse put me in contact with a variety of people throughout the adult age range. Bringing out very many different emotions from me it often became difficult to keep them well hidden. However, I was aware that I had to do just that. Some scenarios would always be more difficult to deal with than others. The overriding painful emotions were always stirred up, when I was part of an assessment team working together with local police. Removing children from their parents or their adult care givers, went against every vibe in my body but often it was our very last resort. That situation would be especially difficult if the children had to go to a foster home, or worse, to a children's home which at times was the case. Attempts to avoid those painful situations often failed me.

Taking my mind back to my own family circumstance and removal from my parents at a very young age, I avoided those safeguarding meetings when possible.

That didn't happen too often either. Having occasional flashbacks to that very awful evening when my mother screamed at visiting social workers and police officers, who had been called yet again by our neighbours.

"Okay. Take her and don't bring her back. Never ever bring her back. She doesn't belong in this family in this house or in my life."

Remembering those words coming from my mother, cuts me almost as deep but not quite as raw, as it did on the day it happened. Her rejection of me was painful beyond any explanation I can muster up to share. As a young adult growing up I often questioned in my own head, where had my mother's desire to work with professionals been. What sort of a person would call themselves a mother and then speak in that manner about their child? My removal from her care on that particular evening did not mean permanence. She and only she made the permanence happen. Remembering how there were no attempts ever made by my mother to hug me, or to show any affection, my promise to myself had been that I would be the one to break that cycle.

Having never seen my father from that day forward, and seen my mother just once when she came to the kids home, I grew up with resentment for them both in my heart. I had and still have no desire to seek them out. Having made the decision that some parents never should be such, I have chosen to live my life with their absence. Being aware that should I ever become a parent I would remind myself of my promise to be the one to break the cycle. I would never be a mirror image of my own parents was the overriding thought which got me through the flashbacks.

Bringing change to the wards

Advertising section of our local paper was where you would find employment back then. Having quite a large portion dedicated to hospital staff vacancies throughout the whole of Yorkshire, I was keen to read the display in Thursday night's edition. A particular one which took my interest read, 'vacancies have arisen at the local Mental Health hospital for qualified nursing staff of various grades.' It was followed by their application details. Consideration being given to obtaining an application paper, I could see many positives for my life and for my career in doing that. Working in virtual isolation in the community had proven to be something of a challenge to me, in terms of how lonely I had become. The wards by comparison would be a constant hive of activity, with challenges often changing I imagined by the hour.

Making that final decision to go ahead, I then stressed over the application and the fact they would be looking at my childhood and my upbringing. Calling Frankie for her opinion felt like a good thing to do. In fact, it felt like the very best thing to do. Knowing we had this relationship where brutal honesty between us would always be the way,

I called my best friend. She was as was usual for her very realistic and very reassuring.

"It'll be fine Helen. You'll be fine. From what I can see you're a great nurse. Your always thoughtful regarding the
needs of others. Mental Health wards needs more people like you. Just get that application in."

Having had that confidence boost from Frankie gave me a feel-good vibe, in regards to my application to the hospital. Wishing she could see relief on my face I hoped she heard it in my voice. The compliment was quickly reciprocated.

"And you're a great friend too Frankie. Don't ever forget that and see you soon."

Positive vibes about my nursing application after speaking to Frankie, it was the road I would be going down. I was ready and prepared to proceed to the next stage of my journey. I ensured my application found its way, amidst thousands of other pieces of mail going through the post office system. Rarely I would be found writing letters or such like. Having knowledge of the postal strike back in 1964, I could see the distress and impact which that would have had on many people, who were urgently waiting for their mail to arrive. I had a great empathy for people who regularly relied on the post office service. There was equal empathy with our post office workers. They considered their striking action to be the only way to rectify their deals, which to them appeared to be very unfair. From an exercise perspective, my postman had told me that he felt like the luckiest man in the world to be doing that job. From a financial perspective he shared how he had felt as though he was almost being violated.

Mental health in the middle 1980s did not have

the best of reputation from 'a caring for the patient perspective.' That fact was evident throughout the whole of our county and in fact the whole of the country. I knew if given the opportunity I could bring about improvement to people's way of thinking. Waiting to hear back from the health authority felt like a tedious time for me. I'd found myself thinking that carrier pigeon might have been quicker. Not confident that others would appreciate my sense of humour I kept those thoughts tucked away privately. Eventually the presence of the letter on my doormat brought me out in a sweat, accompanied with my usual eczema outburst in stressful situations. Opening up the envelope with some caution I smiled at the content.

My application to the local hospital was successful. Waiting period for my interview from receiving that news, seemed to be much longer than it perhaps was. Interview morning being spent rehearsing answers to presumed questions was quite draining on my energy. There being no certainty I would be asked those particular questions and me feeling full of trepidation, I decided to give up. Knowing the nerves had to calm down was the easy part. Knowing how to bring about that calmness I wasn't too sure of. Taking a short walk and the practice of deep breathing both left me feeling nil and void. Nothing seemed to be working for me at that point. Changing my outfit 3 times ahead of setting off to the hospital, the feel of having some confidence in myself and in my own abilities had marginally improved.

Arriving at the human resources office I did my breathing again ahead of knocking the door. Hearing the words "come in" only served to heighten my other senses. The room looked enormous. And probably wasn't. 4 people sitting round a table I felt all of their eyes were on me as I stepped towards them. Managing to stay calm presented me with something of a challenge. Rising to it I met the challenge head on. Hoping the interviewing panel would not observe my nerves, I remembered how Frankie would paint on her fake smile when she might be crumbling inside. I did likewise. Despite the interview not having started at that point, I was feeling the vibes that I was liked by panel members.

    Appreciation to the panel for their time for seeing me was expressed. Having that appreciation reciprocated right back at me, helped my anxiety to take a step back a little further. Thinking how the interview was going quite well, despite very few of my predicted questions being raised as a topic for discussion, my anxiety took a large step backwards. Requested by matron to go and wait outside in the corridor for a short period, left me unsure if I had said something inappropriate. Pacing the corridor rather than sitting, the idea was to keep my anxiety under control. What was a short 10-minute period felt more like an hour ahead of being called back to the interview room again.

    I had shared my vision and my optimism about bringing change to the wards, of what had been sometimes known as institutions. My own experience of institutions from being raised in a children's home, apparently was a positive in the interview scenario. Matron smiled as she reminded me.

"You've got the experience Helen. Life in the children's home had to be hard for you. It's a positive in this interview. You'll relate to institutional life where others may be less able to. You're the last of 7 applicants to be interviewed for this role. You're the one we feel would be most suited to the position. The job is yours if you still want it."

Hearing those words was a very joyous moment for me. My interview was successful. Soon I would be bringing my experiences to a place where they were badly required. There would be no long speeches from me to the panel. I was and am a lady who hears an outcome and acts modestly upon it.

Thanking matron and others on the interviewing panel very briefly, I shut that door behind me ahead of punching the air. Eventually my awful childhood experiences were creating positivity in my adult life. Bursting with excitement I was like a small child on Christmas eve night whilst waiting for father Christmas to arrive. I went directly home and danced round the room like a demon demented. Having no regard to whether my neighbours could see me or not, the volume was switched up a notch. I was elated. Hard to comprehend how the offer of employment could generate that much excitement in anyone. I seriously questioned my own stability at that moment.

Eventually calming myself down it was time to make a phone call. Struggling again to contain my excitement I told Frankie that I had to see her as soon as possible. We shared some time together later that afternoon. Frankie as always was realistic and very supportive too.

"No surprise to me Helen. I knew you'd walk it. Your perfect for that job and we both know it. Here's to the future and to the lovely people-both staff and patients, who are strangers you have yet to meet."

Embracing ahead of saying goodbye with a plan in place for our next meeting, I had a deep sense of gratitude for the true friend which I had in Frankie. Wondering where time might take Frankie and I as we journey our way through life, one thing I had absolute certainty about was the sustainability of our friendship. It was as solid as the rock of Gibraltar.

Rooney's new baby

Preparing myself for my upcoming meeting with Frankie's boyfriend made the nerves a little extra twitchy. Pangs of anxiety were truly showing themselves, in the eczema which had raised its ugly head covering almost all of my right arm. Being unsure what it was all about or why I was feeling that way, I decided that some relaxation was required in order not to let my feelings show. Knowing how Frankie would not be impressed by any of my very negative thoughts about her boyfriend and there were plenty of them, wasn't altogether helpful for me. Situations which felt strongly negative to me always presented me with a challenge to overcome. I would find it pretty difficult to hide my true feelings around them. I could only hope the art of disguise would be effective on this one regarding the boyfriend.

Remembering Mikey, with his many troublesome ways and antics in the children's home made me almost shudder. Him threatening to jump from the window and the outcome of that, were the overriding thoughts in my head at that time. Wanting the best of everything for my friend Frankie, I did not believe that Mikey Rooney either could or would provide the best of anything let alone everything for her. I was also aware that she had made a choice and who was I to disrespect that choice. I needed to stop taking the moral high ground, get off of my judgemental ladder and try to dismiss my thoughts of Mikey's past. Perhaps a little easier said than done but my determination was high up there on the radar.

     Frankie's plan was that we should all meet up at Gerry's restaurant and what a great plan that was. Knowing all staff at the restaurant as well as she did, she was aware we would be taken good care of. On this occasion she had left nothing to chance. A table for 3 was reserved for 7pm on Tuesday the 6th of August 1985. Decisions of what to wear were minimised for me, largely due to my lack of desire to have an abundance of clothing in my wardrobe. Black work trousers matched up with a pale blue blouse, slightly heeled black shoes and I was satisfied with my choice. Gerry's wasn't posh and Frankie wasn't posh. I was therefore confident that my own chosen outfit would be up to scratch and meet their approval, not that I needed the approval of Mikey Rooney but felt the need not to let Frankie down.

     There I was again allowing myself to be quite judgemental. Questioning myself about the fairness of my strongly held view of Mikey, my head told me to be quiet and give the man a chance. Arriving 15 minutes ahead of the designated time I had always been one for being at the very least prompt and often ahead of the scheduled time. Weather was very good to us at that time. I sat with drink in hand patiently waiting on a bench outside under a deep blue sky. Keeping hydrated was important to me, so yes, I had brought my own already half empty bottle of water.

     Watching a black Mercedes car with that year's current plate pull into the car park outside of Gerry's, I could only think how it was all right for some and what lucky person owned such a magnificent car. It was very impressive looking. It was magnificent back in those days and in many ways, still is magnificent today. My eyes almost popped from my head at the very sight of Frankie Chigozie climbing out of the passenger seat. She was followed by a very smartly dressed young man from the driver's side. Our eyes locked as he came towards me.

"Well if it isn't Helen in the flesh- I never did know your last name, but what an absolute pleasure to meet you again as an adult."

Extending his arm towards me, we shook hands which felt a little bit bizzare in the circumstances.

"The feelings mutual Mikey Rooney and I'd recognise you anywhere. Apart from being older you haven't changed a bit in appearance and still seem to have that same charming and suave personality."

Frankie's cheeky grin which lit up her whole face, assured me of the pleasure which she had gleaned from our meeting. I had learned how to recognise her fake smiles – this one was not fake.

Many hours later and lots of information being shared, I had heard lots about Mikey's plans for the future. Having worked as a sales rep within a software company he aspired to build his own business one day. His levels of ambition surprised and inspired me too. Thinking how he deserved to hear my thoughts, I shared with him and Frankie.

"Great to see you building a good future for yourself Mikey and not letting the past define you and bring you down. It's very much to your credit."

His smiling face showed his regard and his gratitude for my comments. Turning to his girlfriend he spoke the words quietly almost like in a whisper.

"Told you how I would impress her Frankie and gain

her approval."

The idea of Mikey Rooney seeking my approval for anything in his life or about him, was quite bizarre in my head. Sharing that thought felt like the right thing to do. We laughed ahead of continuing with some conversation which would take us down quite a different road.

Frankie smiled her sweet smile again ahead of telling me how she and Mikey had plans to be married. The marriage would be happening before the birth of their baby.

"It's not because I'm pregnant Helen. You know when you meet 'the one' and Mikey's 'the one' for me."

"Wow your life's all coming together Frankie and you know I'll always be in it. I'll always be there for you well for both of you from now on."

Mikey expressed feeling a little surprised but deeply gladdened, upon hearing I would include him in that support, alongside an expression of his gratitude.

"Frankie's told me what an amazing adult you have become. Having you in my corner means an awful lot Helen." Smiling, I reached across the table to place my hands on theirs. Words just dropped down from my mouth something like water from a pouring tap.

"Not too many people can have shared our childhood experiences and become productive adults as we all appear to be."

Expression of my true thoughts surrounding their imminent marriage, would seem a little like I should perhaps mind my own business in the eyes of Frankie and Mikey. Accepting that all looked serene on the surface, it still felt a little rushed and hurried to me. Being proud of myself that I had stopped being judgemental, did not mean I shouldn't have feelings of cause for concern. Those thoughts were kept very much tucked away under my hat and would remain to be my secret. They would only ever surface if they're were to be an obvious need for that to happen.

Frankie smiled that all knowing smile as she continued to inform me, that their marriage would be a very small gathering at a registry office in York. She told me how Mikey's situation was very similar to hers in terms of family as far as he was aware. Plans were already in place for the ceremony. They would be married on the 24th of August that year. Their assumption was that it was a given that I would be present at their marriage ceremony. Frankie's place was a one bedroomed rented flat. They would live in Mikey's flat which was a little more spacious, whilst waiting to secure something better something a bit more upmarket. Forever the optimist and seeing the positive in everything, she eagerly told me.

"It'll be fine for the baby Helen. There's a small garden so how lucky does that make us."

A wonderful evening had been spent at Gerry's at the expense of Mikey Rooney. That's a memory which will be forever imprinted on my mind. It was the evening I met the man who would be husband to my best friend and father to her child. Date for their wedding came around very quickly. I often thought in general terms about the passage of time and if there was anything we could do to slow it all down. Knowing there wasn't I made my motto to be "live every day as if it's your last." That appeared to be what Frankie and Mikey were doing. A very small no fuss gathering was duly held at the local registry office. My lifelong friend Frankie Chigozie was now a married woman. She was Mrs Mikey Rooney. Climbing into Mikey's black Mercedes, the next step was back to Gerry's for a celebration meal. Frankie and Mikey aside from the posh car were both very minimalistic people. I couldn't help but wonder when and if that situation might ever change.

Having my own house with two empty bedrooms, my life was beginning to feel extravagant by comparison to my friends. Frankie, Mikey and their soon to be new born baby would all be hold up in a one bedroom flat. Thoughts about how we had all lived together for many years in the children's home, were swirling round and round in my head. Could we do it again? Should we do it again? Should I extend an offer to the Rooney's to come live with me whilst they waited for a house of their own. Knowing that Mikey's savings were mostly tied up in his posh car, I had choices which would ease my own feelings of almost guilt regarding my house in addition to helping them out.

Suggesting to Mikey that perhaps he should sell the car to raise money for better accommodation, I was sure would not be heard very well by either of them. Extending an offer for them to come live in my house was my other option. There was also a third option. Wondering if I maybe should do or say nothing also stretched my thinking. Was it really any of my business? Intuition told me that perhaps it was not. That's where my interference got left. Right there in my thoughts and nowhere else. Knowing my friend was an educated and sensible lady made my decision easier. Commending myself for the improvements I was showing, in not interfering in Frankie's life, just looking after my own affairs was a good feeling. I felt proud of my achievement. I was learning to accept that Frankie had chosen Mikey to be her husband. I was learning that matters such as those would always have to be between them, with the absence of any suggestion or any interference from me.

Knock at the front door I instantly knew who my visitor was. If there's ever such a thing as a signature knock that one was Frankie's. Having a catch up with all news exchanged we went for a stroll through the nearby woods. Walking in the woods always brought a very calming effect to any anxiety either of us had ever felt. Our focus which was partially being on the creatures of nature which were surrounding us, was interrupted only by happy and humorous thoughts. Frankie's smile spread from ear to ear as those happy memories came flooding back. She recalled our days in the children's home and how staff there, often took us out for walks through those woods. We reminisced about Mikey climbing onto the shed roof on more than one occasion. Remembering the fire service being called when as an 11-year-old he got stuck up a tree, brought us both to our knees in laughter.

Frankie laughed a loud belly laugh as she recalled the night when we were kids and the whole house was woken. Local police were once again searching our dormitories in the hopes of finding Mikey Rooney. When Mikey didn't want to be found he ensured that's exactly what happened, until the people hiding him had enough. Having been missing for 18 days solid on that occasion, I'm sure staff were very tired of his behaviour. I'm sure our local police were tired of him too. Eventually being dropped off outside of a police station Mikey gave himself up. Sharing with officers how he had hooked up with a scruffy looking man of whom he had no knowledge, his account of the time away was questionable.

Telling officers how they had travelled to Ireland together on a boat from Holyhead, the adult male had covered all of the travel costs for them both. Mikey had allegedly been convinced by the man that they were related. Whilst being welcomed at the traveller's home in County Cork, the child was assured there was no blood connection between them. He was returned back to England in care of the same traveller man. There was nothing of relevance to substantiate his story or disprove it either. As adults Mikey and Frankie have recalled that scenario. Truth being the Ireland trip had been a fantasy. Mikey had befriended a boy call Tom of similar age to himself. He had stayed there till Toms parents eventually had enough and took him to a police station. We considered how their ethics were surely questionable. In a light-hearted manner Frankie told me.

"Hope this behaviour doesn't come back and bite him on the butt Helen."

Always being up for a giggle we shared one at the very suggestion that it might and then my serious take on it all. Someone had to look at the situation in a serious manner and it wasn't ever going to be Frankie. Mikey had a polished halo. He could do no wrong in her eyes. Having the desire to sew the seed of doubt whilst not wanting to sound judgemental, I continued quickly before I lost the nerve and changed my mind.

"Everyone knows kids inherit traits from both of their parents. Unwanted behaviour isn't always learned behaviour but then you know that already Frankie."

Her expression told me it was time for that unfavourable topic to come to its end. Deciding that enough reminiscing had occurred for one day we planned a weekend together on the journey back home. Our time walking in the woods had passed without any mention or suggestion of any offer for the Rooney's to come live at my home. Still feeling it might be better if I stay out of their accommodation plans- that was it; Deciding to stick with the decision which I had previously made to myself would have to be the best option.

My early morning alarm was very loud. Neighbours complained that it could be heard far away. Perhaps a slight stretch of the truth there but yes it was very loud. If the decibels of Big Ben (Famous London clock) had never been challenged, then my clock was a change for that situation. Pulling open the curtain's and throwing open the bedroom window I felt like I was almost ready for the day and whatever it might present to me. A slightly chilled autumnal breeze with a very clear blue sky, brought hope for a little sunshine and don't we all love to catch the rays when we can. Coffee on the go and I was ready to leave for the hospital. Handovers could often be time consuming. This morning's one would surely be no different. Seven new admissions overnight was also the indicator, that no two days would ever be the same on the hospital wards. I loved it. I loved the variety.

Working as a charge nurse came with many responsibilities. As is still so typical of today's government, my pay cheque did not reward me for those extra hours and many areas of decision making, which had become part of my weekly experience on the wards. In fact, it did not and still does not reward me or others as it should have done, for working regular weekly hours. Never allowing that to be a deterrent for me in taking the extra responsibilities, I was glad to be the person I was. My rewards came from seeing what was a severely ill patient on admission, go home to their families with much improved mental health, combined with a good care plan in place, some weeks or perhaps even months later.

Being on shift and dealing with an especially troubled and challenging patient, wasn't altogether the best of times to receive the phone call from Frankie. She was almost frantic which was very unusual for her. Hearing her strained voice told me there was an issue. Experiencing excitement coupled with strong pangs of anxiety was making her situation hard. Her waters had broken. Mikey was out of town and not expected to be home until much later. She wanted me to be there with her. Her psychology training played no part in supporting her in that situation. Almost shouting the following words at me I wasn't sure I had heard them accurately.

"Helen, I know this is a big ask but I can't cope on my own. Can you help?"

She heard the silence in my voice. The few seconds it takes to think about a situation was probably slightly extended. Very much out of character for Frankie she was then snappy, inaccurate and quite unreasonable towards me.

"Doesn't matter Helen- I can hear you have priorities and surprise surprise I'm not one of them."

That was it- she ended the call quite abruptly leaving me almost speechless. Why would she ever think she is not a priority to me? What had I ever done to cause her to feel that way? I knew the answer was nothing. Almost ready to shed tears and then that little inner voice reminded me how I was stronger than that, I remembered to do some deep breathing. The inner voice reminded me how my friend Frankie was in a difficult situation and not behaving or speaking from a rational perspective.

Internal buzzer going off on the ward, was the cue

for delegated staff to leave when required to do so. No time for questions or discussion they had to run. As had often occurred, a shortage of qualified staff throughout the wards meant we had to pull together, in support of each other in emergency situations. This time could not be any different. How could I abandon my colleagues when I would not allow for them to do that? Double standards would be frowned upon in that particular circumstance or in any circumstance on the wards. Feeling how I was faced with the most awful dilemma my decision was that Frankie would have to understand. First babies often taking many hours to appear from the onset of labour, it was my view that time was on my side. Soon as the wards situation resolved and staff returned back to my ward, I would then cut my shift short and go to be with my friend. Calling her back to share those thoughts Frankie was in a better place in her head. Offering her apologies for her previous outburst I was reassuring that no apology was required.

Arriving at the labour ward of our local maternity hospital I took a long and deep breath in ahead of laying eyes on my friend. Considering her earlier outburst to me I had to be prepared for more of the same. Happy to see me she was well into labour and letting her feelings and thoughts be known. My thoughts of telling her don't be frightened of childbirth as drugs are an option for pain relief, at that point stayed firmly in my head. I couldn't help but wonder why mothers were given drugs to help with labour pain, yet nothing to help them through what often could be the long and lingering pain of motherhood. There would be no drug available when your heart might be breaking in 2 pieces or your frustration levels towards your children are so high you need to scream. Seeing it all in my patients over and over again, deciding to keep those thoughts to myself also felt the better idea at that point.

Time going by and Mikey still absent from the labour ward, she made her feelings known about that situation, to anyone who was prepared to listen. What was coming out of her mouth was very out of character for Frankie. In her circumstance to continue trying for a drug free birth was feeling quite senseless to me. Unable to contain my thoughts any longer, I reminded my friend how there would be no medals given out for her endurance. There would be no martyrs. No words were necessary to let me know her view on that comment. I knew her well enough to understand that her responsive look, told me she wasn't impressed and perhaps I should mind my own business. Signs of intense pain were etched across Frankie's face. Her very unfair annoyance with her husband was expressed with some great volume, but a lot less insulting on this occasion.

"Typical of him never here when he's needed."

That was a side of Frankie which I had never experienced before this day. I'm sure that in more rational situations she would have shown greater understanding. Some hours later with Mikey having arrived their beautiful baby girl had just entered this world. Frankie's anger towards her husband had faded away. That was the point at which I made my exit from the delivery suite. Leaving my best friend forever and her husband to meet their baby daughter together felt like the right thing to do.

"I'm off now Frankie. Congratulations to you both and you know where I am should you need anything."
Knowing Frankie would be in touch as soon as they were settled, I too looked forward to meeting their beautiful baby girl.

Enter Charlie Regan.

Community nursing had put me in contact with the same patients over a lengthy period of time. On occasions seeing them in clinic whilst other times it would be in their own home. One of my saddest and most harrowing experiences of doing a home visit, had to be an occasion when I was in attendance with a social worker. A dear elderly gentleman was suffering from the sudden and severe onset of psychosis. Being unsafe to be left at home his family had expressed grave concern. Overall purpose of our visit together was to arrange an urgent hospital admission. He was refusing to go. A social worker plus a mental health nurse or doctor were required to be present in order to enforce hospitalisation. Request put out for the nurse I drew the short straw.

"It'll be a good experience for you Helen were the words on the other end of my phone."

It was an experience I didn't wish to have. I hated that visit. Only positive outcome from it was the fact the gentleman was persuaded by me to go to hospital voluntary. That is always a nicer scenario for the patient and for their family too. I had on many levels enjoyed the continuity and the routine which community nursing had brought to my days.

Working on the wards of a Mental health hospital was at times pretty much a challenge for me too. However, I was never a defeatist. Patients on the wards came at a relatively fast turnover. Some having as little as a 1night admission whilst others might vary. That could be anything between 1 night and occasionally for as long as perhaps 3-4 months or even more, depending on their condition. Some would present with more serious mental health disorders and on occasions the use of psychical restraint might be required.

       Holding a senior charge nurse position, I would often be the person who would be the decision maker in those painful situations. Staff nurse calling me for consent.

       "There's an isolation situation about to be required can you support?"
Hearing those requests always sent my anxiety flying high. A huge responsibility was what I considered it to be. That action had to be a last resort in the prevention of self-harm to the patient by themselves, harm to other patients or visitors and or to ward staff. All 3 of those rules held equally priority and were rigidly adhered to. Always reflecting and questioning my reason for agreeing to a restraint, was something which I felt was very important. Going home at the end of the day always brought me a great deal of satisfaction. Knowing I had done my best for my patients and supported the nursing team working under my supervision, I could sleep better at night.

       Work calling me whilst being off duty didn't feel the best for me. Needing consent from a senior charge nurse to call in extra agency staff, was a regular policy of the hospital. Staff sickness that morning having reduced the rota by 3, the requirement for agency workers was imminent.

       "Sorry Helen it's not right as your off duty but you know how it goes, so no choice only to call you."

Expressing my consent to go ahead and make that call I also gave assurance I would quickly follow this policy up with NHS management. Having resolved their issue at that time in my view, was the equivalent of no more than placing a sticky plaster over a forever festering wound. The situation required a long-term official solution. Often not having sufficient staff to cover all shifts, held the potential to create dangerous health and safety issues on the wards.

It was a policy which required some change and was something which had held my interest for a long time. Calling a meeting with senior bosses within the health trust, I was instantly frowned upon by Amanda who was my immediate boss. Who was I to dare be so assertive and so forthcoming with my views, was the point where she was coming from. She did however in the name of professionalism dress up her words.

"It's somewhat unusual Helen for staff to avoid going through me in order to bring change to the wards, but you've done it so let's see where it goes."

My response was perhaps a little on the, what some might consider to be 'the cheeky side.'

"Knowing how you always like things the way they are surely equates to avoiding change and I want change, the wards need change, so c'mon Amanda let's move this forward."

Body language told me she wasn't overly impressed with my response. Knowing that on this occasion that the paddles had been removed from her boat, Amanda's choices in the situation were also removed. She was stuck with nowhere to go other than graciously attend the forthcoming meeting. I was and still am a great believer, that if you hope to ensure something happens in this world, there's often only one route to achieve that. It has to be 'to do it yourself.' I'm not sure that people higher up the employment ladder than Amanda, were too impressed either with my approach for getting what I believed the wards needed. There were plenty of whispers going around the wards from their senior nursing staff in surprise of my forth righteousness. The knowledge I would be scorned by some was like water off a duck's back to me. I pursued all aspects of my job with a fierce passion. Being quite outspoken, direct and when required forthright, there was very little that would hold me back where my work was concerned.

Having left no way open to them for denial of that need, they duly pushed my ideas forward for approval from more senior management. I hoped to have my suggestions listened to at top level and looked forward to seeing them implemented on the wards. We had a result with immediate effect from people higher up the promotional ladder. Moving forward whoever was in charge on any given shift regardless of their nursing level, were given authority to call agency staff should they feel it was required. Colleagues throughout the hospital both at my nursing level and below, expressed their gratitude for my diligence in following my head. For bringing about the change everyone except management had known would be a sensible move. Seeing that recognition of me in the monthly newsletter made it all feel even more worthwhile.

Christening of the Rooney's baby occurred when she was around four months of age. Catherine Ann were the chosen names. Being slightly surprised that Frankie went down the road of christening as she didn't have any strong religious views, I pondered on those thoughts and feelings. Mikey had no attachments to religion either which made it even more difficult to comprehend. When asked to be the childs godmother I did wonder if I should maybe speak to Frankie at that point. Express my thoughts. Our plan to meet up at the small coffee shop in town went very well. Catherine had grown since I last saw her.

"Wow she's getting so big they don't stay tiny for very long Frankie."
Smiling she placed the baby in my arms. It felt as though she almost thrust her at me.

"Here - you hold her I'll go get the coffee's in."

The feeling of that tiny little woman in my arms was amazing yet scary at the same time. Such a tiny and fragile creature was how I thought of her. Frankie was so full of confidence around the baby as was her husband. Both were usually very reassuring to me that Catherine was not fragile and how I could be a little less cautious when holding her. I wasn't too sure if I was or ever would be capable of that.

"I don't have your confidence Frankie. Me being cautious surely won't harm her."
Frankie would give me that knowing smile followed by

"Listen to me. I'm not putting my precious child at risk so loosen up a bit. She'll be just fine. You'll enjoy her more if your less stressed around her."

Feeling an extra surge of closeness to Catherine's mother we reminisced again. We had some laughs as we recalled events from years gone by. I felt that Frankie had been reading my thoughts about the christening and wished to assure me. Hearing from her how she and Mikey had a wish to give Catherine the best opportunity to choose her spiritual path in life, very clearly answered my unasked question.

"Becoming any part of any religion requires baptism or christening Helen. We do this now for Catherine then it's her choice as she grows older."

Hearing Frankie's reasoning from that perspective I could only see how thought provoking their reasons were. Knowing and understanding their motives for the christening, I was happy to go ahead and accept the role of godmother. That service occurred some three months later in a local Church of England. Frankie had done her research. They had chosen that denomination above a roman catholic, as the catholic church had too many rules and boundaries for their liking. All they required was a simple christening for their child- and not enrolment into a lifelong commitment of attending Mass every Sunday and every holy day. A short but lovely service which was attended only by the Rooney's, myself and a friend of Mikey's was over very quickly. The friend was there to take the role of becoming Catherine's godfather. The service was followed up by an afternoon and evening back at my home for some food and refreshment's. That was my christening gift to Catherine and to her parents.

Mikey's friend Charlie was a very handsome young man who had also grown up in a children's home. Expressing how he was feeling honoured to share the god parenting of Catherine Rooney with me, was a compliment which I was happy to take. Reminding him of their reasons for the christening of Catherine, he could then see there would not be much god parenting to do. Expressing his disappointment Charlies words were chosen carefully. With a cheeky looking grin on his face he told me.

"There I was thinking how that joint commitment would keep you and I in contact. I'll have to find another way

now."
Both laughing at how forthright this complete stranger was behaving, we enjoyed some further conversation. His speech reminded me of my own forthright and straightforward personality, when I wanted to make something happen on the wards.

  Sharing some stories of our experiences growing up as we all had done in children's homes, helped our understanding of the great importance of having parents and extended family when possible in your life. Charlies own upbringing was with the absence of any family input to his life. Never truly appreciating that loss when he was a child he could now see the value in that which he had never known.

  "Nothing and no one can ever match family life Helen. It's that feeling of being loved and cared for above everything else and that's what this baby has and will continue to have."

We each vowed not to let Catherine ever have any of the experiences which we had experienced in our childhood. We would always be there for her as a family irrelevant of any christening promises. Our vows to each other regarding Catherine, held higher importance to us than those which we had made in the house of god earlier that day.

  Charlie Regan appeared to be a true gentleman. Just like Mikey he also worked as a sales advisor for a software company. Business chat between the men pursued mostly by Charlie, consumed perhaps more than a fair share of our time together that day. Charlie's eyes opened wide as he shared with Mikey his sales figures for the previous year. Being invited to a senior sales conference the following month, he was excited at the idea of how many senior advisors he would come in contact with and what benefits that could bring to him.

"Mikey- you know how we have spoken about starting up together doing our own brand of something, well this could be the chance were waiting for. This meeting should give me some great ideas to help us progress with starting our own business."

Mikey clearly didn't feel like engaging too much in that aspect of conversation. His response was sharp if not almost rude and cutting.

"Yep. See how it goes and discuss on your return."

And then he changed the subject.

Charlies face grimaced from pure shock. Not being a defeatist, he continued with his line of conversation without a flinch or a hint of attempting to leave it there. Sense of embarrassment was felt by everyone excluding Mikey. Timing on Frankie's part was perfect although some might say it was a deliberate tactic. I know her well enough to confidently say that it would have been simply good timing. Her calling everyone to raise a glass to their daughter put something of a new focus on Charlies conversation. Reminding myself how it's so wrong to be judgemental of people, I couldn't help but quietly wonder if Mikey had pangs of jealousy regarding Charlies obvious success.

Charlie by now had some other things on his mind. His expression had changed to a look of almost curiosity. Calling me to one side and suggesting we stepped outside for a minute, I was intrigued. He indicated the need for there being some privacy required for what he wished to say.

"Not sure I want Mikey or Frankie to overhear. You know how protective she is of you."

Well I didn't know that but suggested he continue, as now I

was feeling even more intrigued. Stepping outside together to the garden almost felt rude. As though we were getting our heads together away from the Rooney's in a bad way.
Charlie had a very cheeky looking smile. He grinned widely as he quickly told me.

"I'm booked into an all-expenses paid hotel in Harrogate for a long weekend. I know it's not the usual chat up line for a first date, but here goes, come with me Helen at no expense to yourself."
Almost choking on my saliva, I took in a sharp deep breath.

"Wow you're not backwards at coming forwards are you Charlie Regan. I'll have to think about that one and let you know."
I was then shocked by myself for saying I would give his request some consideration. A man I had met that day and would consider a weekend away with him made me question my own sense of responsibility and my morals.

Not wanting to give me a total get out of jail for free card, he accepted my response ahead of him asking me for a date the following evening. Did I need time to think about that? No, I didn't. Deciding to show him some of the enthusiasm I was feeling I placed a soft kiss on his cheek and told him.

"Charlie Regan you're such a charmer and well yes it would be great to meet up again tomorrow evening."
Pulling me towards him we embraced ahead of going back inside. I knew this man wanted to get to know me. Would the feeling continue to be mutual? Only time would tell.

Ever changing plans.

Frankie's decision to return to the work place challenged her emotions and created some confusion for her. At nine months of age, she was aware that her daughter Catherine would potentially need or at the least benefit, from having her mother's attention as and when she demanded it. The other side of that coin, was Frankie's strong desire to put to good use the education which she had received. She battled with those thoughts however her pursuit of work continued. Sourcing good quality nursery care and not allowing herself to be guilt tripped by other mothers, were further challenges for her to deal with. She faced them in an admirable and enviable manner. Our phone conversation was quite in-depth. Frankie was very clear.

"I'll see how it goes with Catherine at the nursery. If she's struggling then that's the decision made. Work will have to go on the back burner. Have to wait for another day or maybe even 5 years."

Trying a little dry humour in my response with hindsight wasn't going to make a difference on that occasion. I almost dismissively told her.

"Frankie it'll be fine."

There being no facial expression for her to see, I realised my comment may have sounded a little harsh. Her firm and short reaction to that with equal coldness put me back in my place.

"Will it? Will it really be fine?"

And then she changed the subject. Her attention was being required by her baby girl or was it- I wondered? Hearing nothing except my friends voice it wasn't my place to question that. She wanted to end our call then she had her reasons, regardless to having shared the truthful one or not.

"Got to dash Helen. Needed here now and her feeds slightly overdue too. Come over sometime be great to see you."

Expressing a mutual feeling with a plan to visit that evening we ended the call.

Our first ever show of coldness in conversation between us had just occurred. The feeling wasn't one which I would ever like to experience again and hopefully wouldn't. Frankie's work was free-lance thus allowing a variety of scenarios for her. Deciding to provide her services four days per week stretching to five should the need occur, she found herself back in the midst of many cases within social services. She liked family work. Being part of the team and helping to establish what was going wrong within families, she often thought of her own childhood. Thought how it perhaps in some ways, put her in good stead for the career path which she had chosen.

Presenting her new logo idea within those family meetings Frankie suggested renaming of the teams. Her idea was that they should be known as 'Team Child' or in their case 'Team Yorkshire Child.' Everyone involved in the childs life should be included with no exclusions. Knowing how that would be a challenge to managers and social workers, who often to the detriment of the child, excluded foster carers from many of their decision-making meetings, frustrated her immensely. Frankie's determination was rigid. She would make that situation become a reality. She would make it happen was her motto. Presenting her case to management, she was clear and very passionate and very direct with her questions.

"Who knows the child best and who cannot work effectively with a child in the absence of certain information? Who are we setting up to fail by denying them knowledge? It's simple really. Either we trust our foster carers or we don't. If we don't then let's not have them in that role."

Knowing her points were valid, management made attempts to give what Frankie considered to be their unacceptable views to her suggestions.

Being assured that serious consideration would be given to her suggestions Frankie was not accepting of that response. She was assertive. Consideration would not suffice. She wanted commitment and she wanted it there and then and not after they held further meetings to discuss.

"It's sounding as though no one in this room has actually heard a word of what I've pointed out. The facts were presented with clarity. What is they're left to consider? I'm no longer prepared to be part of a team which excludes people who need to be included. You work with me in a respectful manner or you don't work with me at all."

Not wanting to lose her services agreements were made that her view should be upheld. There would be no further meetings with the absence of foster carers. Pleased with her level of success Frankie thanked everyone at the table. She then swiftly left the meeting.

Frankie had always held a strong desire, to help prevent other children and young people going through what she had endured. Memories of her own parents and their lifestyle would at times haunt her. Usually finding ways to deal with and manage those thoughts, on this occasion she was not successful in doing that. Causing me to wake suddenly the phone was ringing out. It was almost midnight. It was downstairs. I hurried. My heart raced almost as fast as I raced to get to the phone before the caller hung up. With fear in my voice I picked up the receiver to hear Frankie's uncontrollable sobs. I was in fear of hearing something pretty awful.

"Calm down Frankie. Stop and breathe tell me what's wrong"

Her emotions continued to run high with her eventually managing to get the words out.

"Everything feels like a very fast-moving train that someone needs to put the brakes on. I'm panicking about being back at work and leaving Catherine at the nursery. She cries every time I leave her. It feels like my thoughts are getting out of control and I'm really sorry to call you so late. I haven't told Mikey how I feel he wouldn't understand but I know you will."

Impressed by my friends' insight to herself- I was able to give her some reassurance. Knowing I'd have to be straight talking with her I was. Any deviation from that held the risk that Frankie might flip. Her flipping would be a picture darker than the clouds which would cause the heavens to open in biblical proportions. It would not be a pretty picture by any stretch of the imagination. Taking a breath so deep it was right from the pit of my stomach, I proceeded with a great degree of caution.

"I know that in some ways Frankie that it's a bit tough on Catherine going to nursery but that's just life. There's many positives around it too."

Initial deathly silence from a non-responsive Frankie, she eventually wondered if I had anything else to say? Again, I was very cautious with the words I used, whilst being honest at the same time.

"Learning some new things which maybe you don't have the ability to teach her, socialising with other babies, toddlers and adults all add up to putting something very positive into her days."

My best intentions backfired right back at me.

Frankie was by now somewhat argumentative which was rather out of character for her. My responses clearly did not have the desired effect. She began questioning why I thought she lacked the ability for teaching her daughter anything. Helping her to understand that I wasn't saying that at all, I took a gamble on giving her some further advice again with great caution and a degree of confidence.

"You'll probably be a better and more patient mum when you are home together with Catherine, after her days at the nursery. Try to remember that being a mother is learning you have strengths you didn't realise you had and dealing with and coping with fears which before motherhood, you didn't realise or even know that they were in existence."

I could hear that her breathing had slowed down and was secretly praying that my comments were being and would continue to be helpful for her.

Checking with me again if they were my honest thoughts, I reminded Frankie how neither of us stretch the truth where serious matters are concerned and it doesn't get much more serious than this. Providing a little more assurance to her, she was happy to hear it from me.

"Catherine will settle soon and will grow to love nursery. I know many mums who are educated as you are and also have a career. All saying the same thing- that they would fester if they stayed home through a sense of duty. I've seen it happen too Frankie and it doesn't make for happy families. The overall point being that if mum is unsettled then the whole family are unsettled and we both know that's the truth."

I could sense the continued calmness in her voice.

"Thanks Helen you're a great friend and as your aware you're my only friend. Love you for your openness and your total honesty."

Knowing that she was feeling more settled I expressed my final wish of the evening for her.

"May peace and contentment be forever yours Frankie just as much as it is already mine and it will soon be Catherine's too. She will settle down in nursery way faster than you can ever imagine."

Acknowledging my sentiment Frankie thanked me. Bidding each other goodnight the whole conversation left me with a feeling of satisfaction. Knowing how my input to her had settled her mind immensely, was truly one of my best feelings ever. A coffee before going back upstairs gave me time to ponder on my own life.

  Continuing to see Charlie Regan at least once weekly had left me wondering, where if anywhere our liaisons might be going. Several months of regular dating with no future plans, suggestion or request from him all felt a little casual for me. Secretly having fallen in love with the man the thoughts of my life without him was looking quite bleak. Having chosen to remain silent about that was becoming a struggle for me. The feeling that no words could explain what was going off in my head and my heart were probably the strongest catalysts for my silence. The busy day which loomed ahead for me, was going to swiftly remove any spare time for thoughts about Charlie. That was always a good thing. Anything which might prevent and stop me from the worry I was feeling in those days had to be good.

Charlie in my view was oblivious to my thoughts of any long-term future together with him. Wondering if that was just a man thing I had nothing or no one to compare him too. Grabbing my casual black trousers and white shirt I took a warm shower. Admiring my fully dressed reflection in the mirror gave me the tiniest of confidence boosts. I was marginally impressed. Coffee on the go and a short drive to the hospital, there I was sitting in the midst of the morning shift for handover. Three new admissions overnight saw our ward to be bursting at the seams. Night nurse in charge was compassionate in her view of daytime staffing levels.

"It's hardly fair Helen. Everyone's so pushed for their time with stress levels almost going through the roof. Surely we can do something to support more than we do." Sharing the woman's view I promised to look at it at the first available opportunity.

Many patients to be seen on the mornings ward round and some staff calling in sick, wasn't an extraordinary situation. It could however be considered to be a challenge for the best of us. My inner resolve would prevent me from panic and guide me towards the best solution to resolve the staffing shortages. Checking the off-duty list would be my starting point. Occasionally there were situations where people would be delighted with the opportunity of an extra shift or two. Pursuing those thoughts, I was quick to get three extra staff onto the ward that morning. The shift was exactly as I anticipated it might be. Almost chaotic at times managing Staff, coffee and bathroom breaks was a challenge. It wasn't an acceptable work situation.

Deciding with colleagues how desk only management would always struggle to understand our predicaments on the wards, decisions were agreed to call a meeting in order to permanently get higher staffing levels to cover all shifts. I was delegated the task of doing that.

"You have great people skills Helen. Remember your actions of previously going to higher management, regarding how we can bring extra staff to the wards on a casual basis. How you made that happen successfully. This job is yours without question."

Taking the compliment with the understanding it didn't come with the absence of extra pressure for me, I organised for a message to be sent out to all senior management. It was for the coordination of a day and time where we could meet collectively. The purpose being to give opportunity to discuss serious safety issues on the wards. Home time and check my private phone time came around fast. Back in the car I was surprised to see a message from Charlie. He wasn't overly fond of text messaging and used it only if the situation was very important.

"I know you can't take calls at work hence the text. Can I see you tonight for dinner? Usual place around 7pm. Let me know. I'll understand if you can't but hope that you can."

That was it. No clues at all given for this out of the ordinary behaviour from him. I was intrigued. Slightly short notice raised my stress levels somewhat. Was something wrong? There had to be otherwise he would not be texting like that. My acceptance response went at some haste through the airwaves to him.

Messaging Frankie was next on my agenda in the

hopes she might have some answers for me. Unlike me she could on occasions take private calls whilst on duty. Breaks in-between her clients were often spacious. This was one of those times. Her response to my text was very prompt.

"I've got time for a call Helen- what's up?"

Sharing with my friend the content of Charlies text to me she was as intrigued as I was, without any possible answers re why he might have done that. She was equally keen to find out if there was a problem.

"Glad you're going to meet him Helen. You know I'm here for you. Be sure to keep me well updated."

Girls being girls and us being almost lifelong friends that's exactly what I had planned to do. There wasn't and isn't much that Frankie and I don't share about each other's lives. Back home after my early shift at the hospital I had the need to shower without delay. Wrapping my long hair in a towel removed the need to shampoo and then a change of heart.

I almost shuddered as I recalled my patient whose hands hadn't said hello to soap and water for several weeks. Those hands had fiercely tugged at my hair that morning. I prayed I wasn't out of shampoo. Squeezing the last drips from the bottle I was left in hope of remembering to buy some more, next time I would be shopping. Time for a very quick nap ahead of my evening date with Charlie seemed like a decent plan. Eventually having decided which outfit to wear I was as ready as I would ever be. The drive to the venue was a little tedious. So many thoughts circling in my head and then reprimanding myself for not keeping my focus on the job at hand. Sudden flashbacks from Frankie's younger life and the car crash gave me a reality check. To remain focused would be my motto going forward. Feeling with some degree of certainty that Charlie would be presenting me with a 'dear

John' letter, taking a deep breath in I tried to regain my composure. A dear John letter would hold the meaning he would be ending things, ending what it was I thought we had between us. Why else would he suddenly want to meet up?

Watching Charlie strolling over the car park at Hales bar in Harrogate, I couldn't help but notice how very handsome he looked. Built like a rugby player is how I would describe his stature. His almost shoulder length dark brown curly hair whisked back from his forehead, was an immense compliment for his green eyes. My heart was melting at the very sight of him, yet I had a great awareness that I needed to be calm cool and collected. I was aware that I needed to prevent Charlie Regan from finding his way into my innermost thoughts. With some degree of trepidation I stood up to greet him. Acknowledging me with a kiss on the cheek he left me feeling even more convinced than before, that he was going to end our relationship and then discovering he was quite upbeat, left me feeling somewhat confused.

"You're looking great Helen. Scrubbing up well after an early shift too."

Taking the compliment, I sort of returned it with a cheeky grin. Trying not to let my guard down too much I told him.

"You're not so bad yourself Charlie Regan."

Pleasing the world with one of his fabulous smiles to that comment, we went indoors.

Fine dining at Hales bar was something we had often done. On this occasion and unusual for him Charlie had reserved a table. Appearing as though he hadn't taking any chances with tables highlighted to me the importance of that evening to him. It also highlighted my fear which I was working incredibly hard on hiding, with the suspicion that I was failing and perhaps making the situation easier for him.

Sharing very similar tastes in food we both picked the sirloin steak with trimmings. Ordering a bottle of a particular brand of red without consultation with me, I was aware how well the man knew my tastes. It felt as though cartwheels were happening in my head with the knowledge I had to outwardly remain calm. That challenge was rapidly becoming a much bigger challenge. Sign for 'The ladies' on the bottom corner wall encouraged me to make my excuse and go. That's where I had opportunity to do some deep breathing in order to calm my anxiety and calm my thoughts.

Why Charlie had made the plan for us to meet up at Hales restaurant still held no clarity for me. End of our evening together almost upon us and still not a word of explanation as to why he summoned me there that evening. With no disclosures being made confusion almost consumed my mind. That scenario had left me even more convinced that he would be ending things with me. Convinced that him being nice to me was his plan for the big build up, in the hopes I wouldn't take it all too badly. I was working on my acceptance with dignity.

Conversation throughout the evening had covered many aspects of our lives in a general sort of way. Charlie had shown particular interest perhaps more than usual, in my work situation. Our evening together being almost over, attempting to secretly read his thoughts by process of elimination questions to him, was futile. There was only one thing left to do so I did it. I relented and raised the topic which was driving me crazy. I would hopefully in a convincing manner, let him see that his absence in my life would be of no real consequence to me.

"What's up then Charlie. I'm guessing your ending things with me so don't worry I won't make a fuss. I'm not like that and It is what it is."

Charlies eyes opened wide. He was as confused looking as I was feeling.

"Ending it with you. Oh, my goodness. No Helen. Never! On the contry!"

Charlie went on to say how he had brought me to Hales that evening in order to share his future plans. I could only wonder that as we had sat there for almost 3 hours and it now being almost time to go home, why had he not raised that throughout the evening? His response to my unspoken question surprised me.

"I'm a little nervous Helen-No actually I'm a lot nervous sharing this, hence putting off speaking about it. I've been working on a side line for a few years. Got some interesting ideas from my weekend away plus the offer of a job working abroad for two years. My request to you and my hope is that you would come with me."

Hearing all about the job offer and how it might work out brought my eczema to the surface again. Anxiety usually did that to me and yes, I was anxious. Thrilled I was wrong in my thinking he would be saying goodbye to me, yet it could be goodbye dressed up in a different fashion, depending on which decision I made. I can't say that I was not tempted there and then to accept his request that we move over to Portugal together. Having visions of potential obstacles was that which created my hesitancy. How would I ever tell Frankie that I'm leaving? How would I tell work that I'm leaving? How would I find work in a foreign country? My head was spinning again. With all else I had going on in life what little space had been left in my head was now fully occupied. The whole scenario had filled me with confusing thoughts. Knowing I had to make some response I gave it my best shot. In the hope I wasn't sounding to self-consumed or to anxious. My tongue went into overdrive reminding me of a small child, not getting their way and putting up protests.

"Sounds amazing Charlie but what about my lifelong friend and what about my work. Have you even thought about either of these things not to mention me finding work in a foreign country and my house what about my house? And what about Mikey and his plans for you both going into business together? You know the plans I'm talking about. The ones you made with Mikey. This feels awful letting so many people down and especially Mikey. He's your friend. How would he feel hearing this is what you're now planning to do?

Charlie smiled that calming yet annoying at times smile. On that occasion it felt annoying to me that he could be so laid back, about a situation which would potentially create so many problems. A sudden lean forward with arms outstretched he took hold of my hands across the table. He was reassuring. Mikey will get what he wants if he still wants it. He had considered Frankie and her family too. There was another factor pointing towards how well he knew me. He knew that leaving them behind would possibly be an obstacle in my way. He cared enough to have thought that through.

"It's not permanent Helen unless we decided we want it to be. Frankie and her family could come to visit. Free accommodation for them. I'm confident that Frankie and Mikey would be delighted for us. I would ensure that Mikey understood how in the long run, this could be a benefit to any potential business we set up together."

Almost sounding ungrateful I questioned Charlie. And my job at the hospital Charlie what happens about my

job?"
Whilst having given that subject some thought, Charlie shared how there was no immediate resolution to that which he was aware of. Hearing that Charlie Regan was in love with me, that he wanted me in his life, wanted me to share a life with him, was more than enough for my brain to absorb that night.

"Charlie, I'm not sure how this has happened but I'm in love with you too."

Another one of his amazing smiles and we left Hales bar holding hands. Back in the car park he took me in his arms. Assuring me that I was all he wanted from life we kissed and embraced.

"Think about the move Helen. I have to let them know by the end of the month so we have three weeks to reach a decision. That's with the view of moving at the end of the following month. I'm not doing it alone. Not wanting to pressure you or anything but I feel like I'm nothing without you. I need you in my life and by my side."

My reaction to his statement had to be visible without the utterance of words from me. I was shocked to have heard Charlie say that. Making promises I wasn't sure I could keep wasn't my style for doing things. Wanting to give him what he hoped for and being able to do that, felt like 2 situations which were miles apart from each other for me. My attempts to be as reassuring as anyone could possibly be in the circumstance weren't the greatest. It showed in his face.

"I'm not sure I could do this to our friends. I'll give it some deep thought Charlie. I won't promise anything which I'm not sure I can honour."

Deciding to leave it there for then we kissed and embraced

again. Eventually having said goodnight I followed his car out from the car park going home our separate ways. Sleeping that night became a major problem for me. Pacing the living room floor early hours my head was pounding. Having gratitude for a few days respite from work I was able to disarm my alarm clock and over sleep without worry.

My planned lunch time meeting at Gerry's restaurant with Frankie, had given me some time to consider the best way to raise the very sensitive Portugal topic with her. Having chosen a weekday for our catch-up meeting, gave me some reassurance that her daughter Catherine would be at nursery. I would be on a day off. There would be no pressure of time for either myself or Frankie. Arriving first I watched anxiously as she approached the front door. Sweaty hands and spotty arms were both there in abundance for me. Having greeted my friend and made our food and refreshment selection, Frankie was eager to hear about my recent date.

"Come on then. What was so urgent with Charlie? I'm bursting to know. Out with it."

Frankie was always so straightforward and direct. That was my honest held view of her going as far back as I could remember. When we were kids in the home, staff regularly commented on how straightforward and direct she was. Same as when she went through therapy. It was like her trademark. This time wasn't going to be any different. Knowing I would hear that question from her and having thought about how I would handle it, everything I planned to say had by now escaped my mind. Only one option left open to me. I let the whole story just drip off my tongue in a disorganised manner. Impressed by my honesty Frankie complimented my straightforward and direct way of sharing such sensitive information.

"Were two of a kind Helen. Get to the point and stick to the point."

Pulling herself further back into the chair whilst arching up her back, said to me that she was preparing to be on the defensive. That vision of her reminded me of my neighbours' cat. That's exactly what it does body wise when preparing for a cat scrap. I often intervene so as to prevent the cats being hurt. Knowing I couldn't intervene in my situation with Frankie wasn't the best of feelings. After a short silence and some breaths in she told me.

"Sharing that can't have been easy for you Helen. Your considering reneging on all the promises we have ever made to each other and the men going into business together."

At that point and much to my surprise, almost shock, Frankie stood up. She picked up her coat and walked out of the restaurant. I was left high and dry. Truth being I would probably have reacted likewise had it been the other way around, so yes, I understood. Remaining seated in the hopes she would come back in, some minutes later she did. She was apologetic.

"I'm sorry Helen for my selfish and over reaction. I know we are always good no matter what. Sure, you'll be worried about our friendship and the men's potential business. Me walking out like I did won't have helped with that worry. But don't be."

The smile on my face would have shown her my sense of relief at hearing that.

To say that Frankie continued verbally to be supportive of Charlies thoughts and ideas would be a large understatement.

"You need to do this Helen. You should enjoy the whole experience of Portugal. We will still be here when you come back. Do remember that regardless to where we are in the world, that our friendship will always withstand the test of time and distance. That's just a given."

Her words melted my heart and were reciprocated. Pushing back my chair away from the table Frankie did likewise in order for us to embrace. She continued with a loving and caring tone in her voice.

"So, it's a done deal then and I'm so happy for you. Come to ours tonight with Charlie. Give him your answer then and Mikey can hear it too. Straight from the horse's mouth as it were."

"It's not a done deal at all but now with your input and your blessing what can I say?"

"You can tell him it's on. Tell him you're going to Portugal and that I'm so jealous, well envious."

Saying goodbye, I watched Frankie go back to her car with a tear in my eye. Knowing how she would secretly be worried about Mikey's reaction to this adventure, she put those feelings to one side. Again, that was a reminder for me of what a special friendship we shared.

Calling Charlie to plan the evening gave me a great sense of excitement. Speaking about the Portugal trip I hastily gave him my decision. Expressing his delight, he assured me.

"You won't regret this Helen. Trust me I'll make sure of that."

I did trust Charlie otherwise my decision would have been a different one. Having arranged to meet him at the Rooney's at half past seven that evening my advice to him was to bring a good appetite.

"Frankie gets very carried away when they have visitors. Presenting enough food to feed the whole of the human race when there's only two of us and she'll never change in that respect. Maybe that's a slight exaggeration but seriously speaking she does provide big dinners."
Charlies response could be seen as a humorous one or some might say a cheeky one.

"Let's bring containers and a bag let's see what she thinks to that idea."
Ending our call, it was then a quick dash to the bathroom for me.

Charlie liked and appreciated the natural look in a woman. No glamour required for his benefit. I didn't care very much for or have any desire for glamour either. Preparing for the evening would be an easy task. Indulging myself with a cat nap that afternoon and early evening I was left feeling quite refreshed for the night. Arrival at Frankie's shortly after my boyfriend I was greeted at the door by Mikey. You could only consider how very smart and handsome looking he was and still is. Mikey was certainly blessed with good looks and a physique to match. My secret thoughts which would forever be my secret, were that Frankie was a very lucky lady.

Our contribution for the evening was a bottle of white wine and some sweet-smelling flowers for the flat. Frankie loved flowers especially colourful chrysanthemums. Going into the winter months they were largely out of season. Being ushered into the dining area our pallets were woken by aroma coming from the kitchen. Complimenting Frankie on her efforts our words were graciously accepted. The size of her heart was surely replicated on the dinner plates. It was as I expected it might be. She presented us with a large three-course meal. Mushroom soup followed by a huge fillet steak served with new potatoes tossed in melted butter with herbs. There was a side dish of green beans and finely diced carrots sprinkled with cut up shallots and spring onions.

Frankie was never one to cut corners when entertaining. Dessert was a choice of homemade strawberry trifle or homemade apple pie with warm custard or ice cream. True to his word Charlie presented her with some food containers ready to take home any leftovers. With his handsome grin he shared with everyone.

"Don't believe in waste Frankie. I'll fill them before we leave."

Recognising his humour Frankie gave him some back.

"Thanks Charlie. These will fit nicely in our freezer."

Expressing his appreciation to her for a fabulous meal they giggled. Seeing how we all got along so well together was a good feeling. It was a solid platform upon which to share the news around the Portugal invitation.

Catherine having settled to sleep ahead of our arrival, gave the Rooney's the space and the time to entertain which they deserved. On the whole she was a well settled baby who was meeting all of her milestones. Watching her grow and develop like you might expect brought great joy to her parents. Having a good sleep routine worked well for all of them. Frankie by now had lost the feeling of inadequacy as a parent, which had been created by her desire for and by her return to work. Enthusiasm showed in her face as she told me.

"It's working great at nursery Helen. So glad I made that decision and thanks to you for your valuable input to it and helping me to see the light."

Dinner eventually done Frankie insisted we leave the pots. Decision was made that we should retire to the lounge with wine, cheese and biscuits. 'More food.' I thought I would burst but be rude to say no. The Rooney's flat was small but compact. Their lounge area was cosy with a small sofa, two arm chairs and a television in the corner. It felt amazing to me how people can manage in confined spaces when they need too. Catherine had a toy cupboard in her bedroom. Frankie was meticulous about storing all toys and books in their rightful place which was in the toy cupboard. She shared how.

"It's the only way to keep this small room free from chaos. Finish playing with it and it's put away instantly."
Thinking how that too would be great training for Catherine as she grew older, I praised my friend for her tidy mind which hopefully would overflow to their child.

"You've seen my bathroom and my bedroom Frankie. Everything has a place and nothing in its place. I could learn from you."
She giggled as did everyone else. Ambience in the room was good.

Charlie had been very disciplined regarding the sharing of his news about moving to Portugal. That was typical of him as per our evening together, when he told me at the last minute and then only after I asked why the urgency to meet up that night. Sitting on Frankie's sofa I quietly weighed up the situation. Deciding Charlie was maybe uncomfortable telling his friend, I considered reminding him he had something to share. At the very point of me thinking maybe I should give a reminder, Charlie began the work-related conversation. Being a person who was sceptical about the idea of telepathy at that point I wasn't too sure of my scepticism.

      Mikey suffered a setback upon hearing Charlies news. His reaction was quite visible on his face and in his body language. Excusing himself for needing the bathroom had been his way of taking a moment to recollect his thoughts. Back to the living room he had a little tone in his voice.

"What about our plans to unite in business and what about Helen? Where does she figure in all of this?"
Flattery felt almost overwhelming for me, in the knowledge that Mikey would be selfless enough to consider my place in Charlies plan.

      Hearing the full story and how Charlie and I would return back to England after the two-year period, it all felt more palatable to Mikey, however he was still worried which showed in his tone. With a degree of humour and a level of solemnity too he told his friend.

"I'll be planning whilst your away Charlie. Looking for some office space for the high fliers we're going to become. It's been our dream and we'll make it happen. Just don't ever forget our plan for that."
Assuring his friend there would be no forgetting their plan I thought how Charlies expression was telling me otherwise. Deciding that only time would tell I kept my thoughts as just mine. Evening having come to its end our plan to meet up the following weekend was put in place. Putting together our ideas for leaving England, was something which now required our full concentration.

      Planning a two year stay in Portugal's capital city, we knew was never going to be the easiest of tasks. In fact, it was going to be something of a challenge for both Charlie and myself. Having Frankie's undisputed support gave us the confidence that she would iron out any fears, which Mikey might be experiencing in terms of his potential private business together with Charlie. Starting point for me was to inform my employer of my decision to go abroad. Despite holding a good position in the work place and the ways in which I had asserted myself there on previous occasions, my behaviour was not consistently like that.

I wasn't always the most confident of people when it came down to meetings with management and people higher up the ladder than myself. I then remembered the meetings I had secured with higher management within the health trust, regarding safety issues on the wards and the need for extra regular staff. Having formed those meetings and successfully gained what I had requested for the wards, I knew I could do this too. Knew I could make it happen. Requesting through the ward clerk that I be given an appointment with the chief nursing officer, my request was granted for the following day.

Preparing myself to have that meeting brought me a few tummy flutters, with eczema appearing again out of the blue. Working in mental health I was very aware of the signs of anxiety and some ways to help counteract that situation. Taking a long relaxing bath ahead of my meeting to serve my notice, eventually I was ready to leave the house. The journey there was something of a mixture of anxiety and confidence in equal proportions. Car parked up near the hospital gave opportunity to have a short walk with time for a coffee too. Being well known in 'Katie's' the coffee shop, my order was always so predictable.

"Having a crafty one today Helen ahead of your shift"

Not wishing to share my plan and not wishing to lie either, a simple smile and the cost of the coffee was all she got back from me.

Walking the lengthy corridors of the hospital once again, for my appointment on this occasion with the chief nursing officer, my hands were beginning to tremble slightly. Eventually being stood outside the door with the shiny plaque saying 'Tom Chesterton's office' I knew there was no turning back at that point. I took some deep breaths in ahead of knocking the door. Deep breathing was something which usually worked for me in those tense situations. Being invited in I was then warmly greeted and in a very gracious manner by the officer.

"Good to see you Helen. I don't think we've met before but your reputation precedes you. I'm Tom Chesterton. How can I help you today?"

Despite being helped to feel at ease by the man's comments, my brain was still doing very fast cartwheels. It was on overdrive. Wondering how he was assessing me at that moment and I knew he would be assessing me, as it went hand in hand with the job, I could only hope he didn't sense my anxiety. I couldn't help but wonder what reputation he was speaking about. I wished he would quickly elaborate and put me out of my misery. What was probably no more than 30 seconds felt more like a week to me. He didn't say another word about that. My trembling hands began to slow down a little. I had to decide from his question that there was no room for the exchange of niceties. Just like my friend Frankie, he appeared to be very straightforward, direct and to the point. I followed the man's lead.

"I'll get to the point then Tom. I'm going abroad for two years so I'm here to hand in my resignation.

"I see."
And then quite a lengthy pause. It seemed lengthy to me but perhaps was no more than half a minute at the very most till he spoke again. Trying to fathom what was happening in his head proved to be futile for me. Suddenly he spoke with interest in his voice.

"Tell me more."

Can't we always tell when someone's genuinely interested or simply going through the motions. With just those 3 words I knew his comment was genuine.

Hearing about Charlie and his adventure out to Lisbon kept his interest. He commended the man's spirit. He highly commended mine too acknowledging how difficult my decision had to be for me.

"Your brave Helen your both very brave taking this chance. That's exactly what it is. It's a chance but your both young so your chances to succeed are greater."

Sharing how I held the same view Tom could see that naivety was not something which I was suffering from. Expressing my thoughts regarding potential employment in Lisbon he pondered momentarily.

"I've got an interesting idea- something which may be of benefit to you."

Tom shared how he had knowledge of a clinic out in Lisbon. Management from there had approached our health trust. There's an opening for a 2-year secondment and hoping to take someone from England. He wondered if that might be of any interest to me?

"It could be a good opportunity for you Helen. Your job here would be safe for when you return in two years' time."

Everything felt as though it was moving so fast. Head was

racing. Did I want to make commitment? Tom continued to tell me how there's another staff member interested in this secondment.

"My view is that you would be the best candidate. Let
me know by the end of this month. If you want it then the decision will be that its yours."

That being a lot of unexpected information to absorb my 1st reaction was to simply smile. Not knowing how to respond to the suggestion, I assured Tom I would give his offer my full consideration and get back to him with my response within 24 hours. Ending our meeting and saying goodbye to the gentleman I paid a visit to my own ward within the hospital. Not scheduled for duty that afternoon staff were pleasantly surprised to have my presence. Placing a freshly made coffee in my hands I was simultaneously told.

"It's great you're here Helen. Staffing shortages on all wards today- we could use extra hands."
Thinking how there was no escaping and feeling as though I was being rail roaded, what was I to do in the circumstance? Yes, I surely allowed myself to be roped in. Wouldn't you have done the same?

Offering four hours of my time was graciously accepted by the staff nurse in charge of the morning shift. She was still there working in the afternoon. That was a regular occurrence throughout the whole of the hospital. Matching me up with a new patient admitted overnight who was on round the clock observation, I felt like I was being useful. Despite being something of a higher rank than the nurse delegating to me, her request and guidance had to be adhered to. That would be the best manner in order to get the best value from my time, with the best outcome for her patient. Getting value for time combined with best patient outcome was something which I had instilled into my staff. The nurse was grateful for my support. Informing me of the hourly rates I would be paid she had a compassionate tone.

"Thanks Helen you will already know from personal experience how much this means to me and to the ward. I'll be sure to add it to your hours for overtime rates. It will be at staff nurse levels and not your usually salary rates."

Overtime rates as a rule wasn't something which I was accustomed to being in receipt of. My nursing grade commanded my presence outside of normal shift hours, as and when the need arose. This time would be an exception to that rule due to me not being on shift duty in the first instance. My 4 hours worked on the ward in a different role to my usual one, was very eye opening for me. Experiencing and seeing the level of responsibility felt and just how hard staff had to work in those 1-1 situations, my mind was made up.

Without question I would be going back to visit senior management again. Would be advocating for a pay raise for staff at all nursing levels. My message, my concern, needed to be heard by all colleagues. Communication books on the wards was always an efficient way to spread news. My intentions to take the task to senior management were clearly outlined in there. Time for home and with two days annual leave ahead, my plan was to spend some quality time with my boyfriend. Opportunity was lending itself for discussions, regarding the best way forward in planning the trip out to Portugal, including my offer of secondment. Charlie would need my utmost support in planning this move. Whilst being a successful business man, organisation skills was something with which he had never been blessed with. Something which he hadn't been at the front of the line for.

Frankie called whilst I was on shift at the hospital. Hearing how I was roped in for a few hours on the ward, she was aware of the need to keep the phone call short. Direct to the point she requested.

"Come on over tonight Helen if you have time?"
Always wanting to make time for my lifelong friend I was there at six that evening. Spending some time with Catherine ahead of her bed time gave me great joy. She was growing so fast and would soon be a year old. Frankie was so confident and so relaxed around their daughter.

"Put her down Helen- just there by the sofa and watch what happens!"

The girl sure had her mother's determination and her spirit. Walking, well perhaps more shuffling herself along holding the sofa, was what Frankie had expected me to see. To our surprise she let go from the sofa and went heading towards her mother. Catherine presented us with her first independent steps ahead of falling to the floor. It felt something like a monumental moment to us both. I was given the honour of fulfilling Catherine's bedtime routine that night. Tucking her in tightly at her usual bedtime she fell to sleep almost immediately. Tiptoeing out of her bedroom and across the landing I heard Frankie's shout for me.

"Come on down now Helen. Catherine has time on her own before sleeping and its good for her. It's in her interest."
Hearing that their daughter was already sleeping I was jokingly complimented on my nanny skills.

"You've got the magical touch Helen she always takes a good while longer to settle."

Frankie's culinary skills were as always second to none. She loved fish as did Mikey. I loved fish too. Aroma oozing out from the kitchen would have you feel you were by the seaside. Oven baked seabass with new potatoes and salad was enjoyed by all. Sharing some information with Frankie regarding the idea of a potential secondment, it was her view that I would be wrong not to take it.

"You'll have plenty to deal with when you arrive in Lisbon Helen. Not to have the worry of securing employment would be such a stress reliever for you and for Charlie too." Acknowledging her thoughts about Charlie and the stress levels it would have been hard to disagree.

"You'll come visit I hope with Mikey and Catherine." Frankie's response was full of enthusiasm

"Try stopping us."

Looking ahead and sharing those thoughts with Frankie raised my levels of excitement. Who'd have known the way our lives would turn out from the days we had grown up together in the kids home. That period of our lives had seemed by now to be so much in the distant past. Bidding goodnight till the next time we embraced. Strolling back to my car my head was a mixture of sadness and excitement. Knowing that seeing Frankie- would endure long breaks in between those visits, had caused my anxiety levels to rise somewhat. Having awareness how that was probably going to be common place going forward for the 2 years. I had to find better ways to exert control. Taking it into manageable levels felt rather like a priority.

Back on the wards after some days annual leave a visit to Tom Chesterton's office had been scheduled by me. This occasion it was minus the stress and anxiety associated with our previous meeting. He was welcoming and professional. Hearing my decision to accept the offer of secondment Tom assured me that there was nothing left for me to do, other than turn up at the Portuguese hospital on the agreed date. In anticipation of my acceptance Tom had prepared some paperwork which he handed to me. It was an English-speaking hospital staffed mostly with English speaking Portuguese people. Maps were included in the paperwork. He would be in touch to liaise with the final plans. I had the need to express some gratitude.

"Agreeing to go out to Portugal with Charlie felt exciting yet stressful at the same time. You have taken that stress out of the situation for me Tom. You have my deepest gratitude and I won't let you down. I won't let the trust down."

Accepting my gratitude, he jokingly told be

"Be off with you and enjoy your life in a foreign land."

Having said goodbye and closing that office door behind me I was feeling as though I was 10 feet tall. The child within me was oozing with excitement making me want to skip along the corridor, a sensation I refused to act upon. Knowing how I was thought of and appreciated at this hospital, was just the best feeling in the world. Knowing I was good enough to be considered for and then offered that secondment in Portugal, was a considerable boost to my self-esteem and to my confidence in my nursing abilities.

Despite Charlies many ways and attempts of expressing his denial about this, he was a person who worried about significant aspects of his life. I therefore looked forward to sharing my news with him which I knew would brighten his day. Not being working on the wards for a terribly long time I was surprised to hear reactions from nursing and all staff, in relation to my fairly imminent departure.

"You'll be missed deeply Helen. You've brought something special to our days on here. Its good that you're going on secondment as opposed to leaving. This supports the idea of your return for which we're all very grateful."

Taking the compliments, I was as girls can be. I was emotional and allowed that to be on display. Tears welling up I made attempts to keep it all under control. Sudden outburst on the ward brought my emotions to an end. Being called to assist with a challenging situation was the diversion my thoughts needed at that time. Offering my support as required I did wonder if Portuguese ward policies might resemble ours.

Charlie called. A brief chat and then plans were put in place to meet up again that evening. Once again, we found ourselves back at Hales bar. Food and refreshments order given to the waiter we sat looking at each other with wondering eyes. I was encouraged.

"Come on then Helen you look as though you might have something to say. I'm sure it's interesting as is always the case."

Sharing news of my secondment with him, brought a great sense of relief to Charlie as I knew it would.

"That's definitely interesting and reassuring. One less thing for us to worry about."

An admission there from him that he was capable of worry as shown by his use of the word us and then in the next sentence he diluted it to cause for concern.

"Leaving your position here and you then finding one of equal responsibility in Portugal, felt like quite a cause for concern to me."

Excluding Frankie, I was not accustomed to having someone, anyone care that deeply for me. The feeling was a nice one. I had the desire to share my appreciation of that with my boyfriend.

"Thanks Charlie it's great to be feeling loved and to know someone's in my corner as I am in yours too."

We held hands across the table.

Returning to work the following day my colleague took the call. It was there in the communication book. I was summoned back to see Tom Chesterton with an absence of any explanation why. My heart racing from anxiety I was convinced the secondment plan had now fallen through. Catching up with the colleague I was informed that his message for me was very reassuring. There were no concerns to be worried about. He had some information which potentially might hold interest for me. Being agitated and intrigued at the same time I did my breathing techniques. Hoping lessons might be learned from my reaction to reading the communication book, the 5-minute meeting I called for with all staff ahead of ending my shift was well attended. I looked at and discussed mistakes relating to any and all information shared in our communication book. Reminding staff that.

"Written handover in the book should be so detailed, that it would allow the next shift to pick up where we left off. Don't let my situation this morning repeat itself. As a team all of us are better than this."

My concerns were duly noted with an all-round affirmation it would not be happening again.

Responding to Toms message I left for his office. Making my way down that corridor did not create the same stress levels as did my first visit to him. I was welcomed warmly. As what was usual for him he was direct and to the point.

"Great to see you again Helen now let's see."

I waited patiently with curiosity as he shuffled through the pile of paperwork on his desk. Thinking how his desk was a bigger mess than mine I kept that thought where it belonged. Eventually he pulled up an envelope. Smiling broadly, he told me.

"Ah at last here it is Helen. It's from my colleague who runs the clinic in Lisbon. Dabbling in real estate has been a hobby for him for the past few years."

Laughing as I told him how I wished I had the available finance to dabble in real estate, he did likewise whilst expressing the same sentiment. I then heard how his colleague has a 2 bedroomed house becoming available shortly and how it's in reasonably close proximity to the Mental Health clinic. He wondered if it might be of any interest to myself and Charlie?

Wondering what else could happen to make my day get any better, I knew there was nothing. That was it. I expressed my gratitude firstly to Tom and then to the Lord. Not being an especially religious type of person, I did nevertheless hold some beliefs that there is a god who looks out for all of us. This was great news. Saying my goodbyes to Tom Chesterton and feeling excitement like a young child might feel, I almost skipped all the way back to my ward. We were sorted. All that remained was to have Charlies approval of the house. Calling him to share information my call was quickly interrupted by a ward emergency. Deciding the news would have to wait for a face to face meeting between us, I pondered out loud on his possible reactions. Colleagues

were surprised hearing the words coming from my mouth. Laughing to themselves at the same time I heard them ask
"Chatting to yourself again Helen?"

Feeling appreciative of the many friendships which had developed for me on the wards, I could only wonder how it will feel when I no longer have that friendship circle. When I'm the newbie and in a foreign country too. How that might feel. Was I having 2nd thoughts or was this the way of thinking that should be expected. Remembering how my work friendships never extend outside of work, helped to put the whole thing in perspective for me. Reminding myself how this will be a short-term adventure where new friendships will hopefully develop on the wards, I called a short staff meeting at the end of my shift. Informing the group of my imminent departure and the plan to live in Portugal brought mixed reactions. Some were a little indifferent whilst others showed their care and concern.

"Sure, you will be missed Helen and missed a lot. Are you certain it's what you want to do? It's such a big step?" Reassurance given that I have carefully thought this through and spoken to Tom Chesterton to serve my notice, helped to ease people's concerns. Hearing information regarding the secondment together with the house offer, allayed their worry and fears. Expressions of my gratitude for their concern were warmly offered by me and much appreciated by my colleagues.

Blessings received from various ward staff my next step was to share my news of the house offer with Charlie. Calling him back again we arranged to meet up that evening back at Hales bar. I did quietly wonder that if in our heads, Hales was the only place in existence in Harrogate. There were many other fine places where we could have chosen to dine, however we appeared to have a pull back to Hales bar every time. Considering how we were currently keeping to our comfort zone highlighted that continuity was important to us both. That thought in mind did place some doubt on our forthcoming adventure to Portugal. Quickly clearing my head, I waited patiently for Charlies arrival.

   Hearing about the house brought some smiles to Charlies face. He looked incredibly handsome when he smiled. His eyes would sparkle and light up. Often secretly thinking how fortunate I was to be his other half, then realising my own self esteem wasn't all that great and required to be raised. I too matched up to making a good other half and needed to remember that fact. Needed to remember my value and my worth. Charlie like myself was a very modest person. Rarely seeing the actual beauty in himself my conclusion was that he too required to discover ways to raise his self-esteem.

   Sharing with him my view of having our accommodation sorted, how it was one less thing to worry about and to arrange. It was a good feeling knowing that all that remained to be done was to book the flights. A trip to our local travel agents occurred that weekend. Flights being arranged for the following Saturday week the whole scenario was by that point feeling very real. Duly informing Tom Chesterton of Charlies approval and our decision to take the house, his smile showed his delight and his comment showed his respect for my experience on the wards.

   "Be sure to stay in touch Helen. We need you back here when the secondment period comes to its end. The wards won't be the same in your absence and that's not meant to guilt trip you. This experience will broaden your nursing experience immensely and then all of us, our patients in particular will gain expertise care, from your knowledge gained whilst you spent time in Portugal."

Acknowledging all which he had said with the promise to return, hopefully with some new knowledge, I also expressed how much I would miss everyone and miss working the wards here. I had to throw a joke in too.

"It's been great here Tom. Initially coming for interview was a big step for me. This now feels like a bigger step but one which I'm looking forward to, with a determination which would be hard to be matched by anyone. Oh and no pressure from you then in your last statement to me."

We both shared a laugh. Hearing my sentiments Tom Chesterton stated that he was right behind me. Ensuring me that he and the whole team had shared those sentiments about me too.

"You're just a great nurse Helen and a great advocate for others. We have every faith in you and your abilities."

I was then provided with full details of what was going to be our new home for the forthcoming two years. Thanking Tom for his support with this transition abroad, we shook hands as he wished myself and Charlie all the best in our adventure.

"Have a great experience both work wise and fun wise. See you back here in 2 years."

Leaving his office for the last time for the foreseeable future I turned once more at the door.

"Thanks Tom. Till the next time."

And I was gone. Taking in all which surrounded me I knew I would never forget the man or the place which was offering me this great opportunity in life.

Life in Portugal.

Never having lived together with my boyfriend presented me with a degree of cause for concern to say the least. Being difficult to know what Charlie was thinking of the forthcoming living arrangements-It wasn't something I was or would have been comfortable asking him. I was concerned that maybe he hadn't thought about it. Knowing how it was going to be such a massive change for both myself and for him, left me feeling what some might describe as a little anxious, or should I say perhaps more like being full of trepidation. Having spent occasional weekends away with Charlie this surely was going to be quite different. My plan was to keep those thoughts to myself. There we were on our way back to Frankie and Mikey's again. Some would say that their home was a 2nd home for us.

Sharing our house news with Frankie and Mikey they joked.

"You're the sort of friends everyone needs. We're on the next flight out there – we'll be right behind you."
Time spent alone with Frankie opened up opportunities for me should I have a change of heart, to share my thoughts and concerns which I did. She was analytic of the whole situation as I knew she would be. Reminding me how I was in love with Charlie and he with me allayed some of my fears.

"Don't over think it Helen. When we do we can ruin good situations. This is a good situation so just run with it and

see how it all irons out. My money says it'll all iron out just great."
Knowing she was most likely right I nodded in agreement and then a change of topic. That was the thing with myself and Frankie when a conversation was done to our satisfaction it was done and onto the next one quickly. No going back as nothing more to be said. It's just how we were and for most of the time we still are.

      Catherine Rooney's sudden presence in the room grasped our attention. Scooping her up into my arms I was taken by surprise. On the edge of feeling almost overwhelmed and not knowing why that was- I shared my thoughts with Frankie. Telling her how I wasn't sure what was happening with me at that moment didn't seem to make a difference. Me being a qualified Mental health nurse who should have all the answers, yet I was panicking for no reason well no reason that I was actually aware of. My thoughts were then diverted to Catherine.

      "Wow she's growing fast Frankie. She's so heavy. I'll miss her when we leave for Portugal. I'll look forward to your visits. You will come out to visit us there - won't you?"
That statement to Frankie was perhaps an answer to my own question of why I was feeling almost overwhelmed?

      Despite me giving her instruction and a question all in the same sentence, the smiles on Frankie's face were enough confirmation for me, that yes, they would do that and very soon. Her smiles were followed up by an instruction to lose my lack of self-confidence and enjoy the time with them whilst we still could. Dinner in abundance was provided by Frankie once again. Seeing Catherine enjoy her mother's home cooking my thoughts were racing. A mixture of almost elation when considering our Portugal adventure, clashing with might we one day become parents ourselves absorbed my mind. Playtime with Catherine and then time for a bedtime story again. At her request I was to be the story reader that night. Bringing out the best of my maternal instincts was something which Catherine did with a total lack of effort on her part. She had to be, yes, she actually was the dream child. I was hooked in my thoughts.

Charlie pacing up and down in their tiny garden was a sight to behold. Looking anxious as he moved over in front of the kitchen window, I caught glimpse of him wiping his brow. My anxiety was heightening at the sight of him. This was not like the Charlie Regan I had got to know. It was hard to figure what his problem might be. Appearing to be speaking to himself felt like another slight cause for concern. Being privately summoned outside by him felt very intriguing. Some might say he was almost bordering on being rude. Knowing how there was very little we didn't share with our friends, I was anxious to know what this was all about. He was true to himself to the point.

"You know me Helen and my ways of no great gestures to anyone for anything. I'm hoping you'll accept this request.

"Let's get married before we go to Portugal?"
I could feel the heat rising up through my cheeks. Hating the thought of blushing raised my anxiety levels. Surprise from his unexpected request filled me with uncertainty. Was he serious or was he perhaps just joking?

Charlies gaze was a very serious one as he made the request for a second time. Confirming speaking quietly to himself earlier, he was making attempts at putting some words together. Something that would look something like a decent proposal and then feeling that he failed abysmally.

"Jeez Helen I'm getting worried here I thought we were rock solid. Will you marry me or not? Let's get it over with?"

Self-confidence was pretty low for me when it came down to boyfriends. Requesting a little more time to think and then changing my mind again, I agreed to us getting married.

"I was shocked Charlie. Your proposal came out of the blue. Thinking you were joking was my first thought. Now I know you are serious. Yes, we are rock solid and yes, I will marry you so stop panicking."

Charlies mumbled proposal was now almost becoming an argumentative situation between us. Taking hold of his hands my attempts to help him to stay calm were successful.

Suddenly Charlies eyes just beamed with delight as I'm sure mine did too. Squeezing me like the world was coming to an end we then went back inside to share our news with the Rooney's. Charlies excitement was very obvious. As stated previously by him there's never any great gestures. It's simply out with it as he thinks the situation through whilst speaking.

"There's a plan in place. Meet the new Mrs Regan to be."

That was it. That was the Rooney's told we would be getting married. Our friends were equally excited and delighted for us. Frankie's response was delivered with almost a quiver in her voice. She was emotional.

"I just knew it. I knew it would happen. Couldn't have heard news that would make me any happier. We embraced. The men shook hands as men do and then they too embraced. No fancy arrangements or wedding plans to put in place other than the legal aspect of it all. Two weeks later we were all down at the local registry office.

That was the day which witnessed us become Mr and Mrs Charlie Regan. Sharing exactly the same scenario as Frankie and Mikey with them being our witness, it was a joyous occasion. Back to Gerry's after the ceremony for a no fuss meal with our friends and that was our wedding day done. Having her first experience of a non-religious registry office marriage, Catherine Rooney would have the visual evidence of that event as she went through life. Avoidance of any confusion on my arrival at the hospital in Portugal was important. Informing Tom Chesterton of my marriage was therefore a necessity. It was the only way to prevent that confusion with names. Accepting his congratulations and good wishes for the future-It was once again till the next time.

Day of departure for our new life in Portugal looming over us, there were some final checks to be made. Reality for us was that we were now doing this. That a new adventure, new beginnings had beckoned us. Suddenly it was both exciting and almost terrifying at the same time. Charlie could sense my anguish. He attempted to throw water on my already well ignited flames.

"It'll be all right Helen. Bound to be nervous at this stage and look if it's not working out we can just come back. We're not shackled to that 2-year secondment. Like you'd tell me-deep breaths in and all that."

Showing appreciation for his understanding we embraced.

Eventually the morning to shut the door of my home for the last time, for what would be a very long time was upon us. We were travelling light. Having grasped the opportunity of a special deal with flights, we were leaving for Portugal a little earlier than expected. The morning of our departure saw an extra visit sneaked in to see Frankie, Mikey and Catherine Rooney. That's when we once again said our final goodbyes. Leaving by train for the airport we boarded that flight from Liverpool to Lisbon International airport with some sense of trepidation. Despite being with the man I loved my tears flowed. Feeling a huge sense of sadness that morning Charlie was quite reassuring.

"It's natural Helen. Despite us wanting to do this It's still a great deal of upheaval for us both, but it'll be fine you'll see."

Sharing my husband's thoughts, we began to settle into our flight. A first time flying for us both, it was mixed with some excitement and some more feelings of trepidation. Hearing the pilot's mid-flight message to fasten our seatbelts didn't altogether fill either of us with confidence. Onset of turbulence as we floated through and above the clouds, sent our blood pressure racing. Charlie gripped my hand so tightly my fingers almost snapped. Trying to gain some perspective on the situation didn't and wasn't going to work either. To say that we were nervous passengers would be something of an understatement. Turbulence suddenly stopped as quickly as it had started and what a great sense of relief.

Arrival at Lisbon International airport also brought us a great sense of relief due to being back on ground level again. Having decided that aviation travel would never be a favourite for either of us, we were relieved to know that no more thinking had to be availed to it for the following 2 years. Regaining our composure ahead of disembarking from the aircraft the feeling was almost overwhelming. The Portuguese airport was big and it was clean. Bedlam of it all felt a little daunting for us both. Public facilities were refreshingly clean especially considering how it was such a large place. We were fascinated by how modern looking the whole place was. Collection of our luggage completed, we were then greeted outside arrivals lounge by an English-speaking staff member from the clinic/ hospital where I would be employed. Seeing our names on the held-up placard felt almost surreal. It was a reminder if we needed one that we were now a married couple. Being driven to our new home which was a 3 bedroomed apartment and not the 2 bedroomed house which Tom Chesterton told me about, it would avail us of more space for guests. Situated in the midst of the area of Saldanaha, the country side views looked very impressive in the sunshine.

Position of our apartment was very central to all of our needs. Our closest coastline being roughly 15 kilometres away it was the furthest of all amenities which we would require. My place of work and Charlies too being the closest to home at 2 kilometres and everything else a distance somewhere in between. Having all that information ahead of leaving our homes in England was beneficial. Wanting and hoping to enhance our levels of fitness our decision was made. We would walk the short distance to and from our place of employment as much as would be possible.

Having rented out my home in Yorkshire to colleagues from the hospital, was one thing less for me to stress about. The two-year lease with a tenant signed agreement insured that mortgage payments would be kept up to date. Charlie for various reasons not being so fortunate, renting out of his flat would need to be done from our new home in Portugal. Being very aware of the power of my own words I was cautious in my reaction to him in regards to his lack of organisational skills.

Eventually getting some response from an estate agent back in Yorkshire Charlie was relieved of his property on a 2-year rental lease. Hearing from his estate agent how his tenants held a significant interest in the purchase of his home, he put his suggestion to me.

"Selling would probably be the best option Helen. We could live in your house on our return and use the money from mine for high days and rainy days? What do you think?" I didn't think a view from me in regards to his home would be appropriate.

"Your flat Charlie so your decision."

Continuing to seek input from me regards a potential sale, there was the feeling he couldn't make that decision on his own. Reluctantly I gave my view in more detail. Thinking it was a sensible idea which would be hard to disagree with, the deal was verbally done between us. Extra reassurance given to my husband that his suggestion made sense he was quick in getting back to his agent's in England. The wheels for a sale were put in motion. Having a joint bank account for daily living plus separate accounts for savings since the wedding, our money would be split between us. Tenants who had taken the 2-year rental lease were delighted to now be able to buy instead. It was a win win situation all round. Soon there would be significantly more money in our bank accounts which would not be touched at that point in our lives.

Life in Portugal was blissful with some trips taken out to Paternoster beach. That was largely where our level of interest lay. There were many water sport activities nearby making it the ideal spot for the tourist who held that kind of interest. A variety of restaurants sprawled along the coastline and further inland too was a delight to behold.

Despite at times having packed up a picnic the restaurants were somewhat irresistible. Natural beauty of the ocean combined with some breath-taking hilly walks in the area, lent themselves to burning up our excessive calorie intake on those days out. Enjoying some great experiences at Paternoster beach memories were being made to take back to Yorkshire.

      Taking in the absolute beauty of the country which we were living in, became almost a daily event for Charlie and myself. Free time after our days' work would find us out and about on our trips for discovery. At times taking a tourist guided trip around Lisbon and surrounding area, we were never disappointed. Both of us holding a keen interest in architecture, we could not leave Portugal without the experience of seeing some of its ancient castles and medieval cathedrals. So many historical places of interest to visit in Lisbon we were being spoiled for choice. One of the most memorable of those places for myself and Charlie, had to be the Museum of Geology of Portugal as seen on the following page. It was quite difficult to find but proved itself to be worth the long search. Looking very humble from the outside the inside is telling us a very different story. Having remained unchanged over the years its the home for thousands of fossils, rocks and minerals.

Isn't it a beauty to behold.

        Another of our favourites was again not the easiest to find. Being snuck in between other buildings and not very impressive at all from the outside, St Catherine's church- Igreja Santa Catarina, could so easily be missed. I'm sure it sadly will have been missed by many. Once inside Charlie and I were in awe of its magnificent interior. Simply breath-taking was our opinion of the building. Information shared inside highlighted to us that Saint Catherine's church shows some of the most beautiful baroque decorations in the city of Lisbon. Having a stucco Rocco ceiling, it was considered to be one of the best in the whole of Europe.

        Paintings by some of Portugal's top 18th century painters hanging in gilded frames adorn the side walls. We were informed that this church was one of the few monuments to have survived the earthquake of 1755. It shows a very strong example of Lisbon's wealth in the 18th century. Plain on the outside as seen in this picture below. Beautiful on the inside as shown on the following page. Its natural beauty can be quite breath-taking for the tourist. I know it was for Charlie and I.

Delighted with our own patience and perseverance to search for and discover such beauty, this church is a picture neither of us are ever likely to forget. Back in Yorkshire we had never encountered anything quite like this architecture, which we were now experiencing in our new but temporary homeland. Emails home to Frankie and Mikey encouraging their visit, were steeped with information about the beauty which surrounded us. Promises were made to share our new-found visions with them both once they joined us for a vacation. Some of the church's interior beauty is shown on the following page.

A close up view of the beauty of the ceiling.

Charlies enthusiasm relating to architecture which we were surrounded by was greater than mine. Wanting to see more and do more was beginning to become his priority over work. Needing and receiving some timely reminders from me of the reasons why we were there in the 1st place, usually quenched his thirst to be out and about more. Taking in the culture of the country we had found ourselves living in felt like an absolute joy for us both. It was a privilege which perhaps not too many would have experienced. Evenings would usually find us hanging around our own area. Having made some casual friendships at the clinic with Portuguese ladies, they became welcomed visitors to our home and us to theirs. Experimenting with traditional Portuguese food we discovered how lunch was the most important meal of the day for Portuguese people.

    Restaurants always having the provision of a varied fish menu, they would be found baking up catch of the day or perhaps making fish into some other more exquisite meal. Beef steaks would usually be served with fried egg on top together with fries. We discovered how a fish dinner would be finished off. Thin strips of beef steak, marinated in garlic sauce and served on a bread roll were automatically brought to the table. The idea of eating beef after a fish dinner held no appeal to either myself or Charlie. Our surprise was that after trying it we could see how it worked. Charlie was upbeat in a mood for suggestion making.

    "Let's surprise Frankie and Mikey on our return. Serve them a fish dinner followed by beef as we've just enjoyed, then watch for Mikey's reaction."
Smiling being my response I wasn't too sure how Frankie would appreciate that combination either. Portugal being a multi-cultural country, diversity was seen and experienced in very many of its supermarkets. Combining our own cultural foods with Portuguese and some other cultures too, made our dining experiences very interesting at times.

Weekends usually found us out and about exploring our new place of residence. One of our most memorable has to be the full day Sintra guided excursion. Being described as the most romantic area of Portugal, Sintra presented us with views which looked as though they belonged in fairy tales. Paying a visit to many of the former castles like the ones on the following pages had to be our favourite. Our trip ended with a drive along the beautiful coastal area of Cascais. Taking in the sea breeze finished off our trip to perfection. Here on the following page are a couple of the beautiful places we took our friends to see and enjoy.

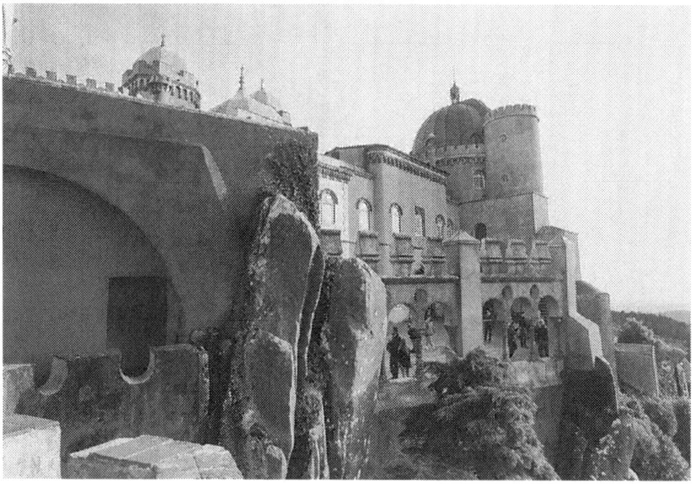

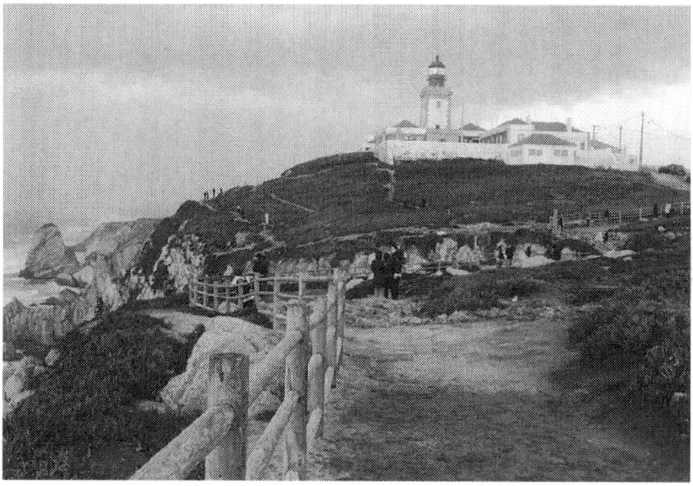

Learning about the culture of Portuguese people was both exciting and enlightening for myself and Charlie. Discovering how they place higher importance on religious values, than those in many other countries felt surprising to us. Their view that relationships and people are much more important than time, thus rendering punctuality to be of far lesser importance than we viewed it to be, was also a new experience for us. It was important to the Portuguese people that the rule was respected and adhered to. I couldn't help but wonder what might the situation be back in England, if the nations people adopted that same rule regarding punctuality. That aspect of the Portuguese culture worked well in favour of Charlie. Always be late for everything was his signature mark. Portuguese traditional music known as Fado was something else we enjoyed having the experience of. This combined with the many styles of folk music can always be found at the countries many festivals. This style of dancing and music is typical of rural areas from Portugal mainland and from the islands too.

Colleagues from the clinic where I was employed arranged for us to attend some of the country's finest festivals. People having fun was just a joy to behold. Other traditions we were exposed to were the Portuguese handicrafts with specialities in ceramics, tapestry and glazed tiling spanning many centuries of history. On the following page you can see some pictures of a typical church exterior and a public building, both having their walls adorned and decorated with tiles. Traditional ceramic tiles which can also be found in many homes in Portugal, adorn the interior of these public buildings.

We were taken on an escorted trip. It was a visit to the museum of embroidery and crafts In Villa de Conde by some colleagues from the clinic. Being around a 4-hour journey from our home in Lisbon, there was much beauty to be seen in the vast countryside of Portugal as we travelled. Making it an overnight stay we set off very early morning. Being driven with canopy down under a bright blue sky and enjoying a traditional Portuguese picnic our arrival time was right on schedule. That's where we saw some bobbin lace textile art as shown on the following page. Some designs were very characteristic of coastal areas, with all requiring hard work and dedication to put it all together. Those as seen on the following page were favourite pieces for myself and Charlie.

Having the experience of seeing shanty towns and being deeply moved emotionally by that vision, is probably a memory which will stay with us both for a lifetime. Seeing the many corrugated iron huts which appeared to be inhabited mostly by people from Africa, made me wonder if they were perhaps illegal emigrants. Laundry hanging out to dry adorned the outside of their small walls, as did tin and iron pots and pans hanging next to the laundry. Despite that vision of what I could only describe as being one of poverty, I was amazed to see how many of the adults and children living in that scenario were so very well dressed.

People walking about minding their own business became quite a curiosity to me. Watching them in branded designer clothing and footwear was not a rare sight.

However, that did not mirror they're living arrangements at all. Having conversations with some who had made their home in the shanty town was very enlightening for us, well perhaps more so for me. We were informed how real estate was financially rewarding the occupants to move out, in order for them to build hotels for tourists. The plan wasn't working greatly as many were taking the money, moving out with a related family moving in immediately. That was the money which financed their modern dress code. Below is a typical view of some Shanty towns we walked through. Charlie initially being unable to see how people were 'using the system' his heart was breaking for the occupants of those huts. Wanting to part with our hard-earned money was high up on his priority list. That was one situation throughout our time in Portugal where I had to keep a tight rein on the purse strings.

Working at the clinic was a whole new experience for me and one which I am glad to have had. Meeting and working hand in hand with a clinical psychologist brought me some new experiences and many great challenges. Perhaps the greater of those, was the fact I learned that we need to give people permission to suffer. Permission to be upset and to be in varying degrees of distress as they process their difficulties. I learned how its mandatory to suffer in some situations and how we all need to understand that. Frankie came to mind in relation to the time she lost her parents. Had anyone given her permission to suffer or had they simply got on with meeting her psychical day to day needs. It's probably the latter due to her need for therapy as an adult. I learned how helping and guiding people into ways of overcoming their distress, had to be much further down the line for them. I learned how that should only occur after they had experienced their time of pain endurance, in the hope they would then be open to the ideas put forward to assist them with their distress.

Learning about what a dictatorship country Portugal had been was interesting for us both. Hearing many stories about how is was opposing to communism, to socialism and to many other groups, the regime was very defensive of Portugal's traditional Catholicism. Discovering how its citizens suffered under that dictatorship, gave me greater understanding of the importance of free speech which the country now enjoys. Welcoming our Friends, the Rooney's, to our new place of abode was an exciting time for all of us. Progressing through the evening we discovered that Mikey and Frankie, just like ourselves ahead of our residency in Portugal, had little to no knowledge of historical Portuguese dictatorship.

"It's a lesson in life for us Helen. Makes us realise how fortunate we are in England with us having free speech. Let's hope our country never goes down that awful road of dictatorship."

Raising a glass to that wish we continued to enjoy the evening with the Rooney family.

Seeing many changes in their daughter Catherine, brought the realisation of how quickly children grow and how easily we can miss their milestones. Taking our guests, Frankie, Mikey and Catherine on some day excursions put new meaning in all of our lives. Just like ourselves the full day Sintra guided excursion was their favourite too. Introducing them to Portuguese cuisine perhaps wasn't the best decision we had ever made. Mikey having a desire for basic English cooking tolerated but did not especially enjoy anything on the restaurant menu. Making his choice he shared his thoughts.

"Maybe you cook for us next time Helen. You know me and my boring ways when it comes to food."

Ahead of their return back home Frankie in particular was anxious to hear about our plan for a return back to England. She was however cautious how she gained that information from us.

"I'm feeling that your both quite settled here. Hoping you don't desert us and don't desert Yorkshire for the eternal blue skies."

Our conversation at that point endured a long pause.

Despite me being on a 2-year secondment and Charlies job being for a 2-year period too, we both had given some serious consideration to setting up our permanent home in Portugal. We were not yet ready to share those thoughts with our friends. Frankie appeared to become a little impatient with our lack of response.

"Taking your time there Helen in answering my question."

Keeping our totally honest feelings to that question to ourselves felt like the best option at the time. Thinking there would be very little to be achieved in giving out news which we were feeling unsure about, was the main reason for our hesitancy. That was especially true if it was going to be news which might or most likely would cause a degree of upset and distress. How would I tactfully and truthfully explain that to my friend, who would easily recognise my transparency.

I was very cautious how I expressed my thoughts without expressing them honestly. Knowing how myself and Frankie had a pact about honesty the situation presented me with a challenge. With a silent wish that I would not be transparent I gave my response. Answering my friend with careful thought, knowing that should we not return to live in Yorkshire, we would at the least be there for holidays so no direct lies were being told.

"Who knows how life might turn out for any of us Frankie. We can never predict what it hides and has in store for us. We're taking it all a day at a time and maybe we'll be back before you know it. I'm feeling it won't be too long till we touch down on Yorkshire soil again."

Charlie remained silent. To say I was impressed with myself for my quick thinking would be an understatement.

Again, that initial smile simply lit up her face which showed a degree of acceptance of and belief in my comment. However, there was a sudden change in her acceptance. Frankie's doubts in what I had said had started scratching away at her thoughts as did Mikey's. Mikey's protests began regarding the plan for himself and Charlie to start a private business together. Wanting to placate them both but Mikey in particular, Charlie gave assurance that we would be home at the end of 2 years as planned and that their business plan was solid. Mikey's response was short.

"That's reassuring Charlie. Thanks."

Annoyance or perhaps more a surge of anger towards my husband, for not thinking as I had done raised my stress levels so much, it brought my eczema to the fore with an instant sense of vengeance. Arms and legs begging to be scratched, my will power with a great sense of resistance came into force again. Annoyance with him for placating them with solid assurance that all would be just fine, I knew was a futile emotion for me and one I wished I had not experienced. Knowing how the spoken word cannot be retracted, the only thing left for me to do was to agree with what Charlie had said. Tactfully changing the subject was my best plan at that time and deal with him later. We would address the situation further down the line, should we decide to remain in Portugal to live.

Driving our friends back to the airport that night was quite an emotional journey. Having said our goodbyes till the next time with everyone acknowledging how fast their 2 weeks holiday had gone by, we watched Frankie and her family go through departures lounge. Despite that journey being emotional, now being absent from their company in the light of Charlies blunder, it also felt something of a relief. It left no time availed to them for further questions or discussions regarding our return to Yorkshire. The drive back to our apartment was mostly a quiet one. Parking up roadside we enjoyed some refreshments. Eventually through a degree of his frustration Charlie broke the silence.

"You did real well Helen by not confirming our

return in 2 years. I let you down and I'm sorry. Not knowing how else to handle what they were saying I just blurted out what I knew Mikey would want to hear."
Understanding how the reality was - that Charlie had been put on the spot I shared that thought with him.

"I get it. You're not close to Frankie as I am. I'm forever alert that she's panicky about our return. Work related situations also make it easier for me to think on my feet when the situation calls for it. I'm well practiced."
Taking my hands in his with care in his voice

"I'm lucky to have you Helen. As I've told you before I'm just nothing without you."
We embraced with assurance that it was the same for me.

Three months remaining on our contracts in Portugal, our thoughts were pushed along. It gave us the determination to explore as much more as was possible of the country. Many hours spent sitting on the beach in addition to the many other experiences we had and would continue to have, would make great memories for us in our later life. Charlie's burning desire to see more architecture would be fulfilled. We had plans which when executed, most if not all of our wants would be fulfilled. Through discussion with colleagues at the clinic my position was made clear by them. They wanted me to stay. Should I wish to take up a permanent role the job was mine.

"You've proved yourself Helen. This clinic has learned lots from your presence. You'd be a real asset long term."
Flattering as it was I had to keep it real in my head. Expressing appreciation for the offer of permanency and not wanting to appear rude, I gave my assurance of my consideration for their suggestion.

Colleagues having previously enjoyed the experience sent some invitations. A whole weekend at a spiritual retreat deep in the forest in Quinta Alada held lots of appeal for us both, but perhaps more so for myself.

"We should do it Charlie. Be a memory to take back to England if we ever go back there. I'm intrigued by the idea of spiritualism and would love to learn more."

Collected by a colleague and her husband early on a Saturday morning, we sped off through the streets and roads leading into the forest. An amazingly enlightening time was spent there over 2 days. Having had a safe place created for us it was easy to then open up and share. It was not however my idea of spiritualism. That was something I planned to research and pursue in later life.

Charlie changed his mind about a long-term business plan in Portugal, as often as the British weather changed from rain to sunshine. With due thought and further consideration from us both, the plan for a permanent future living in Portugal was finally aborted. Sharing our decision with my colleagues at work, disappointment was the feedback I received throughout the clinic. Knowing how much I was appreciated by them I was able to return the compliment.

"All which I've learned here and there's been plenty, I will take back to the wards of the hospital in Yorkshire. Believe me it will be appreciated and thank you to everyone who has made me so welcome. Made the Portugal experience the best it could possibly be for myself and Charlie. Neither of us will ever forget you all."

That being my final day at the clinic a small tea party was quickly organised and put together.

"Can't let you go Helen without a "what is the British way of saying things?" Oh yes, its bottoms up. As we're in a work environment we can drink tea instead of wine."

Colleagues from the clinic gathered together in their staff room. We ate sandwiches and cake and drank tea in abundance. It was a traditional English send off. Waving me off from their front door, I was glad to know that my tears were for "my eyes only."

Back in England

Having had such a great Portuguese experience we both had the same thoughts of how fortunate we had been in having that. Now with the completition of our two-year deal, in the country which had brought us so much happiness behind us, we packed up our belongings, said goodbye to our neighbours and took a flight back home to Luton airport. Leaving sunshine behind we touched down in Luton to quite a foggy and damp late autumn evening. Despite the great experience in Portugal and despite the weather here, it was feeling good to be back on English soil. Gave us both the feeling of belonging which we now knew we could never achieve in any other country. Taking a taxi direct to Frankie's home we remained there for an overnight stay, ahead of moving back into my home the following morning. To say that the Rooney's were delighted to see us back on Yorkshire ground would be an understatement. Frankie was quick with her analogy.

"We all know the expression never say never. Been trying to avoid it in my head in terms of you 2 not returning home. But here you are and it's a wonderful feeling."
The compliment was graciously accepted and reciprocated by myself and Charlie.

Catherine was by now very vocal and very able to express herself quite clearly. Hearing the message from her that she too was happy we were home, I had to decide how that was not child speak. Listening to her parents and what was probably their private conversations, she greeted us with what felt like a very well-rehearsed.

"You're here at last and worried you wouldn't be." Frankie knew me well enough. She knew I would know that was not child speak.

"She's been listening to us Helen so there you are. Our secrets are no longer sacred. Have child no longer have secrets."

Everyone laughed including young Catherine ahead of her tootling off to another room, repeating have child no longer have secrets. Despite Being tired and been given the job of tucking Catherine into bed, once again she brought out my maternal side. Reminding myself how I had to proceed with caution I would keep those urges well under control.

That great energy shared between myself and Frankie had not left our friendship at all. One of her special 3 course dinners, a few glasses of wine and we were set for the night. Charlie joked about the night he arrived at Frankie's with empty containers for leftover excess food. Conversation between the men went smoothly without a hint of work discussion. Mikey Rooney much to our surprise was especially interested in our overall experience of life in a foreign country.

"I know we've been out there to visit you Charlie but that cannot equal the experience of living out there."

Hearing some of our experiences of the Portuguese culture and how we participated in an awful lot of it, I got the sense that his appetite for travel was perhaps a little more awake than had previously been the case.

Sharing with Mikey how that's a conversation to be continued another time and wanting to draw the night to a close, we decided to do that imminently. The sharing of more memories from our foreign experience and hearing the Rooney's experiences over the past 2 years would have to take their place on the back burner. (Wait for another time).

"It's so good to be here Frankie but needs must. Finding travelling awfully tiring I'm all washed out. Come on Charlie Its bed time for me at least."

Looking relieved by my suggestion my husband expressed the same thoughts. Once again Reminding his friend just how good a friend he was, he told Mikey.

"Catch up properly when we're more alert and thanks for tonight and for putting us up."

Morning was soon upon us. Catherine Rooney appearing at the bedroom door was a great start to our day. In other ways it was a very different type of morning to those of the past 2 years. Cloudy skies as opposed to clear bright and blue, covered Yorkshire and covered our small village. Despite being glad to be back home I was now missing the Portuguese climate. Breakfast behind us and being ready to move on I shared with my friend, how once we get settled back in at the house I'll be back in touch. Watching us load up the taxi the Rooney's waved us off till the next time. Frankie had not lost her sense of humour.

"Make it soon you too and bring your containers Charlie. I'm sure they'll fit nicely in my freezer just like last time."

My return to the psychiatric wards was fairly imminent as it was for Charlie going back to his office here in Yorkshire. He was excited. He had many new ideas which could bring huge bonus to the company which as yet did not exist. We both hoped that Mikey's ideas would be beneficial too. Deep down I knew that together they would be something of a force to be reckoned with. My vision for them was usually a vivid one. The sky would be their limit. Timing for commencement of the new company would be of the essence for all of us. There would be no half measures. The view held by all of us was that nothing would be ready until everything was ready.

Being back on the wards of our local hospital I could see that nothing had changed very much over the 2 years of my absence. Despite my efforts to secure higher numbers on every shift ahead of me leaving for Portugal, staffing levels were still a bit hit and miss. Being warmly welcomed back by those who knew me, I was assured that my presence had been sorely missed. Despite having had the greatest time working in a psychiatric clinic in Portugal, I too had sorely missed my colleagues on the wards. Some patients which I had worked with had been discharged and then readmitted.

That was a strong indication of the suffering some people endure and was one of my saddest experiences on my return. I yearned to find better ways for the prevention of those repeat admissions. Through many ward discussions an understanding was reached, that good proactive care being offered in the community would be a strong catalyst in the prevention of readmissions. That care could in part be introduced via phone calls to the patient at home. Care would often be with the provision of financial assistance by a direct payment system. Supporting our patients with the employment of a personal assistant on a delegated number of weekly hours, as per the patient's needs, is how that finance would be used. Research has shown how this system worked well, for a lot of patients in various hospitals throughout the country. I worked hard to successfully have that service implemented within our Mental Health service here in Yorkshire.

Bringing new ideas in the care management of people with Mental Health problems, from my recent Portuguese experience, was very much welcomed by the health trust. Tom Chesterton was especially eager to hear of any differences applied and how and if they had worked in a more positive way. Sharing some literature which I had brought back from Portugal around the various wards, was considered by the trust to be marginally beneficial.

The placement of mental health provision in units or hospitals out in Portugal, would be found mostly at coastal areas. That was leaving the more inland population under served, which would never be great for anyone in any type of mental health crisis. That was an issue which local communities were working hard on in their attempt to have it resolved. They lived in the hope of a good plan being put in place at some point in the near future. Their hopes were for sooner rather than later. Talks given by me to non-medical employees at management levels within the health authorities in Portugal, my hope was that I had sufficiently informed them of the need for mental health clinics and hospitals, throughout the whole of the country not just coastal areas. Colleagues on the wards had promised to keep me updated by email of any progressive outcomes from my talks.

Morning sickness occurring on a daily basis had slowly and unexpectedly crept into my life. Being unsure of the cause as no other symptoms were present, the thought of pregnancy sneaked into my head. Hastily dismissing that possibility gave a strong sense of relief. My dismissal was largely due to the fact that I was menstruating regularly, plus the use of regular contraception was in place. Knowing that should I need to speak to a doctor their first question would be.

"Could you be pregnant? Have you done a pregnancy test?"

That thought in mind I decided to pre-empt an answer to that question and go ahead with a test. That then would allow me to be clear to my doctor that the test had been done and was negative, which is what I would expect the outcome to be.

Preparing myself for the purchase of a pregnancy test kit wasn't the easiest thing I had ever done. Many people hard as it might be to imagine, still saw pregnancy as a taboo subject in those days. Therefore, it was often surrounded by anxiety and embarrassment by those who considered it to be taboo. Some African cultures viewed it as though the mother and baby would be cursed with evil possession and bad luck. Other cultures saw it in a far more positive light. It would for them be the glorious rebirth of their ancestors in addition to being the reproduction of future generations. My thoughts around all of that were, that should I ever become pregnant in the future in a planned way, that would be fabulous for myself and Charlie going through the process of producing our own future generation.

Embarrassment was not mine but often was that of the person behind the pharmacy counter depending on their nationality and their culture. On this occasion my server was a Yorkshire born young woman whose culture and identity was clearly English. It was a lady I had previously known when doing my Mental Health training. The woman serving me without comment fully met my needs. Having taken a bus ride to town and gone to a pharmacy on the high street I eagerly waited for my return bus. Back home I promptly went to the bathroom in order to get my negative answer for my doctor. I was wrong. To my absolute horror and disbelief, that line informing me that yes it was a positive result, brought me out in a cold sweat. Such high levels of emotion I hadn't seen or experienced from myself in an awful long time. How could I be pregnant? How could this ever be possible? Trying to regain my composure I remembered my own advice to others when in a state of distress. Practicing deep breathing techniques duly regulated my emotions for that time. That was not how I had ever wanted to feel on the discovery of my own positive pregnancy test result.

Charlie and I had often spoken about having children at some point in the future. Accepting that being in Catharine Rooney's company always got my maternal instincts raised quite high, it was always a temporary blip for me. Becoming a parent was something which I wasn't anywhere even close to, let alone be ready or prepared for. Calling Frankie with the sole intention of sharing my awful news I held back. I wasn't ready to say it out loud as that would confirm it was real. I wasn't ready to share it even with my best friend whom I knew would be compassionate.

Compassion wasn't altogether what I needed at that time. What I needed was to not be pregnant and who could create that situation for me- Yes no one! There were no miracle workers whom I was aware of and that's what would have been required in order to change the situation. Having the view that we cannot decide who comes into this world and who doesn't, wasn't overly helpful for me either but it was what it was. Being so steadfast in my thoughts against the idea of abortion I was stuck. Stuck in the middle of what felt like an abyss, is perhaps a slight exaggeration but its rather much how I felt at the time.

The phone ringing out at that moment only served to be an annoyance for me. Picking it up in the hopes it might be one of the cold callers I usually hated, this was different as they would be easy to get rid of. Lady luck was letting me down. I was disappointed. It was Cathy the ward sister with whom I was job sharing seeking some moral support. I could hear the strain and tension in her voice. Hear the attempts being made by her in order not to break down and cry. Her voice was low as she told me.

"It's not the best of news Helen. Remember the staff nurse Jackie from ward 17- she got hit by a car today. She's not dead but almost. There's 3 Kids under 9 and an abusive husband. It's just awful. The poor kids. They might as well be orphans for all the good he will be to them if she dies and our hands are tied in so far as giving them support is concerned."

Hearing that awful news about Jackie brought my head back to reality. She was hanging onto her life by a hair's breadth. Hearing how the following 24 hours would be crucial for her felt crucifying. Of what significance was my problem by comparison at that moment? I fumbled for some words which were not coming very easily.

"Yes, I remember Jackie well. That's just shocking Cathy. Does she have any family support? Someone to maybe step up a notch and care for the children?"

Not knowing the lady awfully well Cathy shared how she wasn't sure of the family set up. She had heard more than enough times from Jackie, that the husband wasn't an especially good husband or good father material. When in her lower moments and needing some moral and emotional support, the woman had spoken to Cathy about personal marital affairs. Spoken about her husband's relationship with the brandy bottle and his psychical abuse of her which would follow. Hearing how Jackie was always clear, about there never being any safeguarding issues to be recorded in relation to their children, was good to hear.

    That security for their children was primarily down to Jackie's interventions. Her high levels of protection between her husband and their children never faltered. Always having a plan in place, she insured their kids would be with other family members, whilst she was on shift at the hospital. Cathy's voice was by now almost at breaking point.

"Can you imagine the extra stress she went through Helen. I find it hard enough organising child care when I'm working and kids home from school. Having that awful fear like Jackie had on top of all of that is pretty much unthinkable to me."

Holding back my own emotions my plan to offer support was interrupted. What happened next and how annoying it was at that minute had a high degree of familiarity for me. Hearing the ward buzzer going off as it did I couldn't help but wonder, if maybe the decibels needed turning down a little or perhaps a lot.

    Hearing that buzzer whilst working on the wards you don't think about or consider the volume. Your mind is immediately focused on the fact that there's a problem and someone needs your help and support. Simply realising that you're needed you hurry and run if it's considered to be safe to do so. Knowing how that buzzer meant there would be an incident of some description, it was a sound which none of us cared for too much. Her presence being needed back on the ward, Cathy promised she would keep me updated about Jackie's situation, then she promptly ended the call.

Considering the situation that Jackie's children were now finding themselves in, I had pangs of almost shame regarding my own feelings about my own situation of pregnancy. Knowing how our colleague Jackie would swap places with me in a heartbeat, was what brought me to a more realistic way of thinking. It helped put things in perspective for me. It was at that moment that I decided to embrace my pregnancy. I would share the news with my husband at the first appropriate opportunity.

Figuring out the best way and best time to tell Charlie he was going to be a father, gave me a stress related headache. With a need to speak to him about Jackie and the accident I planned to tell him about our pregnancy first. The unwanted call came that evening from Cathy. It was to inform me that Jackie didn't make it. That she had lived her planned life on this earth and it had now expired. Her time here was up she had now gone to meet her maker. Being a great believer that our life is planned by a higher being ahead of our entrance to this world, in some ways gave me a certain degree of comfort. That belief gave me some understanding at the very least as to why people depart this world at a variety of ages. Yes, it all seemed to make sense. Her psychical body had decimated. Her soul had gone to the next level had gone to the next life.

Being of a Hindu religion and their specific beliefs, the thoughts of another life would hopefully have given her a margin of comfort, at the moment of her death. Her 3 children were taken into the care of our local authority, whilst extended family members were being assessed for suitability to have the children in their care. Hearing how Catherine Rooney would be the delegated psychologist attached to the children made my day slightly better. Her interest in brain trauma had made her the ideal candidate for the job. My thoughts were that she would be the most suitable person to explain to the children, their mother's death through injury to her brain. Catherine's support continuing with the children would hold the best chance in life for them.

Preparing myself for the upcoming discussion with Charlie wasn't the easiest of situations for me. Knowing how his thoughts about having a family were a mirror of mine, I would have to be prepared and ready for whatever came back at me from him. Checking his availability for the following evening the plan was duly put in place.

"We should go out. We've not been to Hales bar since our return back to England. Let's go Charlie see if the place has changed at all."

Hearing his positive response to that took the pressure off me at least for the interim period. He did however express his concern wondering if something was amiss, as it wasn't usual for me to suggest going out and then without question go ahead and arrange it all. I had choices. I could lie or tell him there and then about the pregnancy. Deciding to play Charlie at his own game but not in a vindictive way, my mind was made up to tell him at the very end of our evening out.

Arriving at Hales bar we could see how they're were no real changes to the environment over the period we spent in Portugal. Being remembered and greeted warmly by some staff members was a good feeling too. Wondering where we had been for the past few years Charlie briefly shared about our time out in Portugal. Looks of envy swept across our waiter's face.

"Wish I could have had 2 years in the sunshine Charlie. It would be just what the doctor ordered but having a family make those opportunities virtually impossible. So glad for you and Helen that you've done it."

Charlie smiled. I thought how the gods were looking down on me. Putting that thought from the waiter's comments in my husband's head had perfect timing. Any negative feelings he might have regards our pregnancy would hopefully be turned on their head in the knowledge that we had already spread our wings.

Taking us to the same table we had always shared on previous visits, that reminiscing felt nice. Having made our choice from an extensive menu my mind was racing. Should I really give Charlie some of his own medicine or tell him immediately. Conversation about his work situation was instigated by Charlie. It brought us to almost the end of our evening. Eventually I shared with my husband about the demise of my work colleague Jackie and how her children had been taken into the care of the local authority.

Being incredibly sympathetic to their situation and to me as her colleague, he came to my side of the table for an embrace. Ensuring him that whilst feeling distressed for the family and that whilst there would be a passage of time required for me to fully absorb the news, but yes, I would be all right. Blurting stuff out is something that kids often do when unable to control their thoughts or regulate their emotions. That was me at the very end of that evening. I'm very aware that Charlie having to hear the words with no build up to prepare him for them, was truly unjust of me.

They just rolled off my tongue in a scatter-brained sort of fashion.

"I'm pregnant Charlie."

Rendering him initially speechless gave me some cause for concern. What a huge shock those words were for him. Spitting back his mouthful of wine into the glass, heads turned from other tables as he gasped with some volume in his voice.

"You're what? You're pregnant? Are you serious? Reassuring him that yes, I was very serious. Charlie listened to my drawn-up comparison of what our life was going to look like by comparison to what Jackie's family were now going through and having to endure. That helped to put our pregnancy in perspective for him. Recovering from that initial shock, the smile on Charlies face confirmed to me, his sheer delight at the idea of becoming a father.

"It's not how we planned it Helen but having done so much in our own life's, it's about time we brought more joy into the world. It was a shock and especially hearing it how I did but I'm as delighted as you clearly are."

We embraced to an applause and chants of congratulations from other diners in Hales bar. The moment was and still is a momentous one for us both. Wondering how Charlie would have felt had he known my initial feelings, my decision was that it was not a conversation we would ever need to have.

Business plans between Charlie and Mikey were well in progress. Setting up office in what was a converted barn kept their rental outgoings quite low. Mikey had a passion, a thirst and knowledge for technology which was contagious. He was also a man with huge amounts of ambition. Setting up the forward-thinking company he could see a great future for it and a great vision of a future for them as a company. He was clear with my husband.

"I'm a bit of an entrepreneur Charlie and you should know that. Knowing exactly what I want from this adventure has to be helpful for us both. I'm forever reflecting and questioning myself. Sharing a passion and great energy combined with a great work ethic with yourself, will bring us many financial dividends. I just know it will."
Smiling broadly at his friend's assessment of him and of them as business partners- Charlie told him.

"You need to calm down Mikey and keep things in perspective. I know we're good but are we really that good?"

Charlie would be 2nd in command thus leaving Mikey in charge of the business. Charlie would input ideas learned from our time in Portugal. He would be in charge of web development and digital marketing which was a new and innovative idea. Beginning to know Mikey better from the work perspective was eye opening. Despite his earlier outburst of praise for their achievement, Charlie discovered how really Mikey was a self -deprecating man. His modesty was desirable by all who knew him. Despite having a higher share hold than Charlie, he never used that fact to exert any type of control over him. Always treating him as an equal their company blossomed going from strength to strength. Frankie and I were beyond proud of the men we were married to.

Somewhat like what we all know as 'the American dream' Mikey Rooney and my husband Charlie had their own dream. Together they would provide the world with the latest in software, combined with instructions on how to get the best use from it. They would organise and set up regular teaching sessions for the use of their products. Setting two hours weekly to one side purely for the purpose of teaching and at no cost to the client, would have to be a huge bonus to their sales techniques. They considered how they had the greatest opportunities on this earth sitting there right in front of them. All that was now required to get this company moving further and faster, would be massive amounts of their time, combined with financial contributions of equal proportions.

Charlie would no longer be 2nd in command. They would become equal business partners. Without being reckless they would both need to make considerable financial contributions. Charlie was cautious when discussing the scenario with me. Having chosen his words with some great thought I was enlightened of the following.

"I'm aware we're not super rich Helen but we're not on the breadline either. To get the best from this business situation between myself and Mikey, it will require a financial input from your income in addition to mine. I have a good feeling about how it can turn out to be very lucrative in the long term for all 4 of us. I'm sure Mikey will be having this same conversation with Frankie too."

I trusted Charlie and trusted his judgement on business situations implicitly. I was however initially unsure of the sharing of my own finances. What about this and what about that in terms of needing my money, were thoughts flying through my head at a speed maybe faster than light. Requiring a little time to think through his proposal I took a walk through the woods alone. Calm and serenity gained from those walks was something to be envious of. On return things appeared clearer to me. Reminding my husband of the pregnancy which would give us quite a reduced income for some time, I also gave him my blessings to do what he needed to do. We agreed to do it with great caution, with an inclusive clause that should we need to, that I could withdraw my financial support after a 4-way discussion. We embraced. He would visit Mikey the following evening in order to finalise their plan. This was something to be addressed by the men. As their wives myself and Frankie would input some extra finance to get them off the ground. We would have no further involvement in the business.

Frankie also being pregnant with their 2nd child brought her and Mikey so much joy. Sharing their special news with Catherine required some creativity as it would have for any family in that situation. Frankie and myself shared many giggles at the innocence of their daughter. Catherine's ideas of how their baby would enter this world were humorous on every level. Sheer beauty of innocence demonstrated by her was something to behold. One such example being how she would remove her mother's belly button with a screwdriver, in order for the baby to be taken out. Despite feeling tired throughout the whole period, Frankie's pregnancy otherwise went without a hitch right from the start.

Being pregnant at the same time as my best friend forever felt like quite a special time in life for us both. Unlike Frankie's my own pregnancy wasn't quite so straightforward. Morning sickness wasn't satisfied it had punished my body enough, it came back at evening times too. It continued to be my unwanted visitor up to almost 34 weeks into my pregnancy. Having the need for a short stay in hospital due to suffering the effects of dehydration, wasn't the greatest of times for me. Charlie however found the situation more distressing than I did. His next move whilst with the best of intentions wasn't the best information to share with me.

"I'll talk to the doctors Helen. I'll try to ensure you get the best care."

That really was not one of his best statements to me. Reminding my husband that I was an adult, a capable and independent woman who could efficiently sort out my own health care, he took a psychical step back. Charlie looked somewhat distressed but apologised for his interference. His face however was telling me that an apology wasn't what he wanted to be sharing with me. Further reassurance given by me that anger towards him was not on my agenda- How I simply had the basic need of holding onto my independence, he expressed his understanding of that fact. 4 more days of excellent care on the ward at our local maternity hospital, I was then discharged back home.

Our expected dates for delivery were very close. Just a 4-day difference with Frankie's being the earliest. Supporting each other throughout the following months worked well for us both. Eventually going into labour, we delivered our babies exactly 8 days apart with Frankie being 1st to deliver. Mikey being local on that occasion he brought Catherine to myself and Charlie whilst he supported his wife through the process of giving birth. The phone call from Mikey came sooner than anticipated. Excitement mixed with anxiety almost causing his throat to close up he eventually got the words out. Becoming parents to a new baby boy was idyllic for them. It brought feelings of great joy to their family.

Their baby son would be known as Joseph Kevin

Rooney. Catherine Rooney was delighted to have a brother. Turning into a mini mother almost overnight, she revelled in helping Frankie with the new baby. No questions asked regards his appearance in this world by Catherine was something of a relief for her parents.

"Imagine Helen if she did ask how would we have answered that one? There's no rules book provided and I'm thinking that maybe there needs to be one."

Laughing- Our decision was made. We would need to make it up as we travel the journey so to speak. I too gave birth to a bouncing baby boy whose name as yet had not been chosen.

On admission to the maternity hospital my defences were raised in response to some of their questions. A sense of sarcasm and paranoia, neither of which I was aware to be part of me, were now beginning to consume my thoughts. Being asked what I did for a living I had the very strong urge to lie. My assumption or perhaps with hindsight it may have been my paranoia around that question, was that they needed to know my lifestyle, in order to know what level of respect to show to me. Having the urge to say.

"I drink tea and mind my own business. Perhaps you should try it sometime."

I didn't. My thoughts were suddenly diverted elsewhere. My almost never-ending contractions were by now taking up all empty space in my head. Our baby boy entered this world with no one supporting me other than a midwife. His father was pacing the corridor outside of the delivery suite. Almost quivering and at the last minute ahead of me going into their delivery suite he told me.

"I can't do it Helen I can't be in there for the birth. The risk is too high. I'm sorry but you wouldn't want me passing out and there's 100% chance I would do just that."

I went on to discover how at the very sight of blood that he would be on the floor. How the build-up to the whole anticipation of blood would be enough to bring him down. That would not be a predicament conducive to calmness and serenity, both of which a delivering mother would need. Wishing we had that conversation weeks earlier and not just before I was taken into the delivery suite would have been helpful. I was aware that the time was not right for me to challenge his level of secrecy with me. Eventually after him meeting the new addition to our family. I reminded Charlie how my motto on honesty had always been to.

"Be good enough to forgive people but don't be naive enough to ever trust them again."

That however was something I wasn't too sure I could apply to Charlie in that situation. Anxiety sweeping across his face at the very thought of not being trusted again, I relieved his pain. Deciding we could draw the line on this occasion we made a pact together. We would move forward with a new understanding. Two-way agreements were put in place that should either of us in our future have a difficult scenario to deal with, that regardless of the level of that difficulty we would always share those thoughts. Should either of us break that promise then our life together would reach its woeful conclusion.

Catherine Rooney was quite vocal by this time. She liked to and gained great pleasure from having herself heard. In many ways she was mature for her age. Despite her young years she could be opinionated and liked to have her opinions considered. It was therefore no surprise to us when she made what she called her special announcement. Sharing with her parents and myself how our baby looked like one of her cuddly toys which she had named Charlie, she requested that our baby should be called Charlie too. Not being sure that I was overly keen on that idea I informed Catherine in child speak that the name would be given some careful consideration.

      Deciding to have our son christened- for myself and Charlie was a relatively easy decision to make. It was based on the conversation between myself and Frankie Rooney, in relation to the giving of choices and to the christening of their daughter Catherine. Frankie's thoughts around that had made a lot of sense to me. A double christening occurred some weeks later. Charlie and I were godparents to Frankie's son whilst Frankie and Mikey were godparents to our child. Our friendship circle back here in England was still kept tight to just the 4 of us. Questioning ourselves and reflecting occasionally regarding our social interactions with other people, we all held the view that we were perhaps a little antisocial.

      Mikey was perhaps the most vocal of us about the antisocial scenario. Sharing his thoughts of how having to meet and mix with people, mixing with strangers in our place of work on a regular basis, had kept us and would continue to keep us in contact with the outside world. Chosen employment by all of us made me question, were we really antisocial or just picky about who our friends might be. Deciding his points were very valid ones we all agreed. Mikey poured yet another coffee, then slouching back in his chair he told us he hadn't finished. Reminding myself and Frankie of the chatterbox he was in the kids home, he then continued to share his view that.

"We see and feel for each other and from each other's perspective. The old saying of too many irons in the fire and all that would only confuse things. If this makes us antisocial then so be it."

Being unable to disagree with his sentiments our agreement was secured again. We would continue in our small bubble as just the 4 of us.

Charlie and I were by now the proud parents of Charlie Junior Regan who would be known as CJ Regan. Yes, Catherine Rooney had her wish with picking the baby name. CJ was a delightful baby. He rarely made a sound at night time in the 1st 9 months of his life. Him sleeping throughout the night from day 1 on this earth was a huge blessing beyond our comprehension. Having heard so many stories from work colleagues about their broken nights, my anticipation of having that same experience was very high. Teething troubles brought the 1st signs of any night time disturbance when CJ was around 10 months of age. I was at that point working back on the wards of our local hospital. Being back amidst many other mothers on the ward, there was always someone to share any worries with and always someone to offer their advice.

Childcare was relatively easy to source. Being fortunate to have some work colleagues, who made strong recommendations for nurseries which they had used and found the staff great, gave me confidence in leaving CJ with a stranger. Myself and Frankie used the same nursery. That enabled us to return to the work place when our babies were just 9 months of age. Both children were being weaned off of the breast. Being substituted with formula once daily, plus an introduction to solid food three times daily was working out at varying degrees of satisfaction. Joseph was doing well and C J perhaps not so well. Despite reassurance from the nursery staff I continued to worry about C J and his dietary needs versus his intake. Calling Frankie to discuss this on more than one occasion, I was usually reassured by her input. I struggled however from time to time to hold onto that reassurance. The vision of C J growing in front of my eyes and meeting his milestones, was what gave me the greatest confidence and reassurance that all was well.

Being back on the wards for me in so many ways felt like a blessing in disguise. A blessing in which I was badly in need of. My need for adult company was met as well as the need to increase our financial situation. Having invested a huge amount into the software business, had at times left my bank balance a little on the low side and left me waiting in anticipation of the next pay cheque. Charlie had always been clear with me, that we wouldn't see much financial return if any at all on our investment, for at least twelve months possibly considerably longer. Working three days per week had left the possibility of an option of an extra two days open to me.

Conversations with Charlie, with Frankie, with the nursery and then with my employer, a deal of four days for me on the wards was agreed. Increased income from the extra days work combined with a much-appreciated increase in my overall hourly rates, lowered the raised blood pressure for both of us. Extra money went towards the repayment of our mortgage when possible. Charlie in particular was happy to see that enormous figure being slowly reduced on a monthly basis. Sharing his worries about our financial situation being largely his responsibility, I was once again able to allay those fears. Reminding my husband how we were in this together removed that anxious look from his face.

"Thanks Helen. I feel the guilt due to your money boosting the business, but your great you're so reassuring. Again, thank you."
We embraced.

The men's new software company which was aptly named- 'Rooney -N -Regan Computing Software,' was by this time growing quite nicely. Charlie always had the notion that people invest in people as opposed to investing in their product. With that thought in mind and with Mikey sharing his view, a plan of how to maximise good customer contact was put in place. Charlie shared with me what their new logo might look like.

"We know we're genuine. We know we're the real deal."
Underlined by
"Come chat so you too find the truth in our statement as you will do."
Charlie believed wholeheartedly in their software products as did Mikey. Hopefully now any potential clients would believe in them too. The software business blossomed over the following years. Our family expanded with Charlie and I having 2 more children. When C J was just 3 years of age Identical twins came into our lives. Delighted as we were that was the time when a degree of chaos entered our lives too. The Rooney's once again became godparents to our boys Brendan and Anthony.

Analysing Joseph.

How fast the past years had flown by. The blink of an eye and our children had grown into wonderful adults. Catherine Rooney by this time had turned into a beautiful, intelligent and well-educated young woman. She had many of her mother's traits and characteristics which was great to see. She had also grown up to follow in her mothers' academic footsteps. Studying psychology at degree level she had hoped to work freelance for a variety of agencies throughout Yorkshire. Being the stay at home type and quite unlike her brother Joseph, Catherine appreciated her many home comforts. After graduation she joined up with and became a member of the British Psychological society. Her main interests were in 'the impact of psychological trauma on the brain.'

Catherine was acutely aware of her mother's childhood and the lifestyle which had been led by her grandparents. She was aware of that lifestyle resulting in the awful demise of Frankie's parents and her sister, thus leaving Frankie an orphan. That she said was the catalyst for her keen interest in her chosen area of psychology. Speaking to me with a degree of compassion Catherine told me.

"You've known mum almost all of your life so I'm sure your aware of her intense suffering as a child. I'm trying to establish how much trauma her brain has endured and how much recovery it has made, or not made as the case might also be."

Wanting to tell the daughter of the lady who had been my best friend forever, to just stop analysing her mother was something which I couldn't manage to do. Regardless of how hard I tried the words simply wouldn't come out of my mouth. My attempts turned into a fumble which led to me excusing myself with a false need for the bathroom.

"Sorry Catherine needs must when it's a nature call. Won't be long."

And I was gone through that door- leading upstairs with the speed of a grey hound chasing rabbits. No chance availed to her for a response. Yes, I was feeling quite intimidated by Frankie's daughter and didn't care too much for that feeling. Reminding me of days of being bullied back in the children's home, those were memories which should have been buried deep into my subconscious. Frankie certainly would not be impressed with their child. Despite her statement being made to me with a degree of compassion, in some ways it felt a little chilly too. Growing up without a mother myself I had to wonder how it might have felt should I have had one. My wish at that time was that Catherine was coming from a place of love and not from a clinical research perspective as was the case.

In my estimation she was thinking and speaking more like a clinician and much less like a daughter. Coldness over the years at times oozed from Catherine. Referring to 'her brain' in terms of her mother had felt almost a little on the cold side to me. In some ways generally speaking Catherine had at times been perceived by some as being somewhat cold by nature. Frankie would at times tell me how.

"She's a very smart woman Helen. She knows how our lives are yet she detaches herself a lot of the time. It hurts it hurts a lot."
Knowing there was nothing which I could say or do in those situations to make Frankie feel better, I would simply nod in affirmation of what she had said. Anything else would have seemed false to her. She would be left to wonder how many faces I actually possessed and which of us would appreciate that label?

Years spent with Catherine going through education were a true delight for her parents. She had been a very traditional learner. Having followed the national curriculum to the letter she stood out amidst other students of her age. She had behaved as any parent would hope for and adapted with compliance to the rules and discipline required within the routine of the school day. Catherine had developed meaningful relationships with her peers and her teachers. Always having positive parent evening reports, she had made the status of head girl on 3 separate occasions whilst going through senior school. Catherine was in so many ways very unlike her younger brother. She was the child that gave her parents a great experience, of what parenting could and perhaps in an ideal family situation should be like, both in and out of school.

Being around three years older than my 1st born C J, I had encouraged friendships between our children and the Rooney's children, but especially so with Catherine. Her positive and calm persona could only have brought benefit to my children. Calling Frankie at weekends and throughout some school holidays we made get together plans. Mostly our children went to childminders in school holiday times due to work commitments for myself and Frankie. The

Rooney's son Joseph never got that same deal of encouragement from me. Neither did he show any interest in being particularly sociable with my children or indeed with his own sister Catherine. Frankie and Mikey were both aware of what had appeared to them to be the purposeful void, created by Joseph between himself and his older sister Catherine. I was never sure it was a void created on purpose, but more something which was perhaps out of Joseph's control. The children's mother had often told me.

"It's almost as though they hate each other Helen. Well maybe not Catherine but certainly Joseph has hatred towards his sister. You can hear the silence between them when they're together in the same room."

She continued to share how Catherine makes attempts to engage with her brother which he almost always declines. Simply either ignoring her request or telling her or shouting at her to go away was what often happened. Frankie's belief was that either way it was a concern for herself and Mikey as their parents and also very hurtful for Catherine. That was not to mention how it must feel for Joseph himself. Whilst no one was saying that he's evil yet the situation between them was so sad. Having allowed Frankie to say all of that without interruption was my indication of my respect for and towards her. Again, me acknowledging what my friend had just said and the pain associated with that for the whole family, appeared to lift Frankie's mood a little.

"Thanks Helen. I know you can't do anything. Listening and acknowledging is just great. You know I love you."

Joseph Rooney who is Frankie and Mikey's 2nd child, has grown into a fine man standing almost 6 feet tall.

Built like a rugby player, Joseph at times throughout his life has demonstrated a degree of verbal aggression. Sometimes directed towards Catherine and his parents and almost always towards a person who expressed, or whom he felt had or was attempting to have any authority over him. Joseph was no lover of rules or boundaries and no great lover of education. Having had many school detentions and some exclusions throughout his years in school, becoming or having the status of head boy was never on his agenda. He could be heard telling his parents and often in quite a rude manner too.

"There's more chance of a pig flying past the window than there is of me ever becoming head boy, or having any other achievement in the classroom. Get used to it because it won't change."

Considering the rude manner in which he would often speak to Frankie and Mikey, there was never any surprise for me regarding his lack of conformity in the classroom. In addition to my many other thoughts about Joseph over the years, I had always considered him from a very young age to be a bit of a 'Jack the lad'. He would take himself down the road with that swagger which gave out the message 'you don't mess with me.' The swagger worked for him. It truly worked well in his favour by keeping people away. Keeping people at arm's length from him was important to Joseph.

On occasions I had overheard him speaking to his mother in what I can only describe as the saddest of situations. She would look very saddened and confused as her son told her, how he felt that his heart had no brain and his brain had no heart. That whatever he did he seemed thoughtless and didn't altogether feel that he could have any control over those feelings. Frankie was usually verbally non-responsive in those situations. She would simply be offering an embrace to their child which he always rejected. Was she in his head confirming to him what he said to be the truth? Joseph would take himself out of the equation. The slamming of doors as he went through them indicated a level of his feelings.

Many trips have been made to Joseph's schools over the years, mostly by Frankie but on some occasions by Mikey too. Sitting outside the headmaster's office waiting for their appointment time, the parents would make their decisions. Deciding to be non-accepting of whatever they were about to hear from the school head, could only turn out to be a massive mistake and it always was. Joseph had his issues however he was smart and could see his parents shutting their eyes to those issues. Watching every scenario mentioned playing out in their head, just like they knew it had occurred in Josephs school day, they both shuffled around on their chairs as they denied their child would be responsible for the described behaviours.

For Joseph discovery of their attempts at condoning his behaviours only created more mayhem in his mind. Being unable to understand their decision and despite his confusion over it, he was nevertheless happy to be exonerated by them. The head at times became impatient with the Rooney parents.

"Your intelligent people. Your business people you have to see what's going on with your child before it's too late. One day you may well be having this conversation with a prison officer, if something doesn't drastically change. I'm exasperated with Joseph and his antics. He's going home with you for 3 days. Goodbye Mr and Mrs Rooney and please take your son with you."

Being left with no alternative Mikey and Frankie would do as requested. Collection of Joseph from school reception was never easy. Hearing his protests being expressed to the accompanying teacher, his parents' interruptions were always greatly welcomed by the staff member.

"Thank you, Mr and Mrs Rooney, and see you in a few days Joseph."

Thinking back to his father's days in the children's home with his unruly behaviour, it was very unlike the behaviours presented by their son Joseph, especially into his early young adult years. Mikey had experienced somewhat of a troubled childhood which had impacted his development. He was a damaged child. Through emotional immaturity he had lacked the ability to express himself appropriately. That inability was largely accountable for Mikey's many unwanted behaviours. Everyone who knew Mikey and knew Joseph quite well could see that this was very different.

The situation with their son Joseph was a whole new ball game for the Rooney family. What could possibly be the underlying cause for Joseph's unwanted behaviours, was something which they were not likely to officially discover. Every attempt made by his parents (and there were many) to seek an assessment for their child was firmly rejected by him. Left feeling quite perplexed with their own thoughts around his reasons for rejecting assessments, they decided their hands were tied. There was no more they could do. Feeling they were defeated by Joseph and being unhappy with the situation, they decided to draw a line. Frankie was then serious and emotional with a change of heart.

"It's turmoil for us Mikey we know that, but let's imagine how it is for him, how his head must feel. We can't give up on him. I'm giving it one more go and hope you'll be there with me."
Mikey was there with her expressing how his thoughts were a mirror image of hers.

Joseph was left with a future which was showing potential to be quite a difficult, hard and perhaps at times unmanageable one. Back at the Rooney's home that evening, he was spoken to calmly by both parents once again to no avail. Despite giving him reminders how a psychological assessment would surely open doors for him, the child was not prepared to engage. He was abrupt bordering on rude with his response.

"I'm not talking to anyone about my head. You don't like that answer, you don't like my behaviours, then put me in a kids home like you both were or in foster care. I really don't care."
Joseph then did what was fairly usual for him. Denying his parents any opportunity to respond or to discuss with him further he hastily left the room. The parents surprise was that their house doors were still hanging in one piece.

Catherine Rooney had found herself making attempts to analyse her brother on more than one occasion. Accepting his engagement resistance to her attempts frustrated her immensely. Wanting to fiercely resist the line of potential manipulation in order to have her needs met, she let herself down. Deciding it was the only avenue open to her and it was a very last resort, she would have to proceed. Attempting to buy his compliance with her hard-earned cash, which would ultimately become his with his co-operation in her study of him, again it failed. Joseph was not to be bought and not to be analysed. He was firm and agitated in his response.

"Will you just leave it alone Catherine and leave me alone. I'm me. I'm not one of your patients or your clients or whatever you choose to call them. I won't be manipulated by you or by anyone else and don't go writing your own story of me either, because you'll be wrong."

Knowing how she was yet again defeated she pulled on her old green waterproof coat, her heavy wellington boots and promptly left the house without a further word to her brother. Catherine had inherited her mothers desire to recycle everything which could be recycled. Her old coat and wellingtons had both been pre-loved. She purchased them from a 2nd hand store in the town. Taking a long walk through their local woods was her go to activity when under stress. Knowing from previous experiences that this would give her head some clarity, had strengthened her resolve to brave the weather. Understanding that her brother had many difficult issues to deal with, she failed to understand why her parents had never had this investigated or assessed by professionals when he was younger.

Catherine had made some huge assumptions about her parents. She often wondered why they had as she had considered, buried their heads in the sand. To this point she had never shared those thoughts with Frankie or Mikey, or with anyone. That situation was very shortly going to change. Her decision was made to tackle their parents about what she considered to be wilful neglect of their other child. She was on a mission and she would be heard. She wanted answers which only their parents could provide for her. She was yet to discover that she was wrong and would be quite remorseful for her assumptions and her judgements.

Evening time at the Rooney's she decided would be her opportunity to address her brothers many issues with their parents. Joseph staying with a friend overnight meant there would be no unwanted interruptions from him. Catherine had excelled herself with her culinary skills. Calling her parents to the kitchen table she had set the scene. Having used a little manipulation to hopefully get them on side, she presented homemade apple pie sprinkled with cinnamon. Knowing this was a favourite for Frankie and Mikey she knew how it would set their taste buds on fire. Any compliment from Frankie regarding the baking of her favourite apple pie would be well deserved. Both showed their appreciation of their daughters' efforts.

"It's delicious Catherine you've worked hard to perfect the recipe."

Graciously accepting their compliments and after some small talk, she felt able to follow through her plan. Able to open the conversation regarding her brother Joseph. Jumping in with both feet Catherine was very presumptuous. Telling her parents how she wished to discuss their apparent lack of seeking answers, concerning her brothers issues when he was a child and up to his adult years, she then took a breath. Frankie and Mikey were stunned by what felt like an attack on them by their daughter. Looking shocked and in almost stereo wondered what she was talking about.

"It's about the fact that Joseph clearly has severe problems. His life's a mess and neither of you have done anything to establish what's actually wrong with him. Did he and does he not deserve better than this?"

Both parents initially reluctant to engage with that

conversation, Mikey then broke the ice and was somewhat sharp in his tone to their daughter.

"Don't be presumptuous Catherine. Accusations don't feel comfortable either when you're not in receipt of the facts. Never having discussed Joseph with you in any sort of detail perhaps was wrong of us or was it? Would you want us discussing you with him or with anyone? It's also wrong of you and very unprofessional that you accuse us in this manner. Actually, it feels more like an attack than an accusation."

Her evening, her plan, her attempted manipulation and conversation did not go how Catherine hoped it might and anticipated it would. She was now feeling somewhat deflated. Attempting to leave the kitchen without response to her father- Frankie intervened. Firmly spoken to by her mother the woman was requested to sit back down and listen. Grabbing a chair, she positioned herself away from the table, rather like a spoiled child not getting their own way. She had adhered to her mother's request but now at a distance.

Frankie immediately standing up from the table she looked strained. She began nervously pacing the length and breadth of their kitchen. It was a big kitchen. She was very clearly unnerved by their daughters' questions and not overly sure that she liked Catherine's tone either. This would never be typical behaviour of Frankie around her children. Something in what Catherine had said to her parents had touched a raw nerve with her mother. Eventually responding to Mikey's request his wife sat back down again. Visibly taking in a deep breath she began to share.

"Catherine, I'm not sure that we like the implications

coming towards us from you. We did not neglect our parental duty with a lack of seeking support and help for your brother. Taking him to many professionals over the years has never gained any knowledge for us. I'll explain and perhaps your right that maybe we should have involved you to some extent, but then Joseph understandably so would not have liked that."

Frankie continued to explain to their daughter, how very little support was available for children within mental health services when Joseph was growing up. It feels as though its been swept under the carpet leaving people with nowhere to go, nowhere and no one to turn to. She shared how they both but especially Frankie, had to fight for every appointment which they had been given. How her brother Joseph on all of those professional visits, had demonstrated his lack of desire to be there. In fact, he had not only sat quietly not engaging, but on some occasions, he had been outwardly rude and offensive. Therapists had always felt unable to offer any information or help based on Josephs lack of co-operation. Frankie took a pause- their daughter looked remorseful but remained silent. Standing up from the table Frankie then told her

"So, there we are Catherine there you have it. That's the back story. Despite you thinking we were neglectful parents hopefully now you'll understand how that was not the case. Hopefully now you've also learned not to jump to conclusions in the absence of facts."

Frankie left the kitchen momentarily. Being called back by her husband she was responsive. She returned back to her chair in silence.

Hearing the level of stress in her mother's voice created an unusually strong sense of compassion within their daughter. Somewhere within her soul that high level of compassion had unusually been aroused in relation to her parents. That was quite unusual for her. Feeling remorseful she knew what she had to do. Offering her apology to her parents for her misconception of the situation with her brother came quite easy to Catherine.

"I should never have presumed and should have known you would have taken him for assessments. I'm apologising to you both and feel regretful for having asked the question."

She was fortunate. Her apology for such an awful and hurtful accusation was accepted graciously by both parents. After some further discussion, the conclusion between them was reached, that Joseph was most likely on the Autism Spectrum. That was the thought held by Frankie and Mikey over the years. A lifetime of no support which was his experience to date, would most probably be what lay ahead for him too. Both parents having researched autism and ADHD over the years, they often saw so many of its traits in their son.

Frankie's phone ringing out several times ahead of her picking it up, she then wished she had ignored it. Hearing from Annie the mother of Josephs friend initially felt nice for her. That feeling rapidly changed once she was updated regarding events from the previous evening and from that morning too. Hearing about Josephs unwanted, rude almost peculiar behaviour as it was being described by the caller, was very unsettling for Frankie. Cursing quietly under her breath and being unsure how to respond, she had to think quickly.

Buying herself some further thinking time her decision was made. Despite her immense dislike for dishonest people, she felt there was little choice for her in that situation so she lied.

"Was on my way-out to a hospital appointment just as the phone rang out. I've heard all which you've said and its very important we discuss it. I will call you back later this evening Annie."
The ladies bade farewell and the call was ended. Frankie breathed in a deep sigh of relief. She considered how easily she had lied to the woman and despite her reasons for doing so, she didn't like herself very much at all for doing that.

Joseph being on his way home at that time Annie was breathing in some relief too. She had shared with Frankie how he had been excessively hyperactive, non-conforming and inattentive. Annie had met Joseph Rooney on 2 previous occasions when he paid short visits to her home. She had not witnessed these behaviours previously. Not being very well known to Annie's son either he had never seen these behaviours coming from Joseph. The family had felt almost threatened by the young man whom they invited to stay in their home overnight.

Frankie had a dilemma. Her lies to Annie being out of character and didn't feel comfortable for her, she considered her options going forward. Having never spoken to anyone other than professionals and their own daughter Catherine about Josephs issues, this was a hard decision for her to make. She quietly wondered if now was going to be the time that perhaps being secretive should change. That they should become more open with other people about their sons' issues. Needing to talk it through with me she did what we both did and still do so well.

Calling me in a state of heightened and very

unregulated emotions, Frankie could scarcely get her words out. This was not like her usual way to behave at all. She was one of the people in my life whom I considered to be the greatest at regulating emotions. I was eager to hear what had brought her to this awfully painful state of distress. A little anxious and worried at the same time in regards to what I was about to hear.

"Frankie-Deep breaths in and out but slowly remember."

It's so easy to forget our breathing regime when having a panic attack. I know. I've been there myself and have seen many of my patients in that awful situation too. I could hear her breathing and could hear the lack of her stress with each breath. Eventually my lifelong friend was now ready for some conversation.

"It's Joseph and I've spent my life not being honest with you Helen. It's true that he's never had a diagnosis for his behaviours. It's not true that we haven't tried. We've always acknowledged that he has problems between ourselves despite not speaking about them openly. I should have shared that with you."

Belief on my part for that to be the truth, it surely now had to be the time where we became completely open about Joseph and his issues. Yes, I would answer back to all of that in an honest manner, which I was aware that Frankie might find a little distressing.

My response was something of a surprise if not a shock for Frankie. Trying to pick my words honestly but with caution, I'm not sure I did the greatest job of that.

"From very early years I've known that Joseph has issues."

Interruption from my friend was almost ear piercing.

"What you talking about Helen?"
Sharing with her how we've spoken about it tentatively a few times, she told me to explain.

"You've told me from time to time how he hated his sister and then you would put some humour on that statement. I've seen how he has behaved with Catherine and with and around my own children. I've never thought he hated his sister or hated anyone but more that his issues were out of his control."

Frankie asked with a certain tone to her voice if I had finished what I wanted to say? Sharing with her that my opinion always has been that Joseph has autism and perhaps ADHD too, I heard her take a very deep breath in. I continued to tell her that despite our strong friendship, I always felt that it wasn't my place to tell her what she should be doing about her own child.

Deathly silence fell upon our conversation with Frankie then telling me she had to be somewhere. Her ending the call quite abruptly I was aware she was upset with me. Not wanting to allow anything more awkward than it was at that moment to happen between us, I knew the only thing left to do was that I would go over to Frankie's. I quickly called her back.

"We both know you don't have to be anywhere other than at home. I'm on my way to yours. As always, we'll sort this out between us."

Delighted to hear of my visit Frankie ended that call too but not so hastily. On my arrival I got what many would consider to be the death glare from Joseph. Reality was that he wasn't at that time able to deal with another person being in the house. He wasn't able to politely express with explanation those thoughts either. Telling me in no uncertain terms that my presence there was not welcome, I ignored what appeared to be his rudeness and offered an olive branch. (English expression when attempting to make peace with someone.) Hearing me out but with no response Joseph went to another room. Thinking how it was impressive that he listened I shared that thought with his mother.

"It's as much as he could manage Frankie and better than another angry outburst."

My suggestion to my friend that we go to a café to talk was welcomed by her.

Thorough and honest discussion between myself and Frankie, brought some true light to the matter of Josephs unwanted behaviours. Frankie shared with me through some tears, how she herself had spent a whole lifetime even as a young child, of watching, listening and masking. She would then copy the behaviours of others as she had observed from them. Frankie was clear that her own issues were at a level whereby they could be controlled. She had the understanding that it wasn't quite that easy for everyone.

"I've seen the very positive reactions, behaviours and responses given and shown by others throughout my life Helen. There's the reason I was and continue to be able to be as good as I am. I do have undiagnosed autism. Josephs issues are much deeper much more concerning than mine have ever been, but yes, he has inherited this from me. And yes, I should have shared this with you many years ago but you know how hard it can be to talk about certain situations."

We embraced and then Frankie continued to share her rather sad views.

"The future for Joseph looks very bleak through my eyes. I cannot in any circumstance see him having a decent life, settling down with a good job, having a home of his own and having a family. It feels quite heart breaking."

Thoughts from me were that however difficult it might be for her and yes it would be very difficult, that Frankie should attempt to change her own vision of her son's future.

"Let time take its course. Joseph will be perceptive of your thinking around him and his life. He's still a very young man Frankie and who knows what might happen in the future. These things can have a way of sorting themselves out in ways we could never imagine to be possible."

"I'm not confident that your right Helen but I'll listen to what you've said about my thoughts around him and his life."

I continued to remind her of his ice-skating days and the ice-skating competitions in which he had taken part. She had momentarily forgotten about those days and the positive manner in which he conducted himself whilst doing that. There lay the evidence that it was possible that he could be successful in life. Reminding her how he sometimes said he would be a world class skater one day gave Frankie some badly needed hope.

"He had the inspiration Helen. Had the desire to achieve something for himself. Even if he never achieves much in life that thought still feels positive in my mind."

Who could disagree with that?

Returning back to Frankie's home with her I could sense her caution and anxiety as we approached the front door. Not knowing how we might find her child, she was delighted to see that Joseph had settled a little. He was working in the garden. Watching the look of relief on her face reminded me about the level of difficulty and stress, which the Rooney family have had to endure on an ongoing basis. My thoughts were that this level of difficulty would continue for them at least for the foreseeable future. My sense of admiration for the Rooney parents had crept up the ladder. Hearing an apology from Joseph for his earlier behaviour his mum simply smiled and then she was very reassuring to their son. She was also presumptuous regarding my thoughts; however as usual she was correct.

"Don't worry Joseph I understand and Helen understands too. Don't you Helen?"

Reassurance from me that yes, I understood and that all was fine was very much welcomed by Joseph. It appeared to settle and calm down his anxiety a little more. Engaging in some conversation with us both, Joseph shared his news about a local club which he was attending. Primarily it was an Irish club which held events of other genres one night weekly. Living in the hopes of that going in a positive way for him, he would be there each Friday evening from around 8pm until midnight. Being a club where music and dancing were the main functions, Joseph shared how that would be a benefit for his lack of ability to stay still for very long.

To his mother's surprise he was to a certain extent, acknowledging and talking about his issues to us both. For Joseph that was a very rare and quite unusual occurrence. He decided that he had found a niche in life which would hopefully bring him some solace.

"So, the noise won't be great but dancing allows movement as much as I need to, without looking stupid in front of others."
Reassuring him how he would never look stupid regardless

of the situation, Frankie also gave some acknowledgment that she understood.

Teachings not for everyone.

Catherine Rooney was loving life. Weekends away with some friends had become the normal for her. Continuing to work freelance in her chosen field of psychology allowed her to write her own diary. Never being the 9-5 office hours type, she took work beaks as and when required. Catherine experienced some cross over with her mother on quite a few of their local authority cases. Her keen interest as we know was in the area of Impact of trauma on the human brain. Studying and assessing children who had endured trauma before and during removal from their parents, or from whoever was in the role of being their care giver, whole-heartedly satisfied Catherine's interests. Attending family case conferences ahead of their children being taken into local authority care, she often thought back to her own mother's situation as a child. Having little information about her father's side of the family, Catherine shared with me how she silently wondered if perhaps abuse of some nature had taken place there too.

My own children, C.J. Brendan and Anthony have all been through university. In almost copycat fashion they all had psychology as their chosen subject. All being deep and critical thinkers from a very young age this was not too unlike their father. None of them held any great interest in Charlies shared computing and software business, or in my career of Mental Health Nursing. Finding employment suitable to their level of education was proving itself to be difficult. Knowing some other people who had that same experience the boys were prepared, yet they had understandably hoped it might not be their own experience. C J was perhaps the most vocal about their employment situation.

"It's a sign of the times mam. Being overly experienced or overly educated for many jobs, is a negative through the eyes of many potential employers. There will eventually be something and if not, then maybe some more education and training in a different direction for the 3 of us."

There being no real basis for argument with that comment we shared our approval of our sons' sentiments. Having taken on some casual mundane work as they saw it, they all applied for teacher training college. Again CJ. Was the one with the words.

"There's always going to be kids therefore there will always be a need for teachers. Might mean we have to leave the area. We're old enough to do that if it becomes a necessity."

Being successful in their teacher training the boys next steps was to secure employment in their chosen subjects. Enjoying a good high-end quality of life unlike the Rooney's son Joseph, gave them some appreciation for how life can befall some of us.

Charlie and Mikey's company continued to go from strength to strength. Financially we as a family were by this stage of our lives very comfortable as were Frankie and Mikey. Their daughter Catherine was self-sufficient too. Holding down a good job had given her opportunity to get her foot on the property ladder. Whilst still living with her parents and loving her home comforts, she was also building a nest egg for herself in a small 3 bedroomed house not too far from the Rooney's home. Sharing news of her investment with Frankie and Mikey gave Catherine a huge sense of pride in herself and her achievement. Joking with her mother she told Frankie.

"When you've had enough of the old man you can move in to mine. Rents cheap too."

A small celebration was held that evening at the Rooney's to which myself and Charlie were invited. Raising a toast to Catherine and her new home, much to our surprise Joseph joined in too. His words were so warm and heartfelt they would melt the snow from an Icelanders home.

"To the best sister ever. Behaving the way I do when I'm around you is always the easiest option for me. This announcement about your own house has made me crossover my own barriers to share my pride in you. Love you Catherine forever and always."

And then he quickly left the room. Catherine and her mother reached out for the tissue box. Sharing how that had been a momentous moment for the Rooney family Frankie wrapped the evening up. Leasing of her house to a married colleague paid the mortgage for Catherine with a little left over. She was quid's in on that agreement. Whilst still being single at that time with no near-term plan for that to change, she was secure and happy in and with her life.

Pressure on Mikey and Frankie to support their son Joseph from every perspective, including a financial perspective was building up. The situation had become extra stressful for the parents. Having attempted to secure employment, Joseph was successful on a couple of occasions yet it always ended badly. Filling up shelves in a busy supermarket was his current job. Perhaps that hadn't been the best career choice which Joseph had ever made. Intrusion in his head from some noisy chattering customers meeting up in the aisles, had been more than enough for his differently wired up brain to deal with. At times he found the situation overly stimulating and overwhelming with sensory overload. Those were times when he reacted in ways which would be considered to be childlike, making his behaviour highly inappropriate.

Placing items on the shelves one minute the next he flipped, with no regard to who was in his personal space. Spreading products onto the shop floor then shoving a heavily laden trolley out of his way, Joseph was aware that his behaviour having tantrums was immature and rather childlike. It was however at that moment like many other moments, very much outside of his control. Going swiftly to a private area at the back of the store, a sense of not understanding what was happening washed over him.

That's where he was discovered by another staff member. Seen to be holding his head with both ears covered, and shouting out almost at screaming level, a decision was made not to approach him at that point. He was incoherent. The fact that Joseph was experiencing some emotional pain or trauma was obvious. Immediately his vocal outbursts had ceased he was approached. The staff member was calm in her tone as she enquired.

"Joseph what's wrong? What's going on? I want to help. How can I do that?"

The woman was left in limbo. With virtually no response to her questions Joseph moved over to the staff room. Collecting his coat, walking out of the store and going directly home his decision was made. He had decided he was stepping out of the race he felt he should never have been in.

Thinking he had found his road in life he now knew that yet again he was wrong. That this was going to be yet again another job which he was not at all and never would be successful at. Taking a bus home was a challenge for Joseph in terms of hiding his emotions. Cursing quietly underneath his breath, he wished there were fewer people travelling and that the driver could hasten up the journey back to his area. Trying not to stand up and pace the length of the bus presented him a huge challenge. It was one he was not able to manage. Eventually it was his stop to disembark. No one having paid any attention to Josephs behaviour on the bus, left him with mixed feelings. Whilst on one level it was a sense of relief for him that no one intervened, it also left him thinking how uncaring people could be.

Taken by surprise at her son's return and then his refusal to engage with his mother, she could only wonder what had occurred at the supermarket to create the situation which he had found himself in. Hearing her grown up adult child sobbing in his bedroom, Frankie too became overwhelmed with emotion. She was left with quite a strong feeling of helplessness. Taking herself away from the situation felt something like a good plan. Leaving the house alone to take a walk in their local woods she hoped would bring her a degree of solace. She could only hope there might be some improvement with Josephs situation on her return. There wasn't any.

Joseph continued to be emotional. He remained in his bedroom. The sound of fists punching the wall was overly stimulating on Frankie's emotions. Deciding to go back out again in her attempts to escape her own emotional pain, she quickly changed her mind. Being aware that the thoughts of her doing that, might give Joseph the message she couldn't be in the same house as he was, it was a situation which she wished to avoid. Not wanting to heighten his feelings of hopelessness about himself any further, she felt her absence would surely add further to her sons' distress. Frankie was desperate for help. She quietly and secretly asked god to provide that help and to support them both. Having no religion in Frankie's view did not prevent her from the belief that there is a god. She would continue her day at home and hope that her prayer might be answered.

Psychology training was of little use to Frankie at that point. Putting things into perspective in the work situation, was somewhat different when it came down to the nuts and bolts of family life. However, her knowing she could only wait for however long it might take for her child to calm himself, she would then approach him with the idea of discussion. The phone call in the interim came as something of a surprise to Frankie.

"Hello is this Mrs Rooney? Its Teresa Riley here. I'm the store manager at the supermarket where your son Joseph works. I got your number from his employment records."

Quite unlike Frankie she began to panic. With almost a tremble in her voice her response was.

"Oh, hello Teresa its Frankie call me Frankie please. It feels much less formal and less intimidating."

There went Frankie's differently wired up brain again. Suggesting that Teresa was intimidating her when she clearly was not. The feeling however was very real for Frankie. Knowing she would only mess the conversation up even more with any attempt of explanation, she simply waited for Teresa's response.

"No one's doing any intimidating Frankie. I want to help and I really think that I can do that. Can I visit you to have a discussion initially with yourself and Mikey?"

"Well yes that's so generous of you in the circumstance. Joseph leaves home around 6.30-7pm with consistency every Friday evening for his dancing club. That would be a great time for myself and Mikey. Best you check first that he has gone out. After today's events I'm not sure of anything anymore. Teresa's voice had a soothing tone. She told Frankie.

"Then Friday around 7.15pm it is and yes Ill check ahead of coming to your door. See you then hopefully for everyone's sake."

Teresa then wondering if she had given cause for concern by her comment, she hastily added a further comment.

"By hopefully for everyone's sake I mean it'll be better all round, if Joseph feels able to continue with his Friday night plans."

Reassurance that she understood given by Frankie Teresa there in ended the call.

Frankie wondering to herself how the woman knew her husband's name, she was left to her own thoughts on the matter. Deciding she must have taken a keen interest in Joseph and his family life only caused Frankie more stress. She was fearful and almost tearful. What might their son have told her about the family? What awful impression he had probably given to his employer? Frankie's mind was racing. There being a whole 4 more days before their meeting she couldn't wait that long to know what Joseph may have said.

Calling Teresa back she was glad she couldn't be seen. Having worked herself into a frenzy Frankie sought an explanation for the forthcoming visit. She wondered what Joseph had said which was making the family look bad. Being assured nothing bad had been said and how the visit was purely to initially run an idea by the parents, somewhat reduced Frankie's anxiety. Teresa being reluctant to discuss the matter any further, she said all would be out in the open at their meeting, but nothing for the family to worry about. Reassuring Frankie once more she asked if there was anything else she could help with?

"No thank you, Teresa, and again apologies for having bothered you. See you Friday and I'm looking forward. We're both looking forward."

Frankie was intrigued and delighted at the same time. The fact that their child had his dancing evening plans with regularity, was hopefully going to work perfectly for them. She waited with a good degree of trepidation for Friday evening and for their visitor. Joseph who was unaware of the upcoming meeting, left the house at 7pm prompt almost taking the back door with him. Knowing how his emotions were elevated at that point and how he struggled to regulate them, Frankie's fear then was that he might return home earlier than expected, to find his supervisor in his home. That was a dilemma she had to avoid at all costs. She wasn't taking any chances. In her calmest voice she told him ahead of him leaving.

"One of us or maybe both of us will be there to pick you up just after midnight Joseph."

Hearing his almost grunted response of "suit yourself" she took as the signal he was pleased with her offer. Many Friday evenings had been like that when Joseph was distressed ahead of going out.

Preparing themselves for their visitor who had been kept a secret from Joseph, their wait was very slightly extended. That was a preparation of their mind only. Curiosity was understandably high for both parents. Frankie was relaxed about their home. She had always kept a clean and tidy house so no worries about any judgements Teresa might be making. Eventually arriving at 7.45 Teresa was apologetic.

"Traffic for a Friday night was heavier than usual. Perhaps an accident or something such like holding everyone up but I'm here now. Hope the kettles on."

Those last few words from Teresa reassured her host to a certain degree. Having politely greeted their visitor Frankie's mind once again began doing cartwheels. This time it was in relation to the potential accident which Teresa had just mentioned.

Recalling Josephs mood on leaving the house she knew from lifetime experience that he was capable of almost anything. Could he possibly be involved in an accident? Hearing how Teresa had come to their home, from an opposite direction to that which Joseph would have been travelling felt reassuring for the Rooney's. Having the need to give explanation to Teresa regarding what some might consider to be her irrational thoughts, Frankie spoke very quietly.

"Knowing that Joseph is an adult, expectation from others who don't know him, would be that everything would be all right but it isn't. Every time he goes out in one of his moods, there's always the extra over above and beyond chance, that he might do something inappropriate."

A knowing comforting smile from Teresa was sufficient as an ending to that part of the discussion.

Coffee at the ready Frankie invited their guest to share the purpose of her visit. Hearing how she had empathy with Joseph and the whole of the Rooney family, was a comforting thought for Frankie and her husband. Breathing in a huge sigh of relief Frankie shared with their guest the anxieties she had felt surrounding the visit. Again, she was helped to relax by the lady who was there to offer them a potential solution for their sons' issues. Speaking directly to Frankie Teresa tentatively told her.

"There's nothing to be anxious about. I've got an idea and please don't blow it out of the water without due consideration and then some discussion with Joseph. Not trying to tell you or him how to run your life's, so it's just an idea which I'm hoping that you as a family but especially Joseph might like."

Listening without interruption was typical of Frankie and Mikey when that was called for. That particular situation was one which called for their undivided attention. Hearing how Teresa originated from the South of Ireland and the reasons which had brought her to Yorkshire in England, left the Rooney's feeling almost speechless and full of compassion for the woman. She had shared how being moved out of the family home aged 15 years, due to, their discovery that she had engaged in a sexual manner with someone was her reason for emigration. Yes, she was pregnant. Teresa had been sent over to Yorkshire to a mother and baby unit by her own mother. Her mother's words still brought her some heartache.

"You're a disgrace to the family Teresa. Shift yourself out of my sight and out of the country which your bringing shame on too. May god forgive you for your sin."

Teresa shared how that was the last conversation she ever had with her mother. 3 weeks residing in the unit in Yorkshire and 17 weeks pregnant she lost her baby. Having to deliver her baby in the knowledge it was deceased was a harrowing experience for her. Only comfort came from a kindly woman working at the mother and baby home. That was 22 years previous to this meeting with the Rooney's. Sharing with the Rooney's that despite her awful experience of being removed from the family, that in many ways, she felt it could have been a much worse experience for her. She Spoke about how the catholic church in Ireland had no respect for the unmarried mother. Teresa looked pained as she told us.

"Remember the Magdalene laundries in Ireland. You must have heard of them. The worlds heard of them with their disgraceful ways in the treatment of young mothers and their babies. How those young girls were treated with removal of their babies by Nuns, some at birth and some further down the line. Couldn't have dealt with that so in many ways I'm lucky she sent me to England."

Reaching out to a lady whom she had never previously met wasn't the easiest of tasks for Frankie. She however knew it would perhaps be the expectation that she did that. She offered an embrace to Teresa Riley who was graciously accepting of it. The woman continued to share how her father had died when she was a very young child. How having no memory of him not even a photograph to look at had caused her heightened levels of distress throughout her own life. Teresa continued to share how her mother consumed with guilt for the disownment of her only child, has been in contact with Teresa via letter. She shared how it was an odd feeling how contact was made after all those years apart with nothing.

"The letter was addressed to the mother and baby unit Frankie. When leaving there I left them with a forwarding address for me. Never in a million years did I anticipate it would take the woman who gave birth to me and then abandoned me, 22 years to make her feeble attempts to contact me again. Well I'm really not interested so she can shove her letter where the sun doesn't shine."
Teresa momentarily looked a little distressed then a quick smile with reassurance that she was all right.

Not knowing quite how to respond as this was very personal information being shared by a complete stranger, Frankie simply took a deep breath in. That was followed with a great sense of compassion in her voice by.

"Oh, dear Teresa. That must have been just so awful for you. I can't imagine the pain."
Frankie was a woman who having immense compassion for those less fortunate than herself, often found it a challenge to express those feelings. Teresa could sense how difficult it was for her hosts. She expressed gratitude to Frankie for her compassionate response. The woman continued to share some content of the letter with Frankie and her husband Mikey. She shared how her own mother who was a rather wealthy woman, had purchased quite an old farmhouse over in Ireland. Fully paid for and in an attempt to release her guilt she had given the house to Teresa.

"If she thinks that monetary gifts can erase the pain of rejection, which I feel on almost a daily basis she can think again."

Frankie struggling to find a caring response to that painful comment, remembered the time my colleague Jackie died many years ago. She recalled Mikey reminding me how something as small as a key can open up a whole house and how that analogy shows that a small and thoughtful solution, could perhaps help to solve major problems. Keeping that in mind she offered some home-made apple pie to Teresa.

"Catherine our daughter made it. She likes baking. She's very good you should try some."
Knowing how a slice of apple pie would not take Teresa's pain and hurt away from her, she hoped the touch of kindness might create a feeling of being cared about in the woman's mind.

Again, the woman sitting in front of Frankie and Mikey being a complete stranger, made it difficult for them to be able to respond very much at all to her statements. Facial expressions from them, they hoped would let her see that they cared but found the whole of their conversation a bit complex. Teresa expressed how she had no interest in ever going back to Ireland or in being anywhere close to her mother, therefore she would be renting the property out. Hearing her proposal to them made a lot of sense albeit maybe equally a bit weird. Sharing her thoughts with the Rooney's she told them.

"Joseph has so many contributors to his struggles with city life. Considering what happened at the supermarket this week, he has demonstrated he has little to no control whilst in such a public place and a place of employment. He clearly cannot deal with noise and cannot deal with these types of environments very well at all. My views are that he finds noisy, busy and well-lit up places over stimulating and often overwhelming. His education and employment records ahead of coming to our company support and demonstrate these facts to be true."

Looking to each other Mikey Rooney then stood up as if he was about to leave the room. Teresa was quick to interject with her thoughts. Whilst understanding that Josephs father may not have liked what he just heard, she had not finished what she wanted to say and what she needed to say. She was assertive and polite but quite firm in her tone.

"Mikey don't just walk away when we haven't finished the conversation. I'm aware that I'm a complete stranger to you both and all what I've shared with you, probably sounds very weird and very bizarre, but I could not be more serious. This is a very challenging life which Joseph endures and maybe I could help relieve the way he lives it. Perhaps I could help him to feel less stressed out gaining more enjoyment and pleasure from his days. I'm very serious about this situation."

Mikey had as per Teresa's request sat back down. He and Frankie were totally captivated by their visitors' comments. Teresa went on to say how she could see a potentially good future for Joseph, if he was in a calmer environment where he could perhaps be his own boss. She shared how she had spoken at length to a local farmer.

"He apparently runs the land on my inherited property in Ireland. Being an elderly gentleman, his concerns are his future ability to continue on the land. He has shown interest in and would be prepared to train up a young person, who might be interested in learning a farming way of life. That training deal comes with the house too. The farmer a very generous man has offered his services for free. Having reminded me how farming gives him a purpose in life I was happy to engage with his services."

The Rooney's being very impressed with what

Teresa had just said, still could not lose sight of the fact that she was a complete stranger to them. Frankie was the one to respond.

"That's some understanding your demonstrating about our child but why."

Almost reeling from shock by what came next the Rooney's needed time to absorb what Teresa Riley was proposing to them. Her idea that perhaps Joseph might like to move over to Ireland, rent out her house and farm the land for a nominal rental fee, with the view to becoming a farmer, felt almost preposterous to Frankie and Mikey. Despite initially thinking she knew their son pretty well, they were by that point thinking she didn't know him at all. Frankie was again quick to respond.

"That's way off the scale Teresa. Why would you want to be this involved in the life of a person you really don't know much about at all and you really don't."

Hearing Teresa's explanation, the Rooney's gained better understanding of her desire to show some compassion. She proceeded to request they simply listen to what she had to say without interruption. She got their agreement for that.

"In my head its so simple. As I've told you I've had my own share of stress, anxiety and rejection. I'm aware that Joseph is much loved and also aware that regardless to how much he is loved, that love on its own will never prevent the issues which he is enduring in life. I have a house which I will never live in. I could rent it to someone else quite easily however I can see how it could benefit Joseph. Despite what my mother did, I will say that on the whole Irish people are pretty welcoming and warm. They care and would help and support Joseph. Please don't dismiss the idea without some due consideration. Think about it. Think about giving your son the opportunity to make up his own mind. Time for me to go now. I'll wait to hear back from you."

Promptly picking up her coat Teresa thanked the Rooney's for their hospitality that evening. Agreements were made that yes, they would consider what she had said, ahead of them closing the door behind their visitor.

Catherine Rooney being informed of Frankie and Mikey's discussion with Teresa Riley, was left feeling as overwhelmed as her parents were.

"It's so much to take in but its sounding like an amazing opportunity for Joseph. The peace of farming life combined with the therapeutic aspect of being around animals which we all know he loves, could only work in his favour. It could only be good for him."

Further discussion and consideration between the Rooney's that evening, left them feeling as though their brains had been frazzled. It was time to go out to collect Joseph from the club. Seeing his parent's car parked up outside the club as promised was beneficial for him. The fact they were there, told him there's no bad feeling in relation to how he left the house earlier that evening. He had secretly wondered if the door was still hanging. Having taken a considerable amount of abuse over the years it would be no surprise for him if it wasn't. Discussion between the Rooney parents and their son Joseph in relation to Teresa's visit and its content, would happen but at a very carefully chosen moment. Frankie was clear with her husband how they needed to remain quiet about Teresa's visit and her proposal, in order to give themselves some further thinking time.

Our boys C J and Brendan had taken up teaching positions at 2 local secondary schools. One being in our own village the other was in central Yorkshire. Becoming English teachers had initially appeared to be working well for them both. Taking on extra-curricular activities with their young students, outside of the regular school working day was becoming something of a challenge. CJ in particular was putting in the heavy hours. Often leaving home around 06.30 and not returning till after 7pm was feeling tiresome to him. Those after school clubs were becoming a strain especially for their social lives. Giving extra English tuition to some students who had a degree of learning needs, with little financial reward for C J, was typical of his character. He often shared with us how a portion of his students lacked the confidence to speak out when struggling.

"When someone has explained something to you at least 3 times and you still don't get it, what options are you left with. No confidence to speak up you smile politely, giving out the impression you have a clue when you clearly don't."

That's what he was receiving from some of his students hence their need for extra tuition. As his parents we were extra proud of our son for his compassion shown to the less fortunate.

Brendan had set his sights maybe a little further up the ladder or perhaps on a different ladder. Teaching for him was an all right type of job but certainly not the place to stay, not the place to live out all of your adult working years. He would often tell us in no uncertain terms how he is listening to his inner voice. The voice which is often telling him to ask himself the following question.

"Who wants to stand in front of a class room full of rowdy teenagers' day after day, trying to engage with them or lecturing at them?"

Brendan had reached the conclusion that he no longer wanted that situation. The point being that it can put people off teaching for life.

Working at a school in quite a run-down area where many families were living in poverty, brought its own extra degree of problems to the classroom. Students home situations spilled over presenting many challenges in the course of the school day. Kids falling behind academically so someone needs to be blamed. Parents never taking responsibility for their own behaviour or that of their children, compounded the difficult aspects of a teacher's job. Having blame for classroom issues placed onto the teacher's shoulders was a fairly common scenario.

Parents not always being the most approachable, or the most supportive of their children or of their school, could leave you feeling you were living or working in a war zone at times. Those factors combined, Brendan often found himself doing lots of lecturing about and dealing with their aggravated behaviours. That was not his idea of a peaceful day teaching. He often spoke about the times he was feeling all vexed on the inside towards his students and their parents. How he had at times considered displaying an angry reaction towards them, yet that little voice reminded him to stay calm for which he was eternally grateful for.

Pushing back his brown wavy hair from his forehead, was a lifelong habit for Brendan Regan when under severe pressure. Almost pulling it away from his head on this occasion, here we were, being given the clue that our child was about at his wits end with teaching. Hearing how his stress levels can be and at times are unbelievably high we were helpless in knowing how to offer help or support.

Remembering the ease at which he could be consoled as a child, we wished and longed for that for him to no avail. Sharing how his motto had now become "that if you don't like what you're getting out of life, the answer is to change what your putting in."

Having spent some time within schools myself, whilst working in my capacity as a community mental health nurse, I had often picked up the stressful vibes throughout the whole of the buildings and not just within classrooms. Being in the school environment for the purpose of attendance at childcare conferences, put limitations on my time in that environment for which I was often grateful. We both shared some strong feelings of empathy with our son.

"Teaching and school environments are not for everyone Brendan. Thinking as you do no one could disagree that its maybe time you got out."

Summer holidays for our schools being almost upon us would give Brendan some badly needed thinking time and space. Give him an opportunity to explore his employment thoughts further and perhaps seek out some interviews taking him in a different direction in life.

Our twin son Anthony having moved away from our area we believed he was quite settled in his work. A temporary teaching job covering maternity leave was what he told us. We were again to be proved wrong. Holding a degree in psychology and philosophy combined with a teacher training course, the surprise was ours in the discovery of him travelling on a different path for his career. Interviews had always been the one thing in life where he lacked confidence. This time Frankie's advice had stuck with him. Thinking her a little harsh in her outlook he could see the relevance of what she had said and how it helped him on this occasion.

"Either they like you or they don't Anthony. They don't someone else will so deal with it and move on."

Successfully getting to interview and flying his way through that, Anthony was a happy man. He became an airline host with an American airline company. Being a people's person as he was, with a preference to working with adults as opposed to children he was in his element. Travelling throughout the whole of America and some other continents too, is what was on the agenda for him. That would bring him into contact with people of many different cultures and nationalities. Having a keen interest in various cultures from around the world, his airline position appeared to be perfect for him.

Meeting his needs at every level he would meet the needs of his employers too. Bringing much joy to his days was what every parent would always wish for their child. Life in Pittsburgh appeared to be all and everything he had hoped for. Living in the state of Pennsylvania and being away from home, were both situations which Anthony had adjusted to very well. Calling his parents' home phone almost weekly, they heard how the landscapes of Pittsburgh bore great resemblance to that of England as a whole. Knowing how 2 of our children appeared to be settled in their employment was a great sense of relief for myself and Charlie. Next on our wishful agenda for all 3 of our children, would be to see them settle down, get married and make us grandparents. Reminding ourselves how these would be areas of our children's lives for which we would have no control, we continued with the dream. Where control of our own life choices was in our reach all 4 of us achieved. Having jointly set the bar high with a great sense of determination, was the catalyst for our success.

Frankie, Mikey, Charlie and myself all broke tha awful cycle of inappropriate parenting. Ensuring we would get to keep our children and show them a decent way of life, in the absence of any input from social services, made us proud parents. Where support was required for Joseph it was due to a condition enforced upon him, whereby the best, the most conscientious of parenting skills, would never singularly be enough to address and help his issues. Planned gatherings at Gerry's between the 4 of us, availed us the opportunity to celebrate the many positives in our parenting skills and to acknowledge the let downs too. There were plenty of those shared between us but nothing we didn't take responsibility for.

Despite having Charlie and a valued nursing career in my life, there were times when sadness was a regular visitor to me. Working my way through this particular sad time was proving itself to be something of a challenge for me. The visit from Frankie together with her husband was therefore a very pleasant and badly needed experience. I had looked forward to that evening with enthusiasm. Still being a closed net of 4 in so far as friendships were concerned, they were our only outlet for social events. Our taste buds enjoying the same food flavours was a bonus. Having prepared their favourite meal, it was a favourite for myself and Charlie too. Our evening together went well giving Frankie and Mikey lots of opportunity to discuss with us, their visit from Teresa the supermarket manager. Not having shared their company for almost 3 weeks we had lots to catch up on. The men discussing their software business left myself and Frankie to talk about the children we had raised between us. Their presence raised my mood considerably.

   Catherine Rooney having been in the same job for some time was very settled and had found herself a regular boyfriend. To their knowledge he was called Jeremy and that's all they knew. Sharing with me how herself and Mikey were eager to have introductions, Frankie expressed the thought that a move to live with the boyfriend was on the cards for Catherine.
   "I'm sure she's building up to telling us they're moving in together Helen. Little things like more and more of her clothes and bits and pieces have gone out our front door recently and never returned. We don't ask her questions and she doesn't volunteer any information, so there we have it. We're left to draw our own conclusions."
Reminding my friend how secretive we both were in the early stages of our romantic life, ahead of meeting the men who are now our husbands, there was little else left to say about Catherine's situation? C J and Anthony having reasonably settled lives with one working in education whilst the other enjoyed a career in aviation, played a part in the evening's conversation.

   Main topic concerned the Rooney's son Joseph. Appearing to be uppermost in the thoughts and minds of both his parents, Frankie opened the door for that conversation. A bomb shells been dropped on us Helen and which way to turn, which way to deal with it is proving to be almost impossible. Our brains are frazzled trying to fathom it out. Through discussion that evening of the whole Joseph situation, combined with the offer on the table from Teresa, a decision was reached. The Rooney's child was unhappy. One of our children wasn't overly happy in his chosen employment. The idea of bringing them together to the table with us seemed like a very good idea. We would meet at Frankie's. Keeping Joseph on neutral ground would work in his better interest.

Neither young men being aware of the reason for the gathering, we had their agreement that we should all share an evening meal at the Rooney's home. Eczema and spots and every irritating skin condition imaginable, seemed to aggravate both sets of parents in the week leading up to the meeting. Frankie called me. She was in a frenzy with thoughts of uncertainty about the planned upcoming event between the two families.

"We doing the right thing here Helen because if we are why do I feel so bad? Why do I appear to have lost the ability to survive and regulate my own feelings, thoughts and my emotions?"

Assurance given that my own situation with anxiety was almost a mirror image of hers, Frankie calmed herself a little. Continuing our conversation about Joseph Rooney we had to agree, that he can be both introvert and extrovert to a greater degree than might be expected. Craving attention and the need to be with someone, other times he would suddenly need and want some solitude. Again, both of these needs would be demonstrated in a far more extreme manner than that which you might expect from an adult. Joseph had demonstrated those traits all of his life. They were however more pronounced in his adult life. Acknowledging to her how our son Brendan has also often demonstrated similar traits in his personality surprised Frankie.

Hearing how Brendan's socialising time usually

has an expiration date where he too needs solitude, we both realised how our children were similar in so many ways. Frankie put it all in perspective for us.

"Seeking and finding this solitude is a valuable and deeply needed time for both men to recharge their batteries. It highlights how they can cover up from others just like we do at times."

Ending our phone conversation, we arranged for the meeting to occur at Frankie's home the following evening.

Catherine Rooney had some great understanding of her brothers issues and how they impacted other people. Her attention to everyone present that evening was impeccable. Knowing how stressful it would probably be for myself and Charlie, for her parents and perhaps for the young men too, was the catalyst in prompting her to host the evening. Having prepared one of Joseph's favourite meals, would place the picture in his head that attention was being given to him. Catherine was hopeful that having that picture in his head, would help her brother to remain calm and co-operative for the evening. Knowing how he struggled to deal with loud noise, especially that associated with people talking loudly, Catherine had privately reminded all of us to make attempts to keep our voices relatively low.

Hearing the ideas about a farming way of life in Ireland which had been put forward by Teresa the supermarket manager, Brendan and Joseph but perhaps more so Brendan, showed some appreciation for her thoughtful nature and her deep insight into Josephs problems. Brendan expressed his thoughts about Teresa as a person.

"No idea why she is giving up her house and farm. She's obviously a person who's in love with people rather than power and that's just great. She represents the type of people who should be listened to."

Brendan was quietly applauded by all of us for his very insightful comment. Hearing from his parents how Teresa's plan was to rent out the house and land to him left Joseph feeling a little confused. Having a great love for animals of all descriptions learning to become a farmer did have a degree of appeal for him. That was heightened by his thoughts of the peace and tranquillity of rural life. However, Joseph was still confused. Why would Teresa or anyone want to give him what he saw as such a potentially great opportunity?

Listening to the Rooney's speak about Teresa's own upbringing in Ireland, the pregnancy and the rejection of Teresa by her own mother, Brendan expressed his unconditional respect for the woman. Struggling to understand how any mother could reject their child in that manner he turned towards me. His words were soft.

"I'm sure we were challenging mum well I know we were. Remembering many ups and downs and the headaches we created for you and dad between us. Thanks for sticking by us through it all."

Casting his eyes towards Joseph and with the use of a hand gesture, he was inferring that Joseph should acknowledge Frankie and Mikey's unconditional love for him. Brendan's suggestion did not connect with Josephs brain. As usual Joseph was forthright, right down the middle with no grey areas in his comments.

"Good luck sending me confusing and mixed messages Brendan. I often don't understand direct ones so you'd best try again."

The Rooney family all smiled simultaneously and knowingly, as they inwardly agreed with Josephs statement.

Brendan initially felt a little perplexed. Frankie encouraged their son to share what he had told her had happened at the supermarket earlier that day. Her hopes were that it would allow Brendan to have a better insight into Josephs brain. With no reluctance on his part Joseph told his story again. How a shop assistant at the supermarket was trying to explain to him the value of time management. What she didn't know was that his autistic brain was overly confused, whilst he was still trying to figure out what the heck time actually is. Brendan acknowledged just how hard that must make life for Joseph who once again was very direct in his comment.

"You're wasting your time with looks and gestures Brendan. Just tell me clearly and directly in a simple manner what it is your trying to suggest to me."

Brendan was shocked. The moment was lost- it was gone. There was no point in any further futile attempts with explanations to Joseph Rooney, concerning how he should acknowledge his parent's love and loyalty to himself and Catherine. Furthermore, Brendan knew that Frankie and Mikey were aware of Josephs appreciation of them for sticking by his side, therefore it wasn't necessary to say it again. Having known Joseph over a lengthy period of time, he had the knowledge that the man was to some degree educated. Brendan however had very little to no understanding of how autism impacted Joseph's brain. He felt almost ashamed for his lack of awareness.

Critiquing himself to everyone in the room for that lack of awareness and especially so as a teacher, he would put the situation right. Moving forward in life he would commit to taking steps to discover that knowledge. He continued to express to Joseph in a very clear and direct manner, how yes, his parents Frankie and Mikey had knowledge of his respect for them and his gratitude for their love and care without question. Catherine Rooney was quick to have the subject closed. She interjected with her own thoughts about Ireland and the farm house.

"Could be a great start for you Joseph. You'd learn a new skill doing the job you'd love doing with no bright lights and screaming loud noises. No sensory overloading."
Brendan beckoned to Joseph again with a hand gesture. He quickly remembered the situation so that gesture was instantly followed up by a verbal request that he might go outside. Both men left the table promptly going into the garden.

Frankie's eyebrows did that thing they do when she's curious and confused. Expressing how the men only casually know each other, she joked that maybe they're having some bonding time, or perhaps Brendan is attempting to learn a little more about Josephs autistic brain and how it functions differently to his. Joining them in the back garden some time later myself and Frankie expressed our curiosity. A knowing glance exchanged between the men and we were ushered back inside. Joseph telling his father to get some wine and glasses as they have a celebration to raise a toast to, Mikey was very obliging. Carefully pouring the wine he told their son.

"Come on then lad out with it. Have you both won the lottery?"

The following 20 minutes or so brought deadly silence to the room, with the exception of Brendan and Josephs voice. We all sat in anticipation of what we were about to hear. Having privately agreed and confirmed their thoughts they shared their news. Joseph however said very little. He told us how he felt that Brendan would be better at giving a clear explanation. Knowing that Brendan was unsettled in his chosen career of teaching, it wasn't too surprising for us to hear how he has now planned to quit his employment with the local education authority. How he no longer wants to work in teaching. His moving forward plan however came as a huge surprise to all of us. Brendan making comments about how people with disabilities are not a problem to be solved, but rather how on the contry they are people who need to be understood and nurtured, just melted my heart.

Knowing how that was my boy showing such a high level of understanding of people with their differences, and said by him with such great compassion too, I was proud. Proud of the child we reared to become such a compassionate and caring human being. He told the room how that's exactly what Teresa Riley was hoping to do for Joseph. She was showing him understanding and a way forward in life which would hopefully be much less traumatic for him. How she was showing her knowledge of what it feels like to be a little different or perhaps even a lot different in this world.

Teresa had shared how differently she perceived herself to be, due to the rejection of her by her mother and due to the baby situation. Brendan continued to tell everyone how he didn't have the greatest knowledge or understanding of the autistic brain but was very eager to learn. Both men expressed their gratitude to Teresa Riley for her insightful nature. Looking to Joseph Brendan asked him the direct question.

"Are you ready for me to share our plan."

An affirmation from Joseph to go ahead left the whole house hearing, how Brendan and Joseph would both travel over to Ireland. They would take up Teresa Riley's offer of renting her house and farm land. Brendan was very clear.

"What's life all about if we don't take risks. Joseph will teach me about autism and I will support him in learning a farming way of life which I too will learn."

With the absence of giving opportunity for anyone to respond he turned his gaze to Frankie. He then requested a prompt meeting with Terresa Riley together with Joseph.

"That'll give opportunity to go through the whole process. Get rent books sorted and plans for collection of the keys including an idea of how and when this adventure can commence."

Frankie being the first to respond she spoke on behalf of all of us. Her psychological and rational thinking came into play as she uttered the words.

"Our family and yours Helen- we're all like branches on the same tree. All of us growing in different directions yet our roots will always remain the same."

Mikey Rooney wiped a tear from his eye. We all raised our glasses in a toast to our young men. Everyone always knew that Brendan who was unsettled in his chosen career of teaching, would eventually find something which he was more comfortable with. He held the philosophy that we should never allow anyone who hasn't walked in our shoes, tell us how to tie our laces. He was very aware that Continuity to show resistance to change would only take him down the wrong and harder path. His resistance to change had by this point disappeared. Not the same applied to Josephs life. It was therefore a huge relief to Frankie and Mikey to know how their child had this adventure ahead of him. To know he would start building a life for himself under the guidance of Brendan Regan. Brendan appeared to have found his right path in life. All now left for him to do was to proceed to make a success of their adventure.

Vulnerable brother

Rooney N Regan software company had continued to grow. Going from strength to strength they were branching out creating many jobs for the unemployed. Their services were now getting recognition worldwide. Having started as such a small company and now having sales figures for different continents was beyond their wildest dreams. This experience for Mikey Rooney and Charlie Regan had brought some deep joy to their days at the office. Despite their ever-increasing success they remained to be very grounded. Remained to be the 2 men who were raised in a children's home with a very colourful background, that being especially so for Mikey.

Feeling that their lives were being appreciated by the right people brought them some more deep joy. Having dedicated time and energy into the business, dividends were by now coming back to them in abundance. Mikey was quite emotional as he shared with his friend and business partner.

"Charlie, the day we met was probably one of the luckiest days of our lives. Thinking back to where we were then and looking at where we are now, we are so blessed. Thinking about certain kids at the children's home whose lives were very much on the wrong path like I was and Shaun Jackson is another example"
Charlie took a deep breath in.

"Some people never change. Becoming adults, they pick their own path. Should it be the wrong one as in the case of Shaun, it's no one's place to try to fix it for them. No one can fix it for them. Only they can do that for themselves. We put ourselves in the right direction and yes look at us now. Thank you, my friend, for everything."

Neither man having fear of demonstrating their emotions they shared a warm embrace. Mikey had a long-held wish concerning an activity which he in particular wanted to do. Encouragement from Frankie to go ahead gave him the push required. Calling his work partner who was also enthusiastic about the activity, the men put their plan in place. They duly took a drive back to the children's home where Mikey had been reared. Mikey's need was being met through this visit. Thinking how the interior hadn't changed in all those years felt a little disappointing to Mikey. Not wanting to offend anyone, they were both reserved in their comments about the house. Conversation went back over the past 20 years. Many of the regular staff on duty that day had worked with Mikey when he was a young child. Delighted to see him again this time as a very successful adult, they were forthright in expressing their thoughts to Charlie and Mikey.

Staff wondered if they might be interested in joining their team as independent visitors. Hearing how they would each be allocated to a particular child brought a keen interest in hearing more about that especially from Mikey. They heard how it would involve Mikey and Charlie occasionally going into the unit to give talks on life skills. Mikey was especially interested in taking on that role. Sharing one of his favourite life expressions with staff –

"It was that people who have been through the fires of hell, should carry some water for those still caught up in the burning flames."
He now had an opportunity to put that expression into action and would do so with much enthusiasm. Mikey also considered and shared another of his much-loved expressions.

Reminding staff how we are all aware that life is an unstoppable moving forward of time, his suggestion was carefully listened to. How that's the energy which drives all of us towards our inevitable demise. Mikey's sentiments felt breath taking to the care home staff.

"Thanks for those insightful words Mikey. Life with us at the kids home certainly appears to have instilled some good values into you."

Mikey felt strongly that these expressions were highlighting the importance of grasping every opportunity, helping people along the road as and when we can do so. Charlie perhaps not being so sure or so keen on the idea would let them have his decision further down the line.

Plans for travel to Ireland eventually put in place, the Rooney and Regan families would say goodbye to their young men. Sun beaming down helped to warm up the ambience of their day of departure. Up at the crack of dawn the men would firstly pay a surprise goodbye visit to Teresa Riley at the supermarket. Collection of house keys from Teresa plus all documents necessary had previously been exchanged. Their visit on this day was once again to show her some appreciation. Allowing Teresa to see first-hand that the benefits coming from her sense of caring were immense. How her compassion was being of huge help to Brendan and Joseph perhaps as much as it was for Teresa. The men showing her that her awful teenage experience with her mother, only added up to making her a better person and how that would hopefully help her further, in acknowledging that a damaged child will not necessarily be forever impacted badly by that damage. She thanked the men for their kind words. She wished them well with a promise that maybe she would go visit them on the farm in Ireland one day. Returning back to their family homes for late breakfast they would say goodbye to their families later that morning.

    Catherine Rooney and her parents had come together with our other children at our house. Being Catherine's idea, she was clear with her reasons.

    "My very annoying and very vulnerable brother will not be leaving this country without a proper send off. Such a huge experience for him and for Brendan too. I'm guessing that Brendan may be feeling the lion's share of responsibility for obvious reasons. Its our job and our duty to ensure he's not feeling burdened. Have him know that we are all here for them both should any issues or challenges they can't deal with arise."

    As her parents Mikey and Frankie expressed their pride in their daughters caring and understanding nature. Myself and Charlie having acknowledged Catherine's sentiments with some gratitude and a strong sense of pride, impacted her to a degree which would not be expected. To everyone's surprise Catherine had to make a request for the tissue box. She was clearly touched by the whole situation and especially so by our views of her as a person. Reassurance given from Charlie that we speak as we find Catherine smiled. Brendan Regan and Joseph Rooney having quickly said their goodbyes, they took a long drive to the port and then a ferry crossing over the Irish sea. Brendan having his own car made the journey more palatable for them both. Their arrival on Irish soil would open up a new world to them both. They were yet to make that discovery.

Table for 6 had been booked at Gerry's for that evening. Being fondly welcomed we were taken to a table overlooking the river. Being adjacent to where Frankie would be sat as a young woman she considered how much cleaner the place looked. She considered how much the restaurant had improved aesthetically too, with new furniture and a newly designed bar area since her experience there in her younger days. The scenic view was relaxing, which in many ways we all needed that evening. That's where we reminisced and raised a glass to our 2 young men who had departed on their journey for Ireland. Catherine raised the toast.

"To Brendan and Joseph in their new adventure and to all things Irish. To Teresa for her caring ways. Her absence in our life this adventure would not be happening."

Shaun still being a staff member at Gerry's arrived for duty as Catherine raised the toast. Expressing his best wishes for the young travellers to everyone's surprise he produced a good luck card. Assuring him it would be passed on Catherine graciously thanked him on behalf of her brother and Brendan. Pulling up a chair to our table Shaun joined us briefly. Some small talk about the men having been into Gerry's ahead of them leaving England, was how Shaun got the news of their departure. This led to a short journey down memory lane between Frankie and the waiter. Reminiscing about Frankie's weekly visits there so many years ago, he shared how her presence had never been forgotten. His services eventually being needed on the floor, Shaun bade us all goodbye till the next time. Walking away he told Frankie

"Don't leave it so long till the next time. Everyone here misses you."
She smiled. They exchanged a quick and brief embrace.

    Conversation that evening enlightened us that Frankie was still at times, in pursuit of further information regarding her deceased family. Catching her in the ladies with a tearful face she made no effort of pretence. Back at the table openly sharing Frankie had a few more tears. She continued to share how she needs to know her ancestors yet accepts she never will. Allowing her mum to express her thoughts Catherine then intervened once Frankie had said her piece.

    Reminding her mother that from a psychologist's perspective and one who is little more than marginally detached, that perhaps her mother should seek some counselling again. She spoke compassionately on this occasion and with an obvious degree of love to and for her mother.

"Situations in our head that sting us need to be addressed. As you know yourself that if ignored they will simply fester causing more pain and never go away. I know someone who would be suitable for you and no I do not mean myself."

Leaning across the table Frankie took hold of her daughters' hands. She spoke with an almost broken voice.

"What did I ever do to deserve such a caring child as you are. I love you Catherine Rooney and yes, I will meet with the person you recommend. Let's leave it there for now and enjoy what's left of the evening."

Catherine smiled. Telling her mother how the conversation would continue back home the following day, Frankie once again was reminded that their child shared her parents' very strong levels of persistence and determination. The group raised another toast- this time it would be to our other children, who we believed to be progressing well in life and long may their progress reign. Our evening at Gerry's having come to its end, Frankie's suggestion of a meet up the following weekend between the parents was welcomed.

   Back on the wards of our local psychiatric hospital life was feeling busier than ever. Many of our patient situations on the wards held strong memories of our colleague Jackie for me. She was the lady who had so suddenly and so tragically lost her life. Leaving 3 children and an alcoholic husband behind her, their children were immediately taken into care. The situation had felt just awful. Jackie's husband lost his life some years after her demise. Their children remained in the care of local authority to the point of each reaching the age of 18 years. Having had many deep conversations with Frankie and Catherine Rooney about dysfunctional families, my conclusion always was that these children would struggle with life's challenges. In the case of Jackie's children, I was beyond delighted to be proved to be wrong. Having a professional involvement with social services, the children and I met on a number of occasions over the years. They were never informed that I knew and worked with their mother. I was delighted to hear how all had gone through university education and were now working in successful careers.

   Through respect for our colleague Jackie, myself and the ward sister Cathy had remained in contact at a distance with the children's foster carers. Providing some financial support over the years, this acted as top up for all local authority financial assistance given to them. We had hoped this was us doing our share to show respect to our deceased colleague and her family. Jackie's children had never been made aware of our input or our financial support. Decision making for that fact had laid with the children's foster carers. Not wishing to make the children feel extra stressed or uncomfortable in any way, we had totally respected and abided by their carer's decision.

It was somewhat of a surprise for me, when the eldest daughter of Jackie was given employment on the wards of the same hospital where her mother had worked and where I still worked. Recognition of myself by her from our meetings over the years felt uncanny, especially so when she made herself known to me.

"Well who would have known you work here Mrs Regan. I recall you so well from review meetings. Did you know my mother Jackie?"

"Whoa call me Helen and Yes, I knew your mother fairly well. She was a colleague. I could never share that information with you throughout your childhood. It's just protocol. I'm sure you understand."

Expressing her understanding of the situation Karina went on to share with me, some information of her younger siblings. Both had a University education and working in education, was good news for me to hear. All had a decent foster home and still keep contact with the foster parents. Delighted to hear that and ahead of bidding goodbye till the next time.

"I've no doubt Karina that our paths will cross again on the wards. If you need to hear anything about your mum and you think I can help, you now know where I am so please don't hesitate."

Extending her arms for an embrace I was happy to indulge.

Unexpected situations.

Continuing to be settled in his chosen career of teaching life appeared to be pretty good for our first-born CJ. Working and living not far from the family home he came back to visit on occasional weekends. Loving those visits, Charlie and I always looked forward with enthusiasm. Typically, this would be when he had a need for some extra laundry to be done, or required advice on some new recipe which he had dreamt up. CJ often tried out new recipes- just for the challenge he said.

"Not that I don't love all you taught me in the kitchen mam, experimenting with food is always good. Your opinions and advice have never let me down yet."

Not especially liking some of his ideas sharing the truth always felt important to me. Agreeing to differ CJ would proceed with his experiment. Photographic evidence from him often showed me how competent he was in the kitchen.

The call to ask if he could bring a friend to stay for the forthcoming weekend was unexpected and totally out of character for CJ. I was like the cat that curiosity might kill if I didn't get some answers. Trying not to sound too intrusive I'm not sure I had very much success there.

"Who? Which friend is it someone we know? Deadly silence was the response I received from our son.

My attempts to gain information about the friend fell onto deaf ears. I was intrigued. I wanted to know more. CJ remained very tight lipped where my questions were concerned. Promptly changing the subject, he shared some general news about his days in the classroom. That was typical of him. CJ was like that. He had always enjoyed a mystery. Recalling his school days-He would delight in handing me a letter, requesting that I should call his school to arrange an appointment to visit. Some schools were terrible in those days. There would be no further information included. You relied on your child to inform you of content the letter was missing. CJ always knowing what the meeting was for would remain tight lipped. Knowing me as well as he did he knew I would be eager for information. That perhaps made his game a little more interesting to him. He would always deny it was a game.

Days leading up to the weekend were full of excitement for myself and Charlie, with a sprinkling of apprehension also thrown into the pot. All that said I have to share that never in a million years were either of us expecting the news which CJ brought to us. Meeting Thomas Summers and hearing that our son was gay caused shock waves throughout my body. Charlie was simply silent- he was non-responsive. Suddenly making some feeble attempts to show his acceptance he welcomed Thomas into our home. To say that most of the weekend was difficult would be an understatement.

Not having any particular religious leanings, we were at the least saved from the obvious pain which that news may have brought to some families. Our concern was for the happiness of our child and for no other reason.

Despite being educated people with good life prospects and good careers, Charlie and I shared how we were pretty much ignorant, when it came down to the facts of people's gender and their sexuality preferences, which veered away from what society had considered to be 'the normal'. There was not anyway on any planet that we could ever understand, how a same sex relationship could ever be a happy relationship. We were shattered. We were devastated for our child.

Strong attempts to cover up our fear and disappointment were duly made by myself and Charlie. Those attempts became more challenging for us, with them rapidly fading away as the weekend progressed. CJ and Thomas were both open and honest people. Deciding to temporarily take himself out of the equation, Thomas took a long walk alone through our local park. This giving opportunity for CJ to have conversation with myself and Charlie, we were appreciative of that time. Hearing from our son how he and Thomas had been seeing each other for more than 1 year, coupled with the reality of his happiness, we eventually grasped his situation. Not that he ever said this, we thought about how people in straight relationships could possibly feel wrong and awkward to CJ. How his struggle with that, would be understanding that these people had found happiness with each other. That was the coin flipped to the other side for us. Having the full understanding that our issue was not a homophobic one, but one of pure concern for our childs happiness and well-being, he filled us both with confidence that he was very happy indeed.

Thomas was a young man with a great sense of humour. He would be hard to resist regardless of your view around gender and sexuality issues. It would have been very hard to dislike him as a person. On his return back from the walk he was greeted by CJ in the way which many men greet each other. It was a quick embrace which Thomas immediately reciprocated. Having booked a table for 4 that evening at Gerry's, CJ reminded me of his awareness that Gerry's had special meaning to myself and his father through my friend Frankie. Being seated at Gerry's and waiting for our selected meals to arrive CJ proposed a toast.

"Mum dad raise a glass to the newest member of our family. Thomas and I plan to share our lives permanently with each other. Hopefully we will live together happily ever after."

Seeing the colour slowly draining away from Charlies face was a little unsettling for all of us. The 2nd shock of the weekend was by now starting to take its toll on him. Ahead of responding to our son, we both required a little breathing space with some time to gather our thoughts. There was no way around our need, no way of escaping from the shock other than time to digest it. That was perhaps especially so for Charlie. CJ would simply have to understand. Interruption from Shaun the waiter with our meals was perfect timing- the expression 'he saved the day' comes to mind. Knowing us as well as he did and having heard CJ share the news, he too was aware we would need some time to internalise it all.

Much to our amazement Thomas had that awareness too. Perching himself backwards and more upright on his chair he looked a little anxious. Amazing how in the absence of knowing that young man I could still see that he was anxious. People do say it's all in the body language and perhaps it is. Thomas proceeded with almost a quiver in his voice. The young man had a look of sadness on his face. Clearing his throat, he then told us.

"It's fine. We both appreciate that as CJ's parents it's a lot for you to take in. My parents have known for years that I'm gay with no real acceptance of my gender issues and no acceptance at all of my relationship with your son. Unlike you they are both homophobic as are all my family members and it's awful. You two are totally amazing. Just as CJ knew and reassured me that you would be."

Watching our child sat across the table from us his face was mixed with joy and anxiety. Knowing the panic he had to be feeling inside, whilst placing my hand on his I was secretly willing the evening to come to its end.

Thomas continued to share how his parents but his father in particular, would make jokes about homosexual people, in complete absence of knowledge of how offensive they were and still are being. Thomas had told his parents and extended family that much of the pain he endures comes from oppression. That if they had a genuine want and desire to help him, then they should rethink their attitudes and join the fight against homophobia. My maternal instincts were hovering. Knowing how happy my own child appeared to be in his relationship with Thomas, I had a strong urge to go around the table and hug the young man who was seated opposite me. Controlling my urges somewhat I once again reached across the table placing my hand over his, giving the strong message of approval and acceptance. Delight on CJ's face could not be measured as he now witnessed my warmth towards his boyfriend. Charlie was quick with his comments of.

"That's acceptance from us both and not just from Helen."

Our evening at Gerry's drawing to a close, the plans were that CJ and Thomas would leave for home the following morning. Making their acknowledgement of the intensity of the weekend for us, they shared their joint decision to have changed the plan, they would now be leaving that evening. CJ was visibly emotional as he told us.

"Your both just fabulous. Hearing all of the news you've heard so far this weekend, you've shown your love for me through your acceptance of Thomas as my life partner."
CJ continued to share how the weekend was tense and at times stressful for himself and Thomas too. They had awareness how bias and discrimination was still rife within many families notably the family of Thomas. Keeping all of those factors in mind they had decided to leave for home directly from Gerry's. Give all of us a little time to sit and ponder, ahead of returning to the work place on Monday morning. Their bags already packed up in the car they would drive us back home then continue on their journey. Saying goodbye to our son was probably the easiest it had ever been, when leaving from his weekends home. Knowing he had someone special in his life outside of family was a truly comforting thought for us both.

Calling my long-time friend Frankie Rooney felt like a good plan. Having arranged for a meet up at their house I prepped myself for presentation of the news I would be sharing with her. Gender issues was something we had never spoken about. Not a deliberate avoidance of the matter but more simply and surprisingly the topic never arose. Consideration given to the vast amount of people, which we both came in contact with through our individual employment, made it even more surprising that the topic never arose. I had met and worked with some patients on the mental health wards, who had suffered badly due to their gender issues. Those issues were often compounded for them, by a lack of respect and recognition from their own families. Thomas came to mind with the lack of acknowledgement and acceptance he was enduring from his own parents and family.

Typical of Frankie she had prepared lunch with a feast which would be fitting for a king. There was enough food to feed the 5,000. Deciding to eat first and share my news later we put the world to rights. Sitting outdoors in the sunshine topping up our vitamin D intake was wonderful. Knowing how everyone needs to offload at times, we shared some stories but no name dropping, from the madness we were surrounded by in our respective work situations. It was a little therapeutic for us both. I was very relaxed in the knowledge that we could tell each other anything in trust and confidentiality and not be offended. That thought in mind I just blurted it out.

"CJ was home last weekend with Thomas his boyfriend. What do you reckon to that?"
Expecting her response to be a response of shock I was left expecting. I was the one left in shock.

Frankie smiled with what looked to me to be one of her knowing smiles. I was a little confused. Her comment almost floored me.

"So glad he's found someone Helen. Guessing that he was probably gay and knowing how ignorant some people still are, caused me lots of silent concern for him."

"You're not surprised or even shocked. You knew?"

"Well yes I've wondered about that for years not that he has ever told me anything. His mannerism his body language to me were sort of tell-tale signs. I'd thought about how sometimes they would relate to a gay person but not necessarily so."

Tension if not the beginnings of anger started welling up inside me towards Frankie.

"You never thought about sharing that with me-his mother."

"For the same reasons that you had never shared your observations of Joseph with me. It wasn't my place to raise any issues concerning your child Helen."

Frankie went on to remind me how very similar we were in our ways of thinking through situations. How at times a person outside of the family, is very likely to pick up clues that parents just don't see, where their own child is concerned.

"We can be too busy dealing with the regular stuff Helen and have blinkers where the deeper stuff is concerned. It happens. We have to get over it."

Remembering how I was aware of Josephs issues when his parents were not, the thought placated me somewhat.

"Yes, your right Frankie we can all have blinkers and I'm sorry. Were just praying that he's happy and that this is not just simply a phase."

She went onto share how her observations of CJ did not necessarily mean that he was gay. How some men can present with that type of body language for no obvious reason. How we both had learned in our training sessions, that some people who choose same sex relationships can suffer confusion and do so for a variety of reasons. How it's never a given that a person is gay even if they think they are, simply due to them being close to or having a relationship with another person of the same sex. That where CJ is concerned that only time would tell and how fortunate he was in having parents able to demonstrate understanding of his situation.

Sharing with Frankie how the disclosure from CJ absolutely floored myself and Charlie, I was surprised at my own ease of speaking to another person, about our concerns regarding something so personal. Being able to acknowledge how our negative feelings quickly passed as we heard it from CJ's perspective, allowed me to appreciate that all which mattered to us was our childs happiness. Continuing to update my best friend forever, she got the message that Thomas is a lovely young man with a good and solid career in teaching. Frankie understood how all of that helped us to be more accepting of CJ's potential life partner. She was delighted to hear that our eldest child was perhaps going to settle down with someone. Sharing how a planned-out future between the boys was looking very positive, I was quick to add that yes, I still considered all of our children as our boys. Frankie requesting a meet up the next time Thomas and CJ graced us with their company, the plan was put in place. We embraced ahead of us saying goodbye for that evening.

Post arriving with an envelope bearing the Stars and Stripes of the American flag excited me. Recognising my childs handwriting I promptly ripped the envelope open. It was weeks if not months since our last proper contact with Anthony had occurred. Occasionally he would drop a text message, checking on our well-being and saying very little about his own life in Pennsylvania. Emails from him usually had the same lack of information in their content. Anthony was aware how much we both enjoyed sitting down reading a content filled letter. His letters never

disappointed provided we were happy having pages to read, concerning
the area in which he was living, and wider parts of America. There was always lots of historical news about Pittsburgh. There was nothing personal about himself ever shared. Often thinking how he had been using the avoidance technique brought its own degree of concern to myself and Charlie. Was there a problem in his life which he was not prepared to share? Then wasn't it the same with our other child CJ, who equally had never shared much in terms of his private life, to the point where he had little choice. Was there something about us as their parents which sent out the message we were not approachable?

  Letters from Anthony would also be filled with news surrounding the area in which he was living and what was available entertainment wise, should it be desired by anyone. He often spoke about how other people were making a living and what his views were on their employment choices. This time it was different. On this occasion he had some special news for us. He was coming home for good. He would arrive back in England the following week and was hoping for a pick up from the airport. How about the possibility of him moving back in with myself and his father was a question which was clearly highlighted by Anthony? Flight details were also clearly shown in his letter. Having just discovered what at times felt exciting news and other times concerning news about CJ and Thomas, we couldn't help but wonder if perhaps something similar was happening in Anthony's life. Charlie reminding me that speculation would never be purposeful and how I was over thinking the situation, I gave him my agreement to stop. We would simply wait and see despite the challenge that would set for me.

Quickly responding to Anthony by text message we confirmed that yes, an airport collection would be fine. Reassuring him there would always be a bed with his name on it in our home, I struggled to understand why he had the need to ask. Having had the hope our children would always know, that their place under our roof would forever be a given I was disappointed on that. Acknowledging that he was never one for the over sharing of personal information, that we would wait patiently and with baited breath for his return. That's when we would hopefully discover his reasons for a sudden return back to England. A short response by text message Anthony expressed a desire that we didn't worry.

"Chat when I'm home. All's good see you then."
Attempts on my part to recall favourite foods for Anthony proved to be a little difficult. Charlie and I decided that having been in the States for almost 3 years, perhaps lots of things would have changed in his life including his dietary habits. We would need to play the waiting game then grocery shop accordingly once he arrived back in Yorkshire.

Morning of Anthony's arrival upon us my eczema had reared its ugly head again. Usually occurring at times of stress in my life, it reminded me how anxious I was about the upcoming events of that day. Charlie got the car all fired up and ready. Nipping along the motorway somewhat like a boy racer my advice to him was, that perhaps he should slow down before we might be forced to slow down. How in that event there would quite likely be no airport collection? Visions of Frankie's family on the day she was orphaned so many years ago now, flashed through my mind as though it was yesterday. Sharing my thoughts with him that was a situation neither of us wished for. Charlie promptly and gently applied the brakes.

Our eventual arrival at the airport brought a sense of relief. We walked slowly together from the car park to the airport entrance in silence. With some degree of trepidation our pace became faster as we proceeded towards arrivals terminal. Watching our child walk down the long corridor brought instant tears for both myself and Charlie. Quietly wishing he had given us some warning of the problem, we now had to embrace it without too much fuss. Anthony hated fuss. 3 years was a long time and how his appearance had changed. He looked thin almost frail. A long embrace and then with no one knowing quite what to say next, we walked again almost in silence to the car park. My mind however was racing doing cartwheels as it does in that type of situation. What had happened to our child? What experiences did he endure to cause this situation of what appeared to be almost frailty? And why oh why did he not talk to us? Holding onto our levels of distress, regulating our emotions was hard for myself and Charlie. We did it.

Familiarity breeds contempt was something I was familiar with. Hearing that expression from many distressed patients on the wards, their application of the statement was used when discussing family issues. In particular husband and wife situations, which were usually festering by the time a hospital admission became a necessity. On that occasion for our family it appeared to work in our favour. Back in the car Anthony began to relax a little.

"It's really great to see you both again.3 years is a long time and it's gone so fast."

Anthony continued to share with us how suddenly and with absolutely no fore warning at all, that he lost his job with

American airlines. Could they do that? Could they treat an employee that badly? They were questions which required answers but for another day. Anthony is an articulate and educated man. Our thoughts were that he surely would have asked those questions himself.

Hearing how that situation had occurred almost 9 months previous to our son coming home was hard for myself and Charlie to hear. The whole scenario had quite devastating implications for Anthony. Here's the story we were being told by him. Being removed from his accommodation which his airline had provided, the man had become homeless. Living on the streets in down town Pittsburgh he had hoped from day to day that his situation would change. That life would improve however It didn't. 9 months down the line his decision to go back home to his parents felt like it was quite a sensible one. Were we hearing a truthful account of events? Intuition and my private thoughts suggested not. That however was of low priority at that moment.

Charlie exercised great self-control in terms of restraining himself with the questions and the what ifs. Our priority at that point was to get our child home and help him to become strong again. Smiling to my son and not truly believing in what I was going to share -I told him.

"You know you're not great at the minute Anthony. You also know how that will soon change. You'll soon be back on your feet again."

Pulling me close for an embrace I could feel the moisture on his cheeks. I wiped his tears away with my bare hands. Reminding him how a parent's love for their child never declines, his silent tears became more noticeable and more obvious. Momentarily sobbing into my arms and then an acknowledgement from him, that yes now he was home things would improve greatly in his life.

> Catherine Rooney together with her parents dropped by unexpectedly at our home that evening. Surprised to see Anthony back their initial comments were totally reserved.

A simple expression with acknowledgement of their surprise in seeing him home and how good it was to see him again, was all which was said on the matter. That was much appreciated by myself and Charlie and perhaps by Anthony too. Enjoying a meal which I had already prepared ahead of setting off for the airport that morning, I must have taken a leaf out from Frankie's book. Having cooked enough food to feed very many, I was delighted to hear Anthony express the invitation to the Rooney's to stay for dinner.

> Being that comfortable around other people who knew him, told me that most likely his mental health was at the least reasonably still intact. My most pressing and perhaps somewhat reassuring thoughts throughout the night, were the facts that we had 2 psychologists in our presence. Perhaps that was Anthony's reason for requesting they stay in the hopes of getting some support. He's a smart man. He would have known that despite their initial lack of comments on his appearance, that they would be aware something pretty awful had occurred. With my hope of someone analysing or assessing Anthony I was not left disappointed.

> Frankie was outspoken as was usual for her in this sort of circumstance. She was direct and to the point. Expressing how she was aware that our son would have grasped the idea, of people guessing something being badly wrong from his psychical appearance, she told him.

"We've known each other a long time Anthony. You're an intelligent man - you'll know we can see big changes in your psychical appearance. It would be wrong not to acknowledge that you've clearly had a rough time."
Showing some appreciation for her very straightforward and direct manner he shared his thoughts of how-
"Perhaps a little therapy wouldn't do any harm." Frankie agreed.
"When you're ready to talk about it you know where I am. I'm happy to help and I'm sure you know that I would always be professional and objective."
Tears began falling down Anthony's cheeks. Being visibly touched by her comments which exuded her level of care and concern, he wiped his eyes. With quite a broken voice he told her.
"I'm down but thanks to my parents and to you too Frankie, I'm not out. Book me in as soon as possible I'm anxious to get this situation sorted."

Anthony demonstrating that he had full acceptance of his issues whatever they might be, was the knowledge we all wanted to hear from him. Being a mental health nurse, I was aware that acceptance was a major requirement in order to progress forward. Reminding our son how therapy would not be a miracle cure Frankie equally gave him a sense of hope. That in turn gave myself and Charlie a sense of hope too. Exchanging phone numbers, the plan was put in place. She would contact Anthony once back home and checked her diary for availability.

Catherine Rooney spoke to us with great caution. Being careful not to breach data protection, in quite an overview fashion she shared some of her most painful work experiences. Her purpose was to hopefully allow Anthony to see, how the most damaged of people can and do recover, when they have the right mindset and the right therapy. Everyone present much appreciated her input to the conversation. Not allowing his issues to dominate the evening, Anthony expressed his joy and surprise upon hearing of the young men who had moved over to a farming way of life in Ireland. He too is a person who likes to be direct and straightforward. Demonstrating this he told Frankie

"Sounds like they've both opted for the quieter side of life. That has to be so much better and especially so for Joseph."

Frankie almost shocked by his comment was fast to respond.

"Why better for Joseph?"

"It's obvious he has issues Frankie. Hectic life could never be in his best interest. Remember I did my teacher training. I know Joseph and I know the signs."

Accepting his explanation which I personally felt grateful for, Frankie sought his view on his other brother's life. With a strong sense of compassion, he shared his thoughts.

"Well who would have known? Having grown up with CJ its surprising how I never guessed about his sexuality. Gay people are born gay so it's always been the same for him. I'm delighted he's found a life partner and can't wait to meet Thomas."

Reassured by all of us present that none of us were aware, went someway to helping Anthony feel less bad about his own lack of knowledge about his brother. Showing a genuine interest in the family software business between his father and Mikey Rooney, his comments were heart-warming.

"Looking at your childhood days and where you were both raised and looking at you now, the transformation in your life's is just beyond amazing."
Anthony continued to express his thoughts of who would have thought back then, that this would be your situation today. Hearing him express interest in his sibling's life's and that of his father too, was another reassuring pointer that his mental health could be worse. Having experienced a great end to our evening in the company of our friends, Anthony being tired from travelling. It was time to get his head down.

"It's been a long day for me with a tedious flight. The company here has been excellent but I need to get some shut eye, so, till the next time."
And he was gone. Anthony having left the room was the cue for the Rooney family to also call it a day. Waving them off myself and Charlie had ourselves a night cap. Brandy being a favourite for us both we shared bottoms up, in a toast to all things coming together in our family.

Timing of the phone call from Frankie was what some might call almost perfection. Anthony being at a low ebb he made himself immediately available for her. Meeting up in a secluded spot in the great outdoors was something which he felt would meet both of their needs. Knowing Frankie was a great believer in the therapeutic effects of nature and its many implications for the human mind, the idea seemed perfect to him. Anthony loved being outdoors too. Walking whilst talking was his request.

"I'm not especially comfortable the other way Frankie. I'm not much of a one for sitting down in a room and spilling my heart out."
Giving her approval yet quite unsure that this would be the best way forward she took the gamble.

Thinking about the value of observation and how it should never be underestimated, combined with a person's body language, Frankie wasn't certain that walking and talking would suffice. However, knowing how a client needed to be comfortable, she agreed to have their first session in the woods. That having appeared to have gone well Frankie also was aware she had a professional duty of care to her client. She was calm, polite, yet firm in her tone as she told him.

"It's been quite productive today Anthony. For further sessions however, in order to continue to get the best from them, we really need to meet somewhere indoors privately."

Plans were put in place that going forward they would meet at Frankie's home. Day and time was scheduled for the following week. Deciding to use the Rooney's living room as her office appeared to be the only option. Anthony being satisfied with that arrangement they bade goodbye.

Brendan Regan and Joseph Rooney had settled well into their farming way of life. Enjoying the tranquillity and peace of their new environment, had impacted them greatly. Ireland and a farming way of life had proven itself to be the medication they required in order to rid themselves of stress on almost a daily basis. Time spent with the animal kingdom, had somehow brought a huge impact of calmness to them both but perhaps to Joseph in particular. Being a learning curve for both men, they owed their new-found experiences firstly to Josephs supermarket supervisor Teresa Riley, for giving them that wonderful opportunity and secondly to a middle-aged local farmer. Both men being on the quieter side, they had a great sense of appreciation for the lack of almost daily stressful situations. Mixture of anxiety and stress previously experienced especially in their working life's, no longer was their experience.

Joseph quite unknown to him was being to some degree watched over by his friend Brendan. Yes, the men had gone from just knowing each other through their parents, to now having become very good friends. Charlie and I having experienced and enjoyed an empty house over a number of years, were happy having our child back living with us again. The situation not being great for Anthony, our only hope could be that Frankie would work through painful stuff with him. That he would come out of this therapy a much more balanced and happier person than the one who entered, was our greatest wish for him.

News from Ireland to Yorkshire brought some elements of excitement for myself and Charlie. The phone call from Brendan was short and very to the point. Enquiring for our well-being he then went on to share.

"I've met someone. You'll like her I know you will. I'm bringing her home next weekend for a few days. I'll tell you everything then."

The call was ended- that was it and that was fairly typical of Brendan. Never having had much of a liking for phone calls he had ensured this one was no different. Causing me too often wonder how he managed that situation when working for the local authority, I had never asked our son the question.

Preparing ourselves for the weekend in the absence of any information other than it was a female friend, presented me with something of a challenge. Deciding from Brendan's lack of information that the situation felt so much easier to deal with, made everything feel much less of a challenge. No expectations on either side therefore no plans to be made. Just wait and see what the weekend might bring. There was the question of having had 2 of our 3 children present us with situations which we did not expect, would the visit from Brendan do likewise? We had to play the waiting game. Having shared the news with my best friend forever, Frankie as always had a sensible response. She put it in perspective for me.

"She'll be easy going Helen she must be otherwise he wouldn't have left the chat so casual."

Promising I would update her as would be the expectation from each other our phone call ended. Another call from Brendan to Frankie followed. Just to ensure no one would have worry or concern for Joseph being left alone, he shared how the neighbouring farmer was aware of her sons' issues. He would be keeping a close eye in the absence of Josephs knowledge. Frankie was reassured to hear that.

The weekend upon us we watched from the window as Brendan and his friend climbed out of the car. Thinking how well our son was looking and how the girl on his arm was equally as impressive looking we smiled. Quite tall for a girl she was almost to Brendan's shoulder. Watching as together they walked up the driveway her long wavy hair was blown onto her face from the wind. Looking delighted he did the introductions in the way you might expect Brendan to do it.

"Mam, dad meet Fiona. Fiona meet the parents."

That was it. The blink of a minute Fiona McGeever was at the kitchen sink, kettle in hand. In a broad strong but very sweet Irish accent, she enquired.

"Who's for tea. It was rubbish on the Ferry. I'm gasping for a decent cuppa."

Deciding our son was correct in his statement, we both held onto our thoughts that yes, we already liked his girlfriend.

Seeing his brother for the first time in some years, Brendan was left feeling shocked to the core. Hearing his story about the airline company and being homeless, his reaction was a compassionate one.

"Your home now Anthony. Mum tells me you've made some great strides since your return so that's all positive."

The brothers spending time together in the garden gave us opportunity to chat with Fiona. Chance to discover what type of person she really was, in as much as would be possible to discover in a short period of time. Discovering she was a farmer's daughter from county Cork who had been educated at degree level for teaching, I was mesmerized.

"Isn't that a complete turnaround of situations for yourself and Brendan."

Fiona told us how she had secured employment at their local secondary school. Teaching all 3 of the sciences, with chemistry and biology being her favourites. Smiling she told us.

"I've lived my whole life to some degree, with science-based family discussions around almost every meal. Interest was stimulated for me hence the study and now the teaching of it."

Brendan having given talks at the school about the scientific aspects of farming was how they had met. She shared in great detail how that meeting occurred and the fact it was almost 2 years previous to this visit. Laughing she told us.

"I was starting to wonder if you actually did exist or were you a figment of Brendan's imagination. Me waiting to

meet you both has been a long time coming."
The need to be honest with the girl was a high priority for me. Telling her how that's so typical of our son and how he rarely shares anything very much at all with us, she took it all in good spirits.

"Okay this is how his first school meeting in Ireland went."

Describing himself to his school audience as a fast learner- Brendan shared, that after a life in England and teaching in a secondary school, he gave up the chaos of the classroom for the peace and tranquillity of farming and of Ireland. Sharing how he had been taught most of what he knows about farming, by a neighbouring farmer who is in perhaps the last chapter of his life, brought some funny and some cheeky comments from his audience. The funniest being.

"So glad it's not my auld man your describing sir. Not too sure we'd like that but carry on anyway."

Brendan smiled as he continued to share how the gentleman's farm had been in his family for a very long time, perhaps upwards of 300 years. Being raised on his farm had given him many wonderful life experiences. Having kept up with research there was little he didn't know about the scientific aspects of the land. Brendan had done some research himself too. Once through the initial introductions as described above, Brendan captivated his audience as he tried not to baffle them too much with science.

"And there you have it Helen. Is it ok to call you Helen"? Assuring the young lady how we had both been called a lot worse than our given names in our lifetime she smiled.

Dinner organised with some unrequested support

from Fiona, we could only agree what a heart-warming person she appeared to be. Her humour, her great personality combined with what appeared to be her honesty and her willingness to help and fit in, all round we were delighted our son had met, what appeared to be such a lovely and decent human being. Our weekend coming to its close and nothing extraordinary being shared with us, Brendan's words from the phone call were repeatedly going around in my head.

"I'll tell you everything then."

Having to assume that Brendan had inherited his father's gene for putting important stuff on the back burner, I was left with no option. I would have to ask the question what does "I'll tell you everything then mean?" Otherwise we might be left waiting for news to the point of them leaving for a return back to the beautiful Island of Ireland.

Mikey Rooney gate-crashed the evening. He was our unexpected visitor. Interrupting my moment of thought to imminently question our son, Mikey came bounding in arms extended to our guests. Talk about being saved by the bell -It was Brendan's lucky moment. However, it would be a temporary reprieve to be revisited, the moment Mikey left for home. Delighted to see Brendan again, he was anxious to hear some news of his own child Joseph. No requirement for introductions to the girlfriend. Fiona did it all through some laughter showing her bubbly personality.

"So, you're the famous and I almost said infamous Mikey. Heard loads about you from Brendan and Joseph and no, not all good, I'm afraid, before you ask."

At the speed of lightning she followed that up with.

"Just kidding he's praised you to the highest."

Mikey's off the cuff response was equally funny but true.

"Can't say the same about you Fiona as I've heard nothing of your mere existence. Let's hope that continues to change."

News about Joseph Rooney was shared for the 2nd time that weekend. Mikey heard how well their child was coping on the farm. Learning new skills and doing a part time evening college course in -aspects of Scientific's of the land. Starting with the basics of agriculture and arable farming, Joseph had been on the course for 9 months. In complete contrast to his school days, his attitude for learning had flipped on its head. Managing the noisy environment and his times of sensory overload, he would immediately but politely leave the classroom in order to avoid over stimulation. The tantrums experienced at home or in his previous places of employment, appeared to be dead in the ground. Having put the classroom plan in place with his tutor ahead of joining the course, highlighted to everyone the degree of Joseph's determination to succeed. Brendan went onto share his sense of pride in his friend.

"Speaking to a stranger about his issues had to be hard. Doing so in order to have the best chance of success is admirable."

Mikey was delighted to hear how their child had found his niche in life. How he had progressed since the move to Ireland.

"That's just wonderful to hear and its down to one person who gave him the opportunity and to you Brendan for giving him the confidence to take that step. I'll speak to Frankie. We should have Teresa Riley over for a visit and an update. In the absence of her care and compassion Joseph would not be making these strides today."

That being the 2nd time in 1 day I heard high praise for Teresa Riley, I shared my view that it was only what she deserved.
Mikey stood up from the table. Embracing Brendan and Fiona he said his goodbyes making an especially fast exit. Shutting the door behind him my thoughts immediately reverted back to my son and whatever news he hadn't so far shared with us.

"Okay Brendan were still waiting for your news."
With no chance for him to respond Fiona jumped in with her thoughts.

"We've been here for days and you've not told them yet. What's going on in that head of yours Brendan Regan?
She was as she had been the whole time she was in Yorkshire- She was direct and straightforward. That on a general level was appreciated by all of us. Putting us at ease in her company, making it easier to get along with Fiona had been a bonus. The news she was about to share, I believe deserved a bit more thought going into the presentation of it. The words just rolled off her tongue.

"I'm pregnant 12 weeks gone and we're getting married."

Charlie looked aghast. Remembering his adversity to the sight of blood from days gone by, especially my giving birth days- This was exactly how he looked upon hearing the news from Fiona. Brendan sat silently for a few moments ahead of questioning myself and his father. Wondering what our thoughts were on the matter or should I say matters, colour had begun to come back to Charlies face. Managing to utter his thoughts I'm not sure how convincing he was to our guests.

"You're like me Brendan you find what you want in

life and you go for it. I'm delighted you and Fiona are happy and I'm sure that Helen feels the same."

Thinking how my husband was speaking on my behalf yet again, same as he did all those years ago when I was a hospital patient, left me with a sense of annoyance. Knowing it would be just shameful of me, to correct him for his wrong doing in the presence of others, I didn't. It could wait but would not be forgotten.

"Yes, I'm thrilled Brendan for you both. Be a bit hard not to be. Tell us more Fiona."

Flippant as they had discovered was usual for her – she told the Regan's how.

"Wedding plans are already in place. It's going to be a small event at the local registry office. Joseph will be the best man although he doesn't know that yet. My cousin will be a bridesmaid. Come if you like and don't if that suits you best. It really doesn't matter to myself and Brendan."

Much as we considered that we liked Fiona, Charlies glance across the table to me was confirmation that his view mirrored mine. As our child had sat silently we could be forgiven for wondering if that's how he wanted their marriage to be? My brain had gone into overdrive again. Remembering our emergency situations back on the wards I had to act accordingly at that point. My ability for quick thinking seemed to be spot on.

Taking Fiona out of the equation was important for me at that moment. Her flippant speech in relation to the marriage had given myself and Charlie some cause for concern. Not being able to imagine how Brendan had felt I planned to give him some alone time with his dad. The need to remain calm was important to me. Steering Fiona towards our bedroom it was almost in a whisper that I coaxed her away from the table.

"C'mon Fiona I need to show you something."
She was unsuspecting and compliant. The pretext of needing to show her something seemed like a good plan to me. Having to think fast again I searched out my cosmetics catalogue. Knowing that I don't do cosmetics, it was fortunate a work colleague had passed it to me earlier that week, in the hopes of her getting a sale through me. Plain Jane is perhaps more how I might describe myself when it comes down to cosmetics. With the exception of a bit of lippy every now and again, I would never be seen contributing to putting money in the banks of beauty product makers.

Quickly flipping through the pages, I found myself silently praying that bouts of anxiety would not overcome me. Hoping to sound convincing to the woman I told her.

"Here Fiona sit down on the bed and take a look as these bath bombs. They're very good for relaxation. You'll need something to help you relax as you go through the pregnancy. You choose a few I'll place the order- it's my treat for you."

Fiona's keen interest in the catalogue gave Charlie the chance to speak to our son, away from the presence of the woman whom I had become a little unsure of.

The call from Joseph Rooney to his parents came as something of a surprise to them. His usual preference for communicating had been through email. Sharing information about his evening classes, his parents were delighted to hear about it from Joseph. Likewise, he was keen to seek news about them and about his sister Catherine. Delighted to know that all was well Joseph

Acknowledged many improvements in his own life and shared how much he loved living in Ireland. His gratitude for the woman who got him there was immense. Expressing how we all owe such a lot to Teresa Riley. How her compassion and understanding
has given all of us a fresh start, given us a lease in life, it was good to hear that acknowledgement from Joseph. Not being able to deny a word of what her child had said she shared her view that perhaps they should invite Teresa over to Ireland. Spend a little time on the farm with them. Let her see the fruits of her labour as the saying goes. Joseph not understanding the expression he nevertheless agreed with her in principal.

   Frankie duly attempted to end their call. Some reluctance to do that on the part of her son raised her curiosity. Knowing how he wanted to share some more information she encouraged him to do that. Bringing Brendan into the conversation he was starting to sound a little anxious. Mother's instincts pre-warned Frankie that this would be uncomfortable for her child. Encouraging him further to continue, Joseph shared some news concerning Brendan's girl friend Fiona. Now she understood why the phone call and not an email. Having heard all which he had to say, Frankie's advice to her son was that he should call myself and Charlie.

   "They'll hear it better from you Joseph. I'll go over later when Brendan and Fiona have gone back to Ireland. I know Helen will surely tell me then I can offer my support."
The plan for disclosure in place and ending the call to his mother, Joseph had agreed to make that call to ourselves.

   Fiona having returned downstairs at that point,

she was wanting to show the men her choices from my Avon book. Being their last night in Yorkshire with us it was an anxious one for me. Not enough time remained to allow me to make my mind up about this woman. Despite the late hour of night my phone rang out. It was Joseph Regan which initially gave me cause for concern for his well-being. Requesting I move to a private place I could sense from his voice just how uncomfortable he was feeling. Deciding to tell Charlie and our guests a white lie gave me an excuse to be private for the call.

"It's an urgent call from work Charlie. You know how they can be. I'll go to the car to take it."

Leaving the house quickly gave no opportunity for questions to be asked. Securely inside my car I told Joseph we were free to talk. Hearing how Fiona was a story teller who liked to make up imaginary stories, felt a little shocking to me yet not altogether surprising. What Joseph had shared gave me great cause for concern for our son and his emotional wellbeing. Hearing how Joseph had gone down stairs at 4 in the morning, in order to investigate the sound of voices coming from their kitchen, his discovery was surprising to him. He had remained discreet and unseen.

Knowing Brendan was in his bedroom sleeping, he had to attempt to establish who the male voice belonged to. Many times, having shared with Brendan the need for them to block off the largish peep hole, going from the stairs through to the kitchen, now he was glad it was never closed. It was productive in that situation. Seeing Fiona through that peep hole in an attempt to embrace with another man, Joseph returned back to his own bedroom, leaving the door slightly ajar in order he could still hear. Recognition of the man was easy for Joseph. He was a teacher at the local school, where Joseph was an evening student. The school where Fiona was a teacher and Brendan gave occasional talks there. Hearing an angry male voice there was no doubt in Josephs head what he had heard.

"You've been dating both of us Fiona. Your telling me your pregnant, its mine and we should get married. With your reputation how can you know its mine? I'm not interested and hope Brendan won't be either, or the other men you've slept with recently. It's what you deserve for the way you use and abuse people and their emotion's."

Having to take a moment. Take a deep breath in to absorb what I had been told, I asked Joseph for his patience with me before continuation of the story.

"I'm shocked Joseph. I'll take a minute but don't go anywhere don't end this call."

Having respected my request Joseph then continued whilst I listened intently.

"It wasn't good Helen. He walked out slamming the door behind him. Like I used to when unable to cope with life situations. I thought Brendan might wake up. A sense of relief came over me when the man had left the house. Fiona was just callous in her behaviour. She went back to their bedroom like nothing had happened. That's it Helen that's the situation, the story Brendan's not aware of and now she's telling everyone that she and Brendan are getting married as she's having his baby."

I was deeply indebted to Joseph for sharing all of that with me. I could only hope he understood my reaction. Being undiagnosed as an autistic person as we had considered him to be, grasping another person's perspective could be a little difficult for him. His response did not give me much clarity on his under-standing. Telling me that he had also spoken about the situation to his mother and how she had told him to call me. That I would hear it better coming from him than from her. Reminding Joseph that there's very little Frankie and I don't share- and thanking him again for sharing his grave concern for Brendan with us, we bade goodbye. Some deep breaths in, helped calm my anxiety ahead of re-enter-ing the house.

Brendan and Fiona having settled for the night left me space to speak to Charlie in private. Being a discussion which I didn't want to have, my attempts to get Charlie on board were initially futile. Hearing my philosophy that people should treat everyone with kindness, not because they're nice but because we are, brought that worried look to his face.

"I know there's something up Helen. I don't believe that was a work call so what's wrong?"
Knowing Charlie as I did I knew that accepting his comment had to be the right thing to do. Telling him we couldn't talk in the house for fear of being overheard, we should leave a note for Brendan, then take a drive to the nearest all night motorway service for coffee and conversation. Leaving that note for Brendan took my mind back to his childhood days. The days where I might be a little late getting home, or he might have misplaced a piece of school uniform. In many ways at that point I longed to have those days back.

Sharing the content of Josephs call with my husband left him feeling aghast as I was. From his earlier conversation with Brendan, Charlie had the sense that our son was being at the least coerced and at the worst bullied into their forthcoming marriage. Deciding to say nothing about the news we received for the interim was our agreement.

"Let's talk to Frankie and Mikey for advice on this. 2nd opinions are always helpful Helen. And let's find out from Fiona when the wedding is due to take place. We then know how much time we have to persuade our son not to go ahead with it."

Having to agree with Charlies thoughts we returned back home. Plans in place for Brendan and Fiona to leave early that morning looked as though they would be fulfilled. Bags packed and left inside the front door showed someone had been down after our exit the previous night. To carry on as though all was fine had been our promise to each other. Charlie cooked a full English breakfast for them both. It was hard but successful. Having said our goodbyes there was a promise in place from Brendan. They would return back to England at least once more ahead of their marriage and birth of their baby.

Knocking at Frankie's front door was our immediate activity once we gathered our thoughts. Smiling as was usual for her, I was quick to bring up the subject which was by now burning a hole in our hearts.

"We know Josephs told you Frankie and so glad that he has done. We're here looking for help and advice"
Sharing how proud of Joseph they were as that had to be a hard conversation for him, myself and Charlie agreed. Assuring Frankie, I showed my deep appreciation to her child, left all of us in the hope that Joseph will not have pangs of guilt. Our turmoil was going to become Brendan's turmoil. How and when to speak to him felt like an issue. Mikey sat back in his chair. Pushing back his wavy head of hair from his forehead, I knew he was uncomfortable about something. That was Mikey's go to action when feeling embarrassed or uncomfortable. Looking directly at him Frankie was clear.

"Hard as it is you have to tell them Mikey."

"It's difficult but anyhow here goes. Saying goodbye to Fiona we shared an embrace the same as I shared with Brendan. Fiona pinched my backside laughing at the same time. No one saw but I'm sure you probably noticed how fast I left your house."

Mikey went on to say how after sharing that with Frankie, that their decision was to wait for the visitors to go back to Ireland, ahead of saying anything to ourselves.

"Give us more time to think what that was all about Helen ahead of sharing with you."

Catherine Rooney and Frankie pulled on their psychology knowledge. Holding the same view, they agreed that attempting to have the conversation with Brendan over the phone, in so many ways would belittle the situation. Charlie and myself should go to Ireland with immediate effect was the general consensus. We should be there as a support for Joseph too. He had agreed to tell Brendan all which he had told ourselves. Everyone was aware how that would be a challenging task for Joseph.

Our flight next morning from Luton to Shannon airport was a tedious one. We had deliberately chosen Shannon in order to get opportunity to see some of Irelands countryside, on our journey to Cork. Eczema and awful pangs of anxiety were once again showing themselves to be my enemy. Both being on overdrive presented me a problem I struggled to rid myself of. Charlies reminders to take deep breaths, combined with his philosophy of
'it'll be what it'll be' helped a little. Car hire had been easy to arrange. Outside of the airport and travelling towards Cork everything felt better. The drive allowed us to absorb the beautiful scenery of rural Ireland. It marginally occupied our

thoughts. Booking in at a hotel quite local to where the men were living, we enjoyed a light lunch ahead of surprising our son.

      Struggling to see how we would best approach the topic with Brendan I called Frankie. As was usual for her and I should have known this.

      "You've just got to be straightforward Helen. Tell him everything Joseph has told you and what Mikey has told you too."

Whilst saying goodbye to my friend that annoying ping from the phone came through. It delivered a text message from Joseph. News was, Brendan had been informed of what Joseph had seen and heard in the farm house with Fiona. Not hearing it too well Brendan had taken himself away from the farm. No knowledge of his whereabouts wasn't helpful for any of us.

      Charlies idea of calling Brendan did not feel like the best idea in. my opinion.

      "It'll put him on the spot Charlie. Maybe its best we should message as that will give him thinking time."

Telling Brendan, we were at the hotel and leaving details of it, together with a request he might come and meet us there felt like the best option available to us at that point. Wanting to go out and explore the beautiful countryside which surrounded us, was a want which could not be fulfilled. Eventually Brendan appeared at hotel reception. The man looked broken and was broken. My burning thought was, what was left for us to say to our child. Offering an embrace, it was readily accepted by Brendan.

      Lunch at the hotel then going to our room felt like the best idea. Offering privacy to speak openly Brendan did agree. Him accepting all which Joseph shared he was yet to to speak to Fiona. Uncertain of how he would present the facts to her he listened to our thoughts. I could hear Frankie's voice in my head. "Be direct and straightforward". That was my advice to Brendan. He had sadness in his voice but a level of determination too.

"I'll tell her I need a DNA test when baby is born."

Meeting up with Fiona that evening Brendan held onto the news he received from Joseph. Taking her back to the farm house, it was a difficult situation for myself and Charlie being in her company. Having agreed that if Brendan could do it then so could we, we continued as though nothing was wrong. Fiona expressed her surprise at seeing us there.

"Wanted to see where our son lives and works Fiona. Farming life fills us with intrigue and what better way to address that, other than to come here. It's really as simple as that."

Our explanation was in her opinion -us being over protective parents. She nevertheless accepted what we said. My head was doing cartwheels, in terms of how she was in no position to be opinionated on our behaviour and how dare she be so. Having to keep those thoughts under a lid wasn't the easiest challenge life ever presented me with.

Joseph had prepared an evening meal for everyone including ourselves. His culinary skills had greatly improved. Table etiquette wasn't great however we didn't have expectations. Some might say that was fortunate. I would say its irrelevant. Instructed by Joseph to help ourselves from the large pot, our plates were piled high on the table. There were large spoons and forks on display next to the plates. The best beef stew we had ever tasted simmered very gently on the stove. Highlight of the evening for myself and Charlie was perhaps the meeting with their neighbouring farmer. The gentleman who had been and still was offering support to Brendan and Joseph on their farming journey, was every bit the man Teresa Riley had said he was.

Evening coming to its end Brendan very directly confronted his girlfriend, in the presence of us all. Yes, in my estimation she deserved that humiliation. We were in the hope it might go somewhere towards retaliation for what she had done to our son. Initially in denial she knew she was beaten when Joseph informed her of what he had seen and heard. In her usual flippant manner Fiona was almost dismissive. Uncaring in her tone and what she said next our sense of relief for Brendan was immense.

"Shame I've been caught out and yes Brendan I'll meet your DNA request when the baby is born. I'm sure I'm dumped now thanks to Joseph and the mouth he couldn't control."

Then she walked out almost taking the door behind her. To everyone's surprise, the woman was taking no responsibility at all for her behaviour. Brendan looked a little subdued and then surprised us with.

"I was never sure of her as I'd heard the rumours about Fiona but still I tried with her. Everyone knows that in life, we can lose more through fear than we do by trying. She had me mesmerized. Watching her was like watching fallen leaves dancing on a windy day and now it's done. We're over. I don't feel a loss but I'm glad that I tried."

Wiping tears from his eyes Brendan assured everyone he would be all right. He would not buckle to any further pressure he might receive from Fiona. Knowing our son as well as we do, helped us to understand that yes he would be all right. Sitting down beside me and placing an arm on my shoulder he told me.

"Mam you and dad are the best. Travelling this distance, coming to another country to show your support will never be forgotten by me. Joseph you're the best mate. It had to be so hard for you sharing that information with the parents. I'm not sure if I could have done it so It's very much appreciated."

Joseph had in the call to me, expressed his worry regards how Brendan would perceive him for being the bearer of that news. A sense of relief quickly swept across Josephs face as he embraced our son. His words were spoken softly.

"Thought you'd be annoyed with me. So glad so relieved that you're not."

Seeing how well Brendan was dealing with the baby situation, decisions were made that we would leave Cork the next morning. Saying goodbye to the men till the next time we took a coastal drive along the wild Atlantic way and up to county Mayo. The beauty of Mayo was breath taking. The tourist town of Westport was swimming in a flood of visitors with many gift shops for their amusement. Deciding on suitable gifts to bring back for Frankie, Mikey and our children was a bit of a challenge. Limitations made on us due to flying our decision was made. Our children living at home would each be presented with a small plaque-bearing the words 'Caed Mila Failte' meaning a hundred thousand welcomes. Our friends would receive a framed map of county Cork which highlighted the area where Joseph and Brendan work and live.

Being picked up at Luton airport by Catherine Rooney was both a surprise and a treat. She was delighted to see us back on English soil. Taking us for lunch at Hales bar was a pleasant surprise. It wasn't especially like Catherine to do that. I was verging on the edge of feeling worried.

"Everything all right Catherine?"

Sharing her views and news about Anthony was something of a surprise to us both.

"I know mums a psychologist but don't you think she might be missing something. Don't you think Anthony is maybe being a bit sparse with the truth?"

Catherine went on to share her opinion that there's perhaps something much deeper going on with Anthony and it needs addressing.

"We've been dating Helen and I'm worried."

Wow- To say that I was yet again shocked by one of my children would be an understatement. Before I could hear any further information regarding Catherine's worries, I was compelled to make her aware of my feelings.

"Hearing your dating is a shock in itself Catherine but a nice one. Didn't you have a boyfriend didn't you live with someone?"

Thinking how the woman must be feeling interrogated by my many questions I was quick to offer my apologies.

"I'm sorry Catherine the expression of 'Mind your own business' is quickly coming to my mind. Please forgive me and tell me exactly what it is that you are worried about."

Reassuring me that my questions were fine, she continued to share her thoughts about Anthony's deterioration from allegedly being homeless and how she didn't believe the facts married up.

"He's a great person Helen but his mood changes so abruptly. I suspect he's an addict and not sure that mums support is enough to get him back on track, especially if she hasn't got full knowledge of what's happened for him."

Hearing those words from my friend's daughter was almost a mirror of listening to my own thoughts. It felt as though all my worst fears were being confirmed. I too suspected our child was perhaps a heroin addict. I hadn't been brave enough to confront him with that thought or to say it out loud. Not brave enough to share it with Charlie or with anyone. Hearing that I would speak to Frankie tell her about our conversation was something of a relief to Catherine.

  Charlies phone ringing out was a badly needed and much appreciated distraction from our conversation with Catherine. It was Frankie. She was excited to hear the news from Ireland. She would be at our home that afternoon around 4pm. I had considered how time between our son Anthony and Frankie had appeared to be working pretty well. I was then secretly dismissive of all what Catherine had said. Our arrival home was welcomed by Anthony and at that point Frankie arrived too. Hearing how Joseph was doing so well and looking great pleased her a lot. Her overall concern was for both men in the sharing of the Fiona situation. Assurance given to Frankie that both were fine, she then heard that I would update her fully on my next visit to hers.

  "I'll be over soon Frankie probably tomorrow afternoon."

  Having said our goodbyes to Catherine and Frankie we were called to the living room by Anthony. He appeared somewhat anxious yet interested to know about our time in Ireland. Hearing updates on his brother's situation with the cheating and devious Fiona, he was empathic.

  "This'll be very hard for Brendan. Losing her is no great loss, but I know how much he was looking forward to becoming a father."

Some further discussion about Brendan and Joseph occurred and then the bomb shell was dropped on us both. Anthony spoke about how Frankie had gained a lot of experience throughout her career. How the idea of losing his job, combined with being removed from the company accommodation to be the cause of his current health issues, did not feel real or believable to her. Having taken her straightforward and very direct manner into their therapy sessions, she had shared her thoughts with him.

"Listen Anthony we need to be on the same level here. Either you be honest with me or the sessions come to an end."

Taking a deep breath in Anthony shared with us, that whilst he was a little surprised by what he considered to be her abruptness, he also knew that Frankie says what she means and means what she says. He did not want the sessions to end. He told us how knowing the choice was his, that his first reaction to her was to tell her she wouldn't like it and would be very disappointed in him. Hearing how disappointment didn't come into the equation, that she was his therapist so never to be in a place of judgement, but she needed the facts. Expressing his understanding of that to Frankie he appealed to her not to cancel the sessions. Requesting a few days in order to tell Catherine and his parents first she agreed.

Waiting with baited breath to hear what was coming next, I can't say that I was shocked or even felt surprised. Anthony began to tremble as he uttered the words.

"I'm an addict. Been using almost 2 years before the day I went to work whilst under the influence. It was instant dismissal and instant removal from the flat. The flat was required by the airline for my replacement. Been on the streets ever since using any and all money I had for my fix of cocaine, that's what I did until there was no more money left. A friend paid all charges for my flight home. So that's it that's the whole truth. I'm sure your ashamed of me now."

Watching colour drain away from my husband's face, was the assurance I needed, that he had no idea this would be the problem. Anthony reached out to his father seeking an embrace. Charlie filled us both with surprise and deep sounding emotion. He took hold of Anthony's hands almost as though he was a small child. His words I will never forget.

"Son, in a million years we would never be ashamed of you. Whatever you do in this life, if you end up broken by it, do not ever go back to that or whatever it was that broke you."

Thanking his father for what was probably some of the best advice he had ever been given, Anthony buried his head in his hands. We left the room in order to give him the privacy he needed at that moment.

Catherine's arrival back at our house the next morning had perfect timing. Myself and Charlie left them to it. Taking a stroll through some nearby woods gave us opportunity to calm our thoughts and to destress a little. Both being on a work break not having those pressures felt good. Walking in silence felt good too. So much information to be absorbed about our children and their issues, we secretly questioned our parenting of them. Had we done enough? Could we have done more? Should we have done it differently? Should I have been a stay at home mother? Sharing those thoughts over lunch and a coffee in the town centre, we concluded that we did what we felt was best at the time for all of us. There's no sin in that. What we do now is important in order to help the ones who are struggling.

My phone ringing out caught my attention. It was Catherine. Offering her care and concern for both myself and Charlie, in addition to her caring attitude towards Anthony, gave us the lift we needed at that time. Her voice was breaking slightly as she told us

"He's made a full disclosure Helen. He was into cocaine very shortly after leaving England. Reached the tolerance level in around 6 months and been dependant ever since. As I'm sure he's told you he was a user whilst the money lasted."

Catherine went onto say that as we have been friends with Frankie forever, that we should visit and share this with her and that Anthony is fine for that to happen. She was reassuring that she did not enter a relationship with Anthony on a whim. That she had her strong suspicions and would travel that journey of a full recovery in support of and with him. Hearing the words 'a full recovery' gave us badly needed hope.

Frankie was delighted with our visit. Telling her we had lunch in town didn't make a difference. She piled our plates high as was usual for her. Again, we reassured her that the men in Ireland were doing great. That Joseph had told us how much he was enjoying his night class at the local school. That it was our opinion upon seeing him and talking to him, that the move to a farming way of life in Ireland, was perhaps the best decision he ever made. His neighbouring farmer was highly impressed by progress made by both Brendan and Joseph. Hearing all of that brought deep joy to Frankie and to her husband Mikey. Expressing her thoughts about the relationship between their daughter Catherine and our son Anthony, we all shared the same view.

"They're adults and intelligent educated ones. Let's hope they both know what they're doing."

She went on to say how its her belief that Anthony has not been strictly honest with her, in relation to his counselling needs. That was the door opened, for me to share what we discovered just the previous evening. Frankie heard it all without expression. She thanked us for sharing.

"Your honesty is appreciated Helen. Thank you both. I still need Anthony to tell me himself. I believe he will do that."

She was reassuring that she will be able to offer support, now that she knows exactly what it is she is supporting with. She was clear there would be no quick fix and it would likely be a life long issue for Anthony, sitting there quietly in the background of his mind, raising its ugly head when the chips are down. That we would need to have things in place for support, when life goes wrong for him as it does at times for everyone.

"It'll probably be a long journey Helen. We'll all need to discover the triggers and help him work on them, but we will achieve success. I can say that as I already know he wants that help."

Saying goodbye to our friends that evening Charlie and myself felt reassured about Anthony's future, with one small niggle. Wondering if Frankie being Catherine's mother might become an issue with counselling, she was very clear that it wouldn't. She would keep the 2 issues separate just as she would with any other client. Her expectation was and would continue to be that Anthony would do the same. She did express some joyous feelings around the relationship between our children.

News from Ireland came via an email from Brendan. It was followed by a phone call. Fiona had been in touch to inform that she had miscarried the baby. In the circumstance Brendan felt that wasn't such a bad thing. Not sharing my view with him almost felt wrong. Deciding it was perhaps a woman's way of thinking I had a sense of sadness for Fiona and could hardly tell him that. Miscarrying a baby is never a good thing under any circumstance. I've met many women on the mental health wards who were in precarious relationships, got pregnant and miscarried. Their emotions were severely impacted due to the loss of their baby. Whilst expressing all of that to Brendan might be a bit too much for him to hear, I nevertheless had to let him know it does have consequences for the mother.

"She's done wrong by you and by others Brendan and has being dealt with for that. Don't be too hard on her about the miscarriage. I know from work experience she'll find it hard."

"I hear you mam. I won't contact Fiona but if she approaches me I will show compassion."

Feeling proud of my son and telling him so we ended the call.

Knocking at the front door felt very persistent, or perhaps it was just Frankie's head feeling annoyed and aggravated by other things in life. She quietly wished for the person to be more patient. Their surprise visitor was Teresa Riley. Delighted to see her Frankie made their thoughts known. Hearing updates on how well the men and especially Joseph were doing on the farm she was thrilled. Hearing the men's gratitude for her having given them the opportunity, brought a huge smile to her face. Hearing how Joseph was at night school studying aspects of the land and managing his potential outbursts so well, she was delighted.

"He's found something in life that supports his needs Frankie. What an achievement as opposed to his school days here and his working days too."

"And it's all down to you Teresa we are eternally grateful."

Till the next time the women said goodbye.

Big changes looming ahead

Dawn breaking with a hint of sunshine brought more to our family than the beginnings of a new day. Scarcely out of bed the doorbell felt piercing to my ears. It was CJ together with a whole host of his belongings and a drip-fed line of apologies. Reassuring to him that he was always welcome back to the home he was born and raised in, I helped take his stuff to the bedroom with no questions asked. Charlie had left for the office. He seemed to spend so much time there in those days.

Showered with no time left to take breakfast I too set off for work. Early shifts would always be extra busy with overnight admissions or ward rounds. Handover was very enlightening. I was shocked to the core absolutely beyond belief, to find that CJs partner Thomas had an overnight admission on my ward. How was I to deal with that news? Protocol and boundaries told me I had to keep out of his situation. My heart was telling me to get involved. Knowing I couldn't be involved I spoke to bed management. Explaining my dilemma, they agreed for a move to another ward for Thomas.

"We can do a swap Helen. That will happen almost immediately. Stay in the office till he's moved."

Calling Charlie didn't feel the nicest thing to be doing. No parent wants to hear that their adult child has had to return back to their parents' home. He was as shocked as I was to hear the whole story, which in many ways gave no information.

"I'm sorry Charlie but I didn't feel the time was right to ask questions. CJ needs our support not our interrogation at this time. Maybe he will open up as time goes on."

Ending the call to my husband, I was then informed that Thomas had been moved to a ward at the other end of the hospital. The hope was and could only be that our paths would never cross. Sending out a flyer around the hospital, I was clear with all nursing staff and ward managers, that under no circumstance was information concerning Thomas to be shared with me. I shared my reasons for that request. Not looking for empathy or sympathy in the sharing of that information, I nevertheless received both in abundance. Being grateful for the knowledge of a good staff team who consistently read the communication book I left my gratitude there.

"For everyone who has shown compassion and that's just about everyone who works on the wards, regardless of their job status, I want to show my gratitude. Our current family situation is beyond sad. My main concern now has to be for my son. Thank you again."

Direct to Frankie's from the hospital without asking was where I found myself. With Anthony and Catherine dating and Anthony having therapy with Frankie, the need to inform her of my work predicament plus CJ being back home, ahead of Anthony saying something was important to me. To say she was shocked about our situation would be an understatement.

"When we think things can't get any worse Helen

and then this happens. I'm lost for words."
Frankie had nothing to offer me on that occasion other than the advice to try not to worry too much. Should she hear anything from Catherine through Anthony she would share with me. A reminder was given that should Anthony share anything concerning his brother in the therapy sessions, that would have to remain confidential between herself and Anthony. Feeling as though my nerves were shot I was on edge. My snappy response was not acceptable.

"I'm beyond aware of that fact Frankie."
Feeling terrible for how I had just snapped at my friend, I could only apologise in the hope that she would understand.

"Oh, isn't it the most awful of situations which have imposed themselves upon us. I'm tired. I'm irritable and I'm sorry for snapping at you."
She understood and demonstrated that. Smiling she told me.

"Come here give me a hug."
Appreciating the rules of confidentiality for everyone I was unable to share with Frankie, the fact that Thomas had been admitted to the hospital.

Having said goodbye to Frankie I stopped off at the local supermarket ahead of going home. Pastry was my go to, it was also CJs go to when under stress. No risks of deprivation would be taken. Consoling myself with the thoughts that Charlie and Anthony could not be excluded from our sugar intake, my purchase was in abundance to a normal family shopping. My arrival home found the men of the family congregated together in the kitchen. Realisation suddenly hit me, that should CJ express any concern or any worry for Thomas, that my lips would have to remain sealed. Aroma from our kitchen greeted me outside the front door. Having forgotten what a good cook CJ was we were surprised

Chicken Tika Masala with rice and naan bread was almost ready to be served. Having skipped lunch due to considerable worry for my family, my stomach was now craving food and appreciated the input I gave to it.

Having regained some of his lost body weight Anthony at this point was glowing. It had appeared like a new happiness and contentment had consumed him, consumed his thoughts. Catherine's arrival at the house brought surprise for her. Not having spoken to either her mother or Anthony that day she was not expecting to see CJ back home. Praying she wouldn't fire questions at him on that occasion no one was listening to my prayer.

"Whoa what a surprise CJ. I presume your just visiting or has something happened? No don't tell me that you and Thomas have separated?"

The house suddenly went from laughter to falling into deadly silence as Catherine waited for an answer. The man's response was brief and to the point. I'm here because I can be and wish people wouldn't ask questions. Well its only you Catherine so please don't. Well that put her back in her box. Wishing she'd kept her mouth shut she was apologetic. She was genuine and sincere but the elephant had been placed in the room.

"Ooops me and my big mouth getting me into trouble again. I'm really sorry and it won't be repeated."
Dinner was served and eaten through what was more than a slightly uncomfortable period of time. Praise was duly served on the chef for his culinary skills. Myself and Charlie took care of the pots and pans. Catherine made coffee then herself and Anthony left for the cinema. Pastries were shared out 3 ways which we all enjoyed. Having consumed double portions

what was left for Anthony was minimal and I was feeling almost nauseous.

Being enlightened by CJ with some new information, simply caused us both but especially Charlie, a degree of confusion. Having struggled with ideas and thoughts around his sexuality, the desire not to offend, to hurt, or to cause grievance for Thomas, was the glue which kept that relationship together for so long. CJ was open and honest as he told us.

"People whose sexual preference falls outside the line of what's considered to be 'normal', often struggle with knowing precisely what it is they want. That's the category I fell into and it's no one's fault. It's how my brain works. Well maybe Thomas played a part in it. To say that he coerced me would maybe be too strong a word to use, but he did use some bullying tactics making me think I was willing when in reality I wasn't."

Personally, I had covered some of this stuff in my mental health training. I understood to a degree what our son was sharing with us. Charlie was looking very confused. C J made a further attempt to break it down and to be clear of the reasons why he had to get out.

"Look dad its very personal. If your uncomfortable with the conversation then just say so and I'll shut up. Bottom line is that I was confused. I was very attracted to Thomas in many ways mostly on a spiritual level, yet never shared intimacy with him or with any other male. Never ever."

Charlie was quick to respond.

"So, you're not gay then."

C J had no response to that comment other than he likes the company of men, but likes women in a different way. He reiterated again how for many reasons he was confused and would try to explain. Stating that he was lured into a friendship with Thomas and despite being a fully-grown adult he was kept there. How there were always underlying suggestions of.

"Don't you dare say this is anything else other than a relationship or pay the consequence if you do"

He went on to share how for a long time he had realised that Thomas was quite a toxic person. How him staying in the relationship felt very unfair to both of them. Eventually it all became too much for himself and how it took a lot of confidence for him to leave. Despite the strain that leaving put upon CJ he was successful in doing that. He shared how Thomas had mental health problems with aggressive tendencies, which at times were displayed through his frustration with CJ. Reminding us of the first time we met Thomas and how they had left, straight after our meeting at Gerry's instead of the next morning, CJ shared how controlling Thomas could be at times.

That evening at Gerry's was one of his controlling situations and he could be devious and manipulative too. Whilst I sat silently listening Charlie asked if CJ had been psychically hurt, or if something else had occurred to create the current situation of him having left and come home. I could only think that my husband either hadn't been listening or didn't understand how a toxic person might or would behave.

"Yes, I have been psychically hurt by Thomas many times. I won't ever hit back that wouldn't be me. That's it. That's the whole story why I've left and come back here. Not having the courage to tell him face to face I left a letter for Thomas. He'll have seen it by now and not attempted to

contact me so that's very positive."
Reminding our child that our front door was his front door he acknowledged with some appreciation. Living in what was Thomas's house, he would in time search for his own accommodation.

Rooney n Regan computing software business had blossomed almost beyond recognition. Serving their foreign counterparts had raised the financial stakes considerably. Having 2 of our 3 children living back home with us we weren't sure how to feel on their behalf. Should we be worried for them or should we accept situations as they were and simply leave the men to sort themselves out. As always calling my friend was the go to option. Frankie was full of advice.

"Money is no longer an issue for either of us Helen. Now that's something to be grateful for. Anthony's doing very well in therapy. C.J has made a life changing decision. These young men will sort themselves out and best left to it I think."

Hard to dispute anything which Frankie had said I expressed my gratitude for her sensible input. My suggestion then was that we meet up for dinner. Perhaps back at either Hales bar or at Gerry's. Just the 2 of us or include the men if she wished to. Hearing how Mikey wouldn't be overly keen on cooking dinner for himself surprised me, but not as much as her other news surprised me.

"Catherine's going out for dinner tonight. Between ourselves I overheard her talking to Anthony. Don't freak out when I tell you she has a female friend, which she's bringing on a blind date. C.J. will be the other half of that date. In terms of Charlie you know what he's like Helen. Cooking for one isn't really his thing."

I was stunned. With unintentional volume in my voice I almost bellowed at Frankie.

"Don't freak out. How do I manage that? He's just walked out of a relationship with another man. What else am I supposed to do other than freak out?"

As would be usual for her Frankie put it all in perspective for me. Her voice was soothing.

"Helen, he won't be proposing marriage to her. They'll be with friends and doesn't C.J. deserve the chance to do that- deserve a night out in good company."

Again, it was hard to dispute what I had just heard we agreed a table for 4 at Hales bar for that night and to drop the other conversation. Arrival at the restaurant we were shown to what was considered to be our favourite table. I loved dining at Hales- we all did. Food up to its usual standard as was the company a good night was had. Analysing all of our children was something we found easy to do. Frankie wondered how many other parents knew their kids as well as we knew ours and then wondered if we had too much input to their lives. It was like talking about religion. It was a discussion that could go on for ever more if we allowed it to.

Mikey changed the direction of the conversation. Sharing his view that we spend too many of our thoughts on the kids and that he had a different focus for us, we were eager to hear his thoughts. Discussion around our financial situation was then raised by Mikey.

"We all agree that money is no obstacle to us these days and that's great to know. I have a proposal. You want to hear it?"

Telling her husband to spit it out Mikey surprised us and gave us food for thought. His idea of myself and Frankie opening up a small children's home in Yorkshire had appeal to us both.

"You've both got good professional qualifications in subjects which would allow you to help and support damaged kids and let's face it, any child who enters a children's home, if not already damaged they will definitely be so by the time they leave."

Having been raised in one- none of us could disagree with that sentiment. The men having business experience could be supporting in the background. Leaving it there we brought our evening to its end. Saying goodbye, it was a given that myself and Frankie would be in touch probably the next day. Our journey home that night saw me on a high. My mind was spinning with thoughts of a potential business venture together with my best friend forever. Charlie was hyped up too.

"Could turn out really positive Helen. Imagine all the love you 2 would spread to people who needed it most."

Reassuring him I would give it some great consideration ahead of my next get together with Frankie, we agreed to leave it there for the present time.

Phone call came from Ireland received by the Rooney's. Joseph was calm yet upbeat. Sharing about his college course and how well he continued to do brought Joy to Frankie. Then came the other news which every parent would like to hear about their child. Joseph had met a young Irish woman at a local farmer's market. Her understanding of Josephs needs was immense. She too has the same issues as he does and was undiagnosed. Like Joseph a life on the farm has brought peace and calmness into her days. Joseph had been surprised to hear how she too had worked in a supermarket stacking shelves. He shared word for word with his mother what the girl had told him.

"I couldn't deal with the sensory overload Joseph. Despite being too old to be having what I considered to be childish tantrums, there I was having one right in the middle of the store. Embarrassing beyond belief when I think back to it now."

Frankie heard how reaching the decision together that they would be assessed, those assessments have now taken place. Both diagnosed with Asperger's syndrome, that opened the door for them to gain some financial help from the government. Also giving them some peace of mind and understanding regards what was going on in their lives, they no longer had that immense fear of having outbursts in the absence of explanation. His girlfriend was called Moira Mcguire. Joseph informed his mother they were coming to England shortly. He wanted his parents to meet her and wondered if she could stay with them?

"I'd like her to stay with us. Do you or dad have an
 aversion to that?"
Hearing that it's not a problem to his parents Joseph told his mother.

"See you soon then. I'll send trip details when I've spoken to Moira."

Joseph brought the call to an end. Having taken Brendan on a blind date on his own first date with Moira, everyone got on very well. Having heard all of that news filled Frankie with a deep sense of joy. Deciding in the absence of having met this girl, that their child had probably met the woman whom he would build a life with, was such a presumptuous yet very comforting thought for Frankie. Wondering quietly if she was going slightly crazy as she travelled through the journey we call life, she giggled to herself.

Brendan called his parents. House sitters and farm hands arranged for a week- he planned time away. Would it be all right for him to come back to Yorkshire together with a female friend? He was clear with his explanation.

"She's nothing like Fiona mam. She's a friend of Joseph's girlfriend. Both women are working on farms and both quiet and shy women. We all met up over a year ago. For me it was a blind date and we've been dating ever since. She's called Mairead. I know you'll both be happy once you've met her if its ok to go ahead with the visit from your point of view?"

Reminding Brendan that he's always welcome back home and yes fine to bring the girl friend too, the deal was done. Remembering Fiona and how flippant and loose she was, I could only consider that any girl would have to be an improvement on her. Trying not to, I was unsuccessful in my attempts at not feeling guilty, for having been so judgemental. Sharing those thoughts with Charlie, his response was that as far as Fiona was concerned, that if the cap fits then wear it and how that particular cap fitted Fiona very well. Therefore, I should have no feelings of guilt at all.

Text message came through to both myself and Frankie. Flights were booked from (ORK) airport in County Cork. Our sons and their girlfriends would be with us on the following Saturday morning. Hiring a car there would be no requirement for collection of them from Luton airport. They would be spending 4 days in Yorkshire if that was acceptable to their families. It was very acceptable to both ourselves and to the Rooney's.

␀␀␀␀␀Frankie was excited. Sharing her thoughts about Joseph having a girlfriend, was something which she and Mikey scarcely ever anticipated happening for him.

"We never thought of this as being a possibility Helen. You know with his awful random outbursts and tantrums, but here we are. Ireland and farming have truly done him good."

Arranging a meet up ahead of the weekend our plan was in place for Sunday evening. Booking out a table at Hales bar, for 12 people for the following Saturday evening at 5pm, gave myself and Frankie great pleasure. Being the first time, in which our families and their plus one would all be together, had the makings for either a great evening or one maybe not so good.

␀␀␀␀␀Josephs arrival from Ireland brought surprise to his parents. Not only had he got himself a girlfriend he now held a full driver's licence. Beaming with a pride his parents had never before witnessed, with a good degree of confidence he introduced his girlfriend. Moira being a beautiful young woman was as he had said quiet shy. Long red wavy hair hanging below her shoulders, was a huge compliment to her big green eyes. Those were the eyes that dazzled Joseph every time he looked into them. Now they were dazzling Frankie's family, my family and the people of Yorkshire with whom she came into contact. Joseph felt unnecessarily embarrassed. Being the first girl, he had ever brought home to meet the family and family friends, introductions to everyone wasn't the easiest experience he ever had. A shy girl from County Cork with a soft Irish accent she won the hearts of all of us. Not having had the best education experience, Moira shared how working on the farm in a hands-on situation has given her the peace she needs in life.

Hearing how Joseph and Moira had been dating for more than a year was something of a surprise to his parents. Frankie was quick to react.

"Between the driving licence and the girlfriend, you're a dark horse, keeping that to yourself."

The confusing look on Moiras face showed she did not understand that figure of speech. Quick with an explanation to his girlfriend, Frankie's surprise was that Joseph actually understood it. That being yet another sign of how much his life had improved since leaving his life in Yorkshire behind him.

The very moment they entered the house, Brendan's arrival with Mairead brought a sense of joy to the family. No one could explain it yet everyone felt it. Mairead too just like Moira was a shy girl who wanted to blend in. That was obvious from her attempts to engage in conversation with myself and Charlie and with Brendan's brothers. A little on the chubby side with long red curly hair, she shared how delighted she was to be in England for the first time. Being a farmer's daughter, she told us how much she loved the land, but got herself an education too, in order to do something else in life should she wish to.

Mairead had taken a degree course in Psychology. She was trained as an educational psychologist should she ever desire to take that path. She had baked a fruited soda bread as a gift from Ireland for us. A little squashed from her luggage being thrown around it was nevertheless very tasty, and what a thoughtful young woman. She appeared to be a person who would fit right in with our family. Being unable to resist the private sharing of that thought with Brendan he beamed.

"Your right mam isn't she lovely. We get on great.

I want her in my life forever. I'm going to propose to her but not sure when or where yet and please keep that to yourself. If you think dad can keep the secret then you can tell him but no one else."

Being more eager to tell Frankie that she'd need to buy a hat, than I was to tell my husband, felt just slightly strange to me but needs must. I had to keep Brendan's secret. I did share with Charlie who felt as delighted as I did. Our families gathering together down at Hales bar that evening, turned out to be the most wonderful evening we shared in a very long time. Everyone getting along really well, was a big stress reliever. Irish women sharing stories of their childhoods growing up and CJ's girlfriend Alice, mingling perfectly with everyone, the whole evening was perfect. Ending at almost 11pm and saying our goodbyes, Anthony joined the Rooney's back at their house. I was forever amazed at how Frankie could separate her therapy sessions with Anthony, from her friendship with him as her daughter's boyfriend. She did it with style. In fact, they both did it with style.

Life gave the impression it was surely starting to come together for both ourselves and for the Rooney's. Back on the wards I was informed that Thomas Summers was still a returning patient to the hospital. Having had 6 admissions since the point of his separation from CJ, felt like a lot. Wishing for a complete avoidance of the gentleman's information that wasn't always a possibility for me. Being requested to offer my assistance at a ward round was a challenge I had not anticipated. Making a video of my suggestions as a way forward with his treatment, was the best I could do. I could not psychically make myself available in that meeting. Hearing that Thomas was not managing his medication in the community, my idea for that issue was that perhaps long-term injections could be the best way forward for him. Being informed of the previous relationship between myself and Thomas through CJ, the ward consultant was sympathetic. Accepting my reasons for non-attendance at the ward round, she worked from information given by me in the video. Not wishing to know any outcome of his ward meetings my wish was respected.

Our family, together with Frankie and her family continued to enjoy the presence of our children, who were back from Ireland with their girlfriends. Mairead with her obvious show of love and care for Brendan continued to win our hearts. Almost time to return back to Ireland our young men organised a night out for all of us. This time it would be at Gerry's restaurant. The Rooney's and ourselves were delighted to see, that Teresa Riley the supermarket manager had been invited to join us that evening by Joseph and Brendan. Proud of the respectful young men we had raised those comments would keep until we were more private.

The table was taken by surprise as Brendan and Joseph took turns to share their news. Both having found the woman they want to be with and who understands them, as they do their girlfriends, they both planned to put down roots in Ireland. Brendan made the first announcement. Looking a little nervous he stood up from the table. Moving to stand behind his girlfriend he placed his hand on her shoulder. Beginning to speak then stopping again he was nervous. Eventually telling everyone.

"We need to raise a glass to Mairead who will be the newest member of our family. I've proposed and to my delight she said yes."

Brendan returned back to his seat. Calls of congratulations

came from around the table with questions of any potential dates in place. Charlie and I already having that information we too were beyond delighted. Extending our welcome to Mairead into the family, she informed us how her family love Brendan too and how they want for all of us to meet. There was no further information to be shared regards the wedding at that point. There were no engagement rings. Brendan and Mairead shared the same view that rings would be an unnecessary expense.

Our evening continued with excitement and many questions being fired at Mairead. The very shy girl who entered our lives a few days previous, was now losing that fear of being with new people. Sharing about life growing up and being a farmer's daughter, her experiences in many ways felt enviable. Her having freedom from the restraints of city life and being part of what in many ways was a self-sufficient family, was something which many would crave for.

Joseph Rooney called for attention. Turning to his mother he told her.

"I know Gerry's has been a place you've liked to go to when you were younger. Help you get some news or some memories back about your parents and their lifestyles. That had to be so awfully sad for you mam. We've brought you and everyone here tonight, in order you hear some nice news. Something that will make you happy. Give you the happy memory you deserve in relation to Gerry's"
Frankie took hold of her childs hand. In a soft and caring voice, she told him.

"No idea you were aware of my trips to Gerry's. I am happy Joseph. Seeing how well your doing in life has made your dad and I very happy indeed."
She shared an embrace with their son who then turned to

Mikey.

"Come on dad we can have hugs too."

The Rooney parents beamed with shock with pride and delight in seeing the changes in their child. Joseph spoke again reminding his mam, that they were in Gerry's for both parents to hear some nice news, but especially so for Frankie due to her younger years going there. He took a deep breath in and then.

"So, in the same way that Brendan has shared his news I will share mine. Welcome Moira as the newest member of our family. I got on one knee and am delighted that she said yes."

The table shared a loud applause. Frankie wiped tears from her eyes. For a lady who wouldn't want anyone to see her emotions, she surely put on a display. Again, there were no rings for the same reasons as Brendan and Mairead. Guests seated at other tables joined in with congratulations to both couples. Sean who was still employed by Gerry's was one of the waiters on duty that night. Joseph had made that a special request. Knowing how well Sean knew his mother and her family and the sad reasons which had brought Frankie to the restaurant as a young woman, it was his thinking, that it would be nice for Sean to see her have the good news too. Moira shared some brief information about her family back in Ireland and how delighted they were to know about the forthcoming marriage. How they loved Joseph and had a great desire to meet the Rooney family. Brendan, Joseph and their girl friends returned back to Ireland the following day.

Mikey Rooney assessed the business accounts again. There being so much more finance available to them than their requirements, he once again raised the topic of myself and Frankie potentially starting up a business together. Doing our research, we both concluded, that there was a gap in the market for a small specialised children's unit, right there in the centre of Yorkshire. Both being super qualified to run such a unit, we also knew other highly qualified people whom we could seek to employ. Our immediate plan was that Frankie would speak to Catherine. Establish if we went ahead would she be interested in doing some ad hoc work. I would speak to Jackie's (colleague who died shortly after being hit by a car) daughter Karina, with the same question only on a regular weekly basis. She was definitely interested and very keen to join us should our adventure go ahead.

  Life had changed a lot and was continuing to change furthermore, for the Rooney and the Regan families. Searching for premises which would be deemed suitable for our new business adventure, a 5 bedroomed house in a very quiet cul -de- sac (For my foreign readers - Road which is closed at one end thus leading nowhere) appeared to be worth investigation. Where the property was sited would be as good as we could hope for. Being detached with spacious gardens all round, would reduce possibility of neighbours making complaints about noise or any other disturbances. Our viewing was arranged together with our husbands. They would provide their business expertise in terms of securing the property or not, should myself and Frankie feel it was appropriate. That particular property was at least a twenty-five-minute drive from our homes and slightly more from Catherine and Karima. Distance being an important factor for all of us, all risks of young people discovering our home address would be reduced, the farther away we were from the unit. Jointly reaching an agreement on the suitability of the house we decided to go ahead.

Having contact through work with our local authority social services, fostering and adoptions teams, proved itself to be useful. They shared a little information about 3 potential young people, whom they felt could benefit greatly from our expertise on a 1-1 basis. Meetings were set up between Frankie, myself, and the children's social workers over a period of 2 weeks. Reading about and hearing some issues endured by the children, we agreed to take time out for discussion and consideration. Being very clear with social workers, that should we ultimately go ahead with those children who were aged between 13 and 15 years, that all information regardless of how personal it was about the children, would be shared in full with staff members who might come on board with us. All staff ourselves included would be bound by the data protection act. Confidentiality would be respected and adhered to

Reporting back to social services Frankie informed them, that yes, we would like to proceed to the next step. Plans made for myself and Frankie to meet each child individually, together with their social worker in a public place, those meetings occurred and went very well. The plan agreed was that should we be interested in offering accommodation after our meetings with the children, that 1 person at a time would be admitted to our care. There would be a gap of 7 days between each admission. Catherine and Karina had by that point agreed their interest in working with myself and Frankie should the whole procedure go ahead. Suddenly I wasn't sure. My head went on one of its overdrive scenarios. Alright for Frankie as she was already self-employed- I had an employer to think about. What if working together spoiled or ruined the relationship between myself and Frankie? What would happen then?

Mikey and Charlie busy in the background. Them sorting finance on a deal for the property brought me back to reality. How could I ever question my friendship with Frankie? Surely it was as solid as the rock of Gibraltar. Snapping myself out of my unsettling thoughts my decision was to share with Frankie how I had felt. Picking up the phone to call her it rang out in my hands. Not giving me opportunity to make that call it was Frankie calling me. Being a bit sceptical about the idea of telepathy I was increasingly starting to believe in it, as these situations happened with increasing regularity.

Having a heart to heart with Frankie she shared her thoughts of wondering how working together might impact our friendship. Reassuring to hear that she had a moment, it gave me confidence to share my thoughts. Deciding that nothing could come between us in life, we discussed our potential way forward with opening our own business. In addition to our husbands negotiating a property deal they negotiated our fees with social services. Being relieved of those jobs saved us a lot of headaches. Their accountants became our accountants with no input from myself or Frankie. We had an extra sense of appreciation for our husbands support on the business side of our adventure.

Invitations came from Ireland via email from the parents of Moira McGuire and Mairead Dooney. Frankie received theirs same time as we received ours. Sharing our thoughts Frankie and I were amazed how much the world had moved on. How much technology had moved on since our younger days. Having to acknowledge our own part in that development, we reminisced about our husbands and about their computing business. Requests were that we should all visit and bring the kids with their partners too. Share our travel dates and times they would book out rooms at the local hotel. That our children had some dates in mind for their weddings and would like all of us to discuss. We could only consider how warm the Irish families appeared to be from their email content. Charlie would liaise with our children for their availability to travel then make bookings based on that. Frankie and I held the view how this trip to Ireland which we were eager to do, should occur ahead of our new adventure with the children's unit.

Discussing and the securing of some temporary staff for the unit was high up on our list of priorities. Decision was made that I should speak to Tom Chesterton inform him of my future plans. Seek his views of how best to put a bank full of temporary staff together, which we could fall back on for the unit. Charlie informed me that the house deal had gone through. Himself and Mikey would get it set up as a running business, with the creation of an office in there for us. There would be a sleep-in room for overnight staff in order to support working overnight staff should that need become a requirement.

Large communal rooms would be created by the removal of internal walls thus providing ample space for the young people to socialise and relax. There would be a smaller communal room where people could go for quiet time. The provision of furniture could be sourced from local charity shops who had pride in the decent quality furniture they sold. That would be a huge bonus for Frankie as she still held her keen interest in pre-loved everything. The house was decorated in neutral colours throughout. It had laminate flooring which would be a breeze to keep clean. Each bedroom had its own en-suite which was a bonus. There was a separate bathroom on the first floor which would be locked and used by staff only. In order to personalise their rooms our young people would choose their own bedding and and curtains. It was all coming together.

Our family's trip to Ireland was productive. Spending time at an upmarket hotel in county Cork, we were exposed to and treated to traditional Irish music and dance. Our surprise was to find that the girls Moira and Mairead, belonged to a traditional Irish dance group. Seeing them on stage dressed in their dance dress, our young men beamed with pride. A rapturous applause went up from the large audience. Being the first time for Brendan and Joseph seeing them perform, they were mesmerized by the challenging level of footwork performed by the dancers.

The girl's fathers in addition to being farmers were great local musicians too. Hearing them play the flute and button accordion was magical to listen to. Having no affiliation with Ireland or anything Irish other than Moira, Mairead and now their families, we all felt a certain level of closeness and a desire, to discover more about what we were told was a beautiful country. Saying goodbye to our boys, to their girlfriends and to our host families, brought a mixture of sadness and joy. Sadness as we had to leave and joyous as we knew we would be back. Our young men would be getting married in Ireland. That would be our next visit across the water. Soda breads unknown to us were packed into our luggage by the girl's mothers. We were bringing a little bit of Ireland back to Yorkshire.

Anthony and CJ had both shared a keen interest

in history. Spending time in Ireland and especially so in Cork, was the catalyst for them going down memory lane. Sharing their stories about events of long ago, associated with the Irish Statesman Michael Collins, they captivated us as their audience. They shared how Michael was born in 1890 in County Cork. Who as a mere 16-year-old he went to work as a clerk in London. Returning back to his native land in 1916, he became a fighter in the Easter Rising. He was arrested, kept in detention and released in December 1916. December 1918, he became an elected Sinn Fein (Irish government) member. They told us how Michael became famous through his role as director of intelligence of the Irish Republican Army. Organising attacks on police and the assassination of some of Britain's intelligence officers in Ireland, he became very much a wanted man. He was eventually shot to death in 1922 in an ambush in County Cork. A huge loss to the people of Ireland Michael Collins is still mourned and respected by many to this day.

Holiday in Ireland

Return back to Yorkshire and back to our new adventure, was an exciting time for myself and Frankie. There were still many plans to be put in place. Back on the wards of our mental health hospital I secured a meeting with Tom Chesterton. Hearing how the trust would be losing my services, Tom wondered what he could do to persuade a change of mind on my part. Ploughing his way through some work options with suggestions of an increase in my salary, he eventually got the message that I was not to be persuaded. With a degree of sadness on his face he told me.

"You're a great asset to this hospital Helen. Losing you just feels wrong."

Accepting the man's compliments I had the need to express my gratitude, for the many opportunities which the trust had availed to me. I also had the need to thank Tom personally for having believed in me all those years ago in relation to the secondment to Portugal. Hearing about my business adventure with Frankie, he was delighted I would still be supporting people, albeit children as opposed to adults.

"Having a mountain of experience in mental health Helen, hopefully between yourself and other staff members, you might be able to do some prevention work with the young people who cross your threshold. Save them from serious mental health issues and ending up in here further down the line."

Advising me that myself and Frankie whom he had also met in ward meetings, would be given access to the trusts register of competent and reliable supply nursing staff, was the best leaving gift I could possibly have received. It was another box ticked off on the to do list for Charlie and Mikey.

Our families were making some great waves as they navigated their way through life. Anthony's health had improved immensely. His body weight had now increased to what would be a healthy weight for a man of his age and height. Being unemployed through ill health since his return home from the States, he had worked hard at making his recovery as good and as swift as could be possible. Frankie and his doctor both having given him the green light, he spoke to myself and Charlie about his thoughts on a return back to the work place. What he wanted to pursue as a career or how he wanted to pursue it, was unclear to him at that point.

Having kept our friendship circle tightly closed to the 4 of us, had worked to perfection. Frankie Mikey and Charlie would share that view too. That aspect of life was very different for our children. They had spread their wings with each having their own individual friendship circle. Some great, some not so bad, some bad and some very poor choices, were made by all of them throughout the years leading into their adulthood and their adult lives. Positives are, they all appear to now be settled in life with each having a reliable and positive partner. Their blessings to ourselves on our new adventure opening up a specialised unit for severely damaged children, meant a lot.

Further news from Ireland brought all of us some

deep joy. Dates, a church and wedding venue were all in place and set for a double wedding. Being three months waiting period to the point of the weddings taking place, we decided to put the children's unit on hold. Property deal being sorted and finalised, the house was almost ready. All that remained was to secure furniture for the bedrooms, the office and the communal rooms. In so many ways that was the most difficult part of the adventure ticked off. More intricate aspects of the plan, such as negotiations with and speaking to social services, selecting children whom we felt most able to help and interviewing staff, were roles myself and Frankie would fulfil on our return after the trip to Ireland.

This trip to Ireland would see us taking our own cars. Travelling by Ferry would be albeit the longest journey, it would also be the easiest. Attempting to shove wedding outfits into a case, which everyone knows would be thrown around at airports, didn't seem the best plan to anyone. The journey was long. All of us were relatively young. Each car having 2 drivers allowed sharing of that task from home to the ports and back. Whilst stretching our test levels for endurance, the challenge of staying awake did not prove itself to be too much of a challenge. What did present all of us from Yorkshire with a challenge was the order of the marriage ceremony.

Brendan and Joseph had no affinity at all to religions of any description. Their brides to be Moira and Mairead were both raised as Roman Catholics. Being non-practicing in their adult lives, they still wished for a catholic church marriage, mostly in order to please their parents. Mairead Dooney was especially adamant that's what would need to happen. She shared with Brendan her parents' views and especially her fathers.

"He'll be devastated Brendan if we marry outside of the Catholic church. Mum would be okay with it but not him."

Hearing her words said with such passion Brendan held her in even higher esteem than he had previously done. To hear how she had such deep respect for her parents he felt was heart-warming. Similar chats had occurred between Joseph Rooney and Moira McGuire.

Charlie and Mikey showing some grave concern regarding the aspect of religion, were very much reassured by the young women who were to become their daughters-in-law. Brendan had explained how the girls, himself and Joseph held meetings with the parish priest. How the priest had insisted on 6 months pre-marriage course, in order the couple were prepared adequately for married life. Ourselves and the Rooney parents having been married for a very long time, had to wonder how a catholic priest could ensure couples were prepared for their commitment to each other. A man who has such little experience of family life, giving marriage advice was beyond our comprehension. It was too far off the wall and not something you can do from the book in our view.

Dispensations from the church had been granted by the Bishop for both couples in order to allow for the weddings to go ahead. Joseph had shown an interest in listening to bible stories and perhaps having some teaching sessions with the priest. Moira had stressed upon her husband to be, that any children born to them, that she would wish them to be raised in the Catholic religion. Hearing and respecting those wishes Joseph had felt that the best way to offer his wife support in that, would come from him perhaps becoming a Catholic. With a sense of confidence, which they had never seen from Joseph he told his parents.

"You brought us up to do the right thing. Doing this to me feels like the right thing to do and who knows I might actually start to believe it all myself."

Being proud and showing it, wasn't something either of the Rooney parents were especially practiced at, where Joseph was concerned. Perhaps that was a reflection of the difficult time he gave to them throughout his life in Yorkshire. This occasion was the exception to that. Reminding their child of all of his good points, they shared how very proud they were feeling at that very moment.

"Your just amazing Joseph. Your putting your wife to be and any children ahead of yourself and your own needs, and like you said you might become one."

Smiling, Joseph again unusual for him embraced his parents.

Eve of the wedding day was a beautiful sunny summers day. Wet leaves from overnight showers glistened on an overgrown holly bush. Glistening in the morning sunshine they were a sight to behold. The view from our hotel windows was a mixture of beautiful trees in their extensive gardens, combined with some stunning views over the city of Cork. Time to stroll before breakfast, Charlie, myself, Frankie and Mikey set off to investigate the countryside of rural Ireland. The vision surrounding us was truly breath taking.

Having enjoyed a late breakfast, we took a drive over to Dooney's farm. There being 2 houses on the land we felt was quite a luxury. Possibly a strong indication of their finances. The biggest house was set up for the pre-wedding day. Having 2 large rooms which opened out onto a delightful looking garden, scent from the flowers and shrubs penetrated the house. Wooden decking situated just off side from a large patio area, was where activities using the feet would take place. The whole day from mid-morning through to late evening, was filled with fun, with laughter and with traditional Irish music and dance. Moira McGuire with her parents and siblings joined us there. Teresa Riley joined us there too. Amazed that almost everyone present was aware of who she was and how she fitted into the equation she felt respected.

Everyone got along well, sharing tales from our childhood days and listening to tales of Irish folklore. Scarcely any alcohol in sight was not what the world might imagine or be led to believe, would be the regular scenario of an Irish pre-wedding celebration. Brendan and Joseph the grooms to be were not in attendance. Being invited out for the day by some teaching staff from the school where Fiona McGeever had worked, they never did share where they were taken. It was a matter of where they went in Cork or elsewhere, stayed in Cork or elsewhere. The mention of Fiona's name on the eve of our son's wedding day pierced my heart. Having previously heard from Brendan that she had resigned at the school and moved abroad was good news for all of us.

The double wedding took place in a beautiful church in Ballintemple, County Cork. Weather was good to us with beaming sunshine. Ireland being unpredictable it would often and unexpectedly present people with many rainy days. I found myself joining in with others in their thanking to the lord for being spared the rain on that day. Everything went well and to plan for the newlyweds. Observing a church wedding with all the rituals of the Catholic church, was a new experience for Frankie, Mikey, Charlie and myself. We had to wonder how it might impact on Brendan as he goes through his marriage. Knowing Joseph had plans to learn more, the Rooney parents considered it may be helpful in the event of their son and his wife being blessed with any children. C.J. and Alice Nixon together with Anthony and Catherine Rooney completed our families. There were 13 of us in total at the event including our children's partners and Teresa Riley. Teresa had taken a flight from Luton to Cork for a 4 day round trip. There were almost 200 guests from Moira and Máiréad's family and friends.

People gathered together for the wedding reception at a beautiful location close to our hotel. Set in the hills of County Cork it offered some stunning views of the Island of Ireland. Local pipers had been hired to greet the brides and their grooms as they entered the venue. Listening to Amazing Grace being played on the pipes provided an extra sense of relaxation and a topic to focus discussion on for everyone. Wine and food flowed in abundance at the tables. There was no cost incurred to ourselves or to our sons. This was the ultimate in Irish hospitality, combined with the traditional view that the bride's parents would finance their weddings.

Having booked ourselves a 2-week trip in order to see more of Ireland and after having said goodbye to everyone, we headed north West from County Cork. Travelling together with Frankie and Mikey in their car, we left ours at the Dooney's farmhouse. It felt like the sensible thing to do. We could then explore Ireland together. Being advised to see Mayo that was our first stopping point. Booking ourselves into a hotel in Westport made us central for the whole of that beautiful county. The town being in high tourist season, to say that it was busy would be an understatement. Purchasing sandwiches made with soda bread from a local supermarket, we sat in the sunshine by the river to enjoy our lunch. A visit to Matt Molloys (famous Irish flute player) pub in the town finished off our day nicely.

      Places of interest in Mayo recommended to us were Knock Shrine in the village of Knock. Meeting some elderly locals down by the river in Westport brought great feelings of joy mixed with some degrees of sadness. We heard their stories about that village. Hearing that in the late 19th Century, conflict of land and land ownership was rife. We heard how West Ireland in 1879 was an awfully bad year. Excessive rain combined with a fast and devastating potato blight added to the fears of the people. They shared with us how rations were implemented as another famine loomed over the people of Mayo, threatening them with further starvation. Many still had memories and suffered from the very painful famine of the 1840s, where around 1 million people throughout Ireland had lost their lives, either from starvation or hunger related disease. We heard how around a million more left the country many losing their lives as they travelled. Ireland had lost around a quarter of its population. A heart-breaking statistic which many people still remembered. Eventually with so many lives lost we heard how the famine eventually reached its end in 1952. That was probably the saddest story any of the 4 of us had ever heard.

      Charlie expressed his many negative thoughts in relation to why we had not been taught about the famine in our history lessons at school. No one could nor did attempt to disagree with him. People who shared information with us told us the story of Knock in fuller detail. They shared how in the village of Knock there was a small church. It's been said that on a typical working day in the village, something miraculous happened. That on Thursday August 21st 1879, that an apparition of the Virgin Mary with a cross and a lamb on an altar, was seen by some of the villagers. It occurred on a wall of the church. It's been said that the crown on her head was the most beautiful they had ever seen. Despite having no affinity with any religion, we had a great sense of respect for the story we had just been told.

Having greatly appreciated and enjoyed the company and storytelling of the people who joined us at the bridge, we wanted to hear more. Having our first holiday in Ireland we had already learned so much and wanted to expand on that knowledge. Mikey was clear and so right too.

"You want to find knowledge of a local area who better to ask, other than the older generation who have grown up there and still live in the area."

Those ladies would not be offended by Mikey's reference to them, as being of the older generation. Having short grey curly hair their clothing too was in indication of their era. Having introduced themselves earlier in the conversation, we learned that Eileen and Margaret were both retired secondary school teachers. They were happy to accept our invitation for them to join us for dinner that night. Meeting up at the Best Western Hotel we all enjoyed dinner, wine and great company.

Eileen and Margaret appeared to be an absolute fountain of knowledge. They enjoyed the opportunity to enlighten us as much as we enjoyed hearing it all. Further historical information shared with us was in relation to Croagh Patrick and the climbs which occur there with pilgrimages going up yearly. How some people have gone against advice and done the climb in increment weather conditions. How some of those people have had to be brought down by stretcher. Hearing all of that and being non-religious, was difficult for ourselves and the Rooney's to appreciate a person's needs in those situations. Hard for us to comprehend the mentality of people, who would take such serious risks in the belief they would be closer to their god. Sharing those thoughts with our dinner guests, the ladies who themselves were staunch Roman Catholics expressed full understanding of our view. They expressed gratitude for out straightforward and direct views as we did of theirs.

Ahead of saying our goodbyes to Eileen and Margaret I had discreetly shared a message via text with Charlie and both of the Rooney's. Should we invite the ladies to accompany us on a trip to Knock Shrine or maybe meet us there the following day? Both being car owners and drivers travel would not be an issue for them! My responses came back and yes, a great idea were the thoughts from everyone. The ladies were delighted to know we were keen to meet up at Knock Shrine. That was our plan for the following morning. Travelling from Westport to Knock we choose to take the old roads. Providing some idyllic scenery enroute, we also saw some roadside shrines containing statues of the Virgin Mary. We were very strongly getting the message of how Ireland was on the whole a Catholic country.

Our meeting place reached we were warmly greeted by Eileen and Margaret. We took refreshments in a small roadside café ahead of entering the chapel. Commercialism in abundance selling a variety of things but mostly religious artefacts, lined the streets surrounding Knock shrine. Eileen and Margaret shared with us that in many ways, the shops were a necessity in order to keep finances up for the whole of the area. That in some other ways they did not especially like the idea of a place with

many religious connotations, being so commercialised. We went inside the very special chapel where the now church approved apparition had occurred. There's no denying that all of us felt a sense of peace and tranquillity inside that chapel. We made our entrance full of scepticism and left with the thoughts that something special had occurred within that chapel. Not able to explain what exactly made us feel that way, advise from Margaret and Eileen was that no explanation was required.
and we should accept what we were feeling.

"Accepting we're two very old ladies who's seen a bit of the world, Knock Shrine is our peaceful go to place and its never let us down."
Mikey being the quick-witted person that he could be when needed, his response was.

"Old ladies never. Spring chickens well maybe not but at around 65- 70 your little more than middle aged."

Eileen and Margaret smiling broadly expressed their appreciation for his compliment. They also shared how they were lifelong friends from 1st class school and now both aged 87 years. That information had the shock factor for all of us. Again, Mikey was the witty one.

"Well what can we say it must be the Mayo air doing you good."
Everyone laughed at his comments but we knew the ladies secretly felt delighted and what lady wouldn't? Sharing our home address and phone number with Eileen, there was an open invitation for both of them to visit our homes in Yorkshire, should they ever travel that way. We bade goodbye to the first people we had ever met as strangers, the previous day, and now considered them to be our friends. Thinking about our group of 4 we wondered what

had just happened in our heads, to have allowed the idea of those ladies being our friends. No one having a response to that thought, the decision was made to leave as it was and see how it looks in the future.

Achill Island being another place which had been recommended to us it did not disappoint. It was in our eyes more beautiful than we could ever have imagined. On arrival we considered it to be the most beautiful place we had ever seen. In order to see and experience as much as was possible of the island we stayed over a few nights. Finding a guesthouse almost on the beach seemed like perfection.
Myself and Charlie felt that this place was nicer than the nicest places we ever saw whilst living in Portugal. Being allowed to join a cycling club for a day we were provided with bicycles for hire. Taken through the many coastal and hilly roads, Achill's scenery was breath taking. Our day having reached its end we felt painful muscles in places we didn't realise we had muscles. Time to move on from Mayo our next pit stop was Donegal ahead of our return back to Yorkshire.

Discovering how Donegal is the largest county in Ulster, how its bordered by the Atlantic Ocean on 3 sides with the 4th being bordered by county Tyrone which is in Northern Ireland, we absorbed all of its beauty. Discovering some facts, we were told how the actor and writer Sean McGinley was born in Donegal. Hearing from locals how the Port of Killybegs is the largest fishing port in Ireland, serving its fish to other parts of Ireland and to European countries, also to some parts of Africa and to the middle east, was information we were appreciative of hearing. We were broadening our horizons without going very far at all. We discovered that married men often refer to their wife's as "Herself" Staying in a guest house for 2 nights gave us ample opportunity to see lots of the county. High proportion of the population we discovered were speaking in Gaelic in addition to English. Meeting some lovely people, we made attempts to speak in Gaelic following their guidance. You know the old adage – When in Rome do as the Romans do. We failed miserably but had many good belly laughs in our feeble attempts. We fell in love with Donegal and with Ireland.

Time to leave we travelled back down to Cork and to the place where our adventure began at the Dooney's farm. Discovering the newlyweds had gone to Dublin for a few days, then to the North West they would most likely be covering our tracks. Moiras parents joined us at the Dooney's home. Both parents shared how as a family they had never been out of Cork. How this would be as much an adventure for Mairead and Moira as it would be for our sons. Preparing for our Ferry trip back home we were laden with food and fluids for the journey, which had been provided by both families. Being served a traditional Irish dinner of boiled bacon, cabbage and potatoes boiled in their skin, ahead of leaving we were in awe of Irish hospitality. Saying goodbye to the people whom we had jointly considered, would be let into our circle of 4, the Dooney's and the McGuire's were now our new friends too. Heading along the road singing Irish songs we had learned form our trip, we also as you'll see on the next page said.

GOOD-BYE
For Now

TO

What a small Island it looks like and it actually is!

Decisions to be made

Our journey back to England and to Yorkshire was a tiresome one. Charlie feeling quite exhausted from a lack of sleep in conjunction with hectic days, he slept for most of the car journey, from Dooney's farm in Cork to the Ferry port. Joking that he was a light weight he took my humour in good spirits. Charlie was and is like that. It's one of the reasons which attracted me to him in the first instance. Meeting up with Frankie and Mikey in a roadside café just outside of the port, we insured that our cars went on board together, with the Rooney's being marginally ahead of ourselves. On board the ship we enjoyed some refreshments. Reminiscing about our children and how they were building up their lives brought all 4 of us some deep joy. Catherine and Anthony living together was the connection which would keep our families connected for evermore. Arrival back at our own homes in Yorkshire a plan was in place to meet up the following day. There being no time to be wasted the children's home would be up for discussion, amongst any other issues that may have arisen in our absence from England.

Catherine Rooney decided not to renew the lease on her house. Current tenants moving out imminently she would live there once that plan was finalised. Much to the surprise of his parents Anthony with his approval and agreement had been discharged from therapy with Frankie. The Rooney's and ourselves congratulated ourselves for our resistance and our ability to be friends and never once mentioned the therapy afforded by Frankie to our child. He was pretty much wrecked when they commenced. He has now blossomed and made a full recovery. Hearing that Anthony has secured some work as a supply teacher in our local Secondary school was very reassuring. Having done that in the absence of a mention of his plans to his parents, showed how well adjusted he now is. Anthony shared with us his other special news.

"Mam and dad prepare yourselves. Our families are increasing two-fold."

Hearing how Anthony and Catherine would soon be parents to twins, was perhaps the most exciting news we'd heard in a long time. How special that myself and Frankie would become grandparents, at the same time to the same baby or perhaps I should say babies. To say we were elated would be an understatement. There being no mention of marriage was not a cause for concern. We are open minded people who believe in live and let live. They would live together in Catherine's house, with him contributing his half share of the mortgage fees. Having his name added to the house deeds was something which they both desired.

Our oldest child C J together with his girl friend Alice had taken their annual holiday. Flights abroad were pretty cheap at that time. They had secured 3 weeks in Florida. Having flown out there 2 days previous, we received messages of their arrival and how wonderful the whole place looked. No further contact expected until their return back to England. Again, having the knowledge that our families were building their own lives gave such a sense of freedom to ourselves and to the Rooney's. Plans in place for meetings with our local authority, hopefully the children's home would be opening very soon. With Catherine's pregnancy and the birth looming, another staff member with her qualifications or similar, would need to be secured before we could go ahead with our adventure.

Having helped each other to cope with life's ups and downs, sharing many joyous and sad moments, our circle of 4 was how we had always planned to keep things. Having let the Irish ladies Eileen and Margaret into our friendship circle, to our amazement they took up our invitation. Arriving in Selby to stay with family members they made contact with Frankie. A daughter was happy to deliver them and collect from Frankie's home. 2 very fit and agile ladies from Mayo appeared at Frankie's mid-afternoon. Arriving shortly before myself they were delighted to see me too. Dropped off there by a daughter they were the bearers of 2 loafs of soda bread containing treacle and fruit. That being traditional Irish bread its not everyone's favourite but was ours.

Hearing many stories of their upbringing in West Ireland, Eileen and Margaret were a delight to listen to. Presenting us with a CD containing traditional Irish dance music, we were shocked to see the ladies get up and dance an Irish reel, as we listened to the music. I called Charlie

"Yourself and Mikey should come home now if you can- to Mikey's that is. I'm already there with Frankie. You 'll be surprised to see who else is here."
Pushing me for more information didn't work. Charlie should have known it wouldn't. Telling him to get off the phone and collect his coat and car keys I ended the call. Seeing the ladies from Ireland surprised the men beyond belief. Seeing them

dance surprised them even more. Eileen's daughter arrived at 9pm prompt. Hearing how they were then going to the local Irish club which shut its doors at midnight, we were all in awe of those lovely ladies with their abundance of agility and energy.

Declining their invitation to join them we were left feeling like light weights. Charlie was the one to respond. A quick check in with myself, Frankie and Mikey he shared.

"You women are beyond amazing. Were usually asleep by 10 so maybe next time. Let us know you're coming over so we can rest beforehand."
Everyone laughed. Eileen opened up her handbag pulling out a small plastic bottle.

"Here Charlie. Its water that's been blessed at Knock Shrine. Its known as holy water. A few drops each on your forehead before bed and you'll be as fit as a fiddle in the morning."
Surprised by her kind gesture he thanked Eileen ahead of us saying goodbye till the next time. Our first ever decision to have let others into our friendship group we were already having regrets. The ladies lovely as they were it didn't feel right having them arrive at Frankie's. Charlie was to the point with a little tone in his voice.

"We've done it now Helen between the 4 of us we've created this situation and I don't like it."

Rethinking our friendship circle was something which would need attention from all of us. Questioning ourselves and our attitudes to people coming into our lives, was starting to cause some strain. Are we weird and if so then by whose definition? Frankie due to her being a psychologist, was the person delegated the task of unpicking our feelings on that. Needing time to think it through, she was adamant that however long the process might take, that no one would be heard till everyone had been heard and nothing would be agreed or decided till everything was agreed and decided. Her words were reassuring for all of us. All 4 of us having work colleagues and will continue to do so, that's quite different to how we have invited and allowed Eileen and Margaret into our lives.

Alice and CJ back from Florida and returned back to their workplace. C.J. loved his teaching job yet not so keen on the many difficult teenage students he encountered on a daily basis. Sharing once again about poor quality parents as he described them and how his teaching day would be so much improved, if only he had parents support when that was requested. Alice being an educational psychologist she had good understanding of the stresses of a busy and perhaps a dysfunctional classroom. Placing like with like, appeared to be the logic of the school head. In the view of CJ, it could never be a workable plan. His view was that children who are maybe vulnerable for a variety of reasons, have tendencies to behave the same as their peers. Having his attention focused on the best of the group, would and often did create a great shortfall for the more disruptive students. CJ lived in the hopes of better understanding and better practice from the school head.

Frankie's phone rang out several times. Being in a children's case conference made it quite difficult to respond. Eventually picking up the voicemail she made her way to the hospital. Calling me as she drove she discovered I was already there as was Anthony. Catherine had gone into early labour at 32 weeks. Priority at the maternity ward was to try an attempt at stopping labour. Medication given to Catherine was fairly quick to stop contractions. Buying her maybe another week or at least 5 or 6 days, before the onset of labour again, that would give opportunity for babies' lungs to develop a little further. Catherine was sent home on complete bed rest. Anthony being at work full time their decision was that she would go back to Frankie's. She would remain there for the duration of the respite from labour period. Anthony would visit but go to their home over night. Remembering Anthony with his health issues, his addiction, on his return from America, it was feeling almost like a miracle had occurred. Everyone super excited in anticipation of the twins, we were super disciplined too in our purchase of gifts for them.

    News from Ireland was sparse but perhaps a little more regular than had occurred previously. Having women in their lives had to be the catalyst for that more regular communication. It made a difference and a difference which myself and Frankie in particular were grateful for. Never having the experience of in-laws, ourselves, we could only imagine how our daughters -in-law considered us as theirs.
Our boys now our young men had never been great with communication when away from home. Lots of news was shared regarding their farming life's and how much pleasure they all gleaned from it. There was never any mention of pregnancy or babies or our families expanding any time soon. Both girls' parents did share how their other sons and daughters were in their 30s before they had children. Perhaps we would have to wait a bit longer in that case, or maybe accept the fact they might never have children.

A journey of discovery

A never before occurrence, Frankie's arrival at the hospital unexpectedly whilst I was still on shift, raised my stress levels a little. Being somewhat short of glowing looking and that's me being kind, I heard how she didn't want to take chance of me going elsewhere after work, as she needed to see me urgently and then told me.

"But don't worry "

That statement made no sense at all. How was I supposed to not worry in that unusual circumstance? Fifteen minutes left to the end of my shift, for me to focus efficiently and effectively was a challenge. My mind kept on straying back to Frankie and what could possibly be so badly wrong. Passing the handover lead to a ward staff nurse who was more than capable, I left to meet my friend outside of the ward doors.

We walked to my car in almost silence. I could see her hands were shaking slightly. Anxiety of that level had never been an issue for Frankie since the days we first met in the children's home. I was in dread of what she was going to tell me. She had taken a bus to reach the hospital yet no explanation why. My mind doing cartwheels again I had visions of Catherine having lost the babies. The thought was too painful to comprehend. I had to ask. Reassured it was nothing to with any of the kids, my anxiety was somewhat relieved. Suggesting we go to a café rather than either of our homes, I wasn't too sure if that was a good plan due to her level of anxiety. Frankie was sure.

"We might get visitors at either of our homes. This has to be a very private conversation."

Knowing a small café which was usually quiet that time of day, we found it to be so. Not having eaten since breakfast I was in the need of some food. Frankie declined saying she hadn't eaten since the previous evening and no feelings at all to do so.

As always Frankie was direct straight forward and to the point. Tears dropped from her eyes. She almost sobbed as she told me.

"I'm broken Helen. Mikey's been lying to me and keeping secrets. How could I have been so blind not to notice?"

Hearing those words sent shockwaves piercing their way through my whole body. Feelings which were new to me had taken over in my head. How should I respond how could I respond to what I'd just heard from my best friend forever? I was speechless and Frankie could see that. She could also see that trying to have the conversation in a public place was not going to be possible. Suggesting we left the café and go back to mine, on the promise any door knockers would not be responded to, she agreed. Being very unlikely that Charlie would come home, we would simply be on our way out to a meeting should that happen.

We travelled that car journey in almost silence. Not wanting to ask questions I would wait for Frankie to share further information. Sweet tea with some toasted bread was always a favourite for Frankie when in times of distress. It was a comfort food for her.

"You know this always helps settle your nerves a

bit. I don't see the logic in it but as it works for you, eat and drink then if you want to we can talk."
Reluctantly she honoured my request with occasional sobs in between. Leaving Frankie to partake of her food I went to the bathroom where I too had some tears. Thinking how could Mikey have done this, yet I didn't know what he had done. What had actually happened and what and how had Frankie made the discovery which had clearly distressed her so much.

Her voice her words lacked the strength usually shown by Frankie at times of distress.

"Going on for 30 years we've known each other and married for most of that time. I'm broken just like my laptop is broken."
Telling her to remember her deep breathing it did give her time to recollect her thoughts with great clarity. Ready to continue she told me how

"Needing to access emails I went to the office to use his computer. Himself and Charlie were out with clients for the whole day. I knew I could work in comfort and not be disturbed and she stopped again."
Passing the Kleenex box (Paper Tissues) to Frankie she did some more deep breathing and then she continued.

"Passwords always being shared between us he would never guess I would gain access to his computer, as it never left the office and I had never been there. Smart as Mikey is he wasn't smart enough to hide the password for his office computer. Thinking that for such a smart man he had behaved quite clumsy in that situation. Discovering how he had several email addresses gave me cause for concern. All appeared to be work related except one, so yes, I went snooping."

Frankie shared how that's the one which relates to the time he told her he was on a business trip in Holland with Charlie only he wasn't. Wanting to find his roots and any potential family members, he was aware that having a surname like Rooney most likely meant he had to have some Irish connections. Travelling back to Ireland he had made plans to meet with a gentleman who can you believe the deceit of this too, the man was a guest at Josephs wedding. Michael Dooney who is a distant cousin to Mairead's father was the man in question. They had obviously had a conversation of a certain nature whilst we were there for the weddings. My heart was racing wondering what I might hear next. No words were required from me at that moment. That felt fortunate as I didn't have any to justify my thoughts. My face would have shown Frankie how I was feeling. She continued

"Michael apparently is quite an elderly man who is well known throughout the pubs in Cork for his story telling. Some refer to him as the man with so much information, he's like a walking encyclopaedia. Some of his stories are made up and some are painfully true. And that's not all Helen. According to this information Charlie went with him to Ireland too, on exactly the same adventure."

I could feel colour draining from my face with all of my anxieties being triggered. Struggling to understand how my husband, how either of our husbands could be that deceitful and then wondering what else they may have been deceitful and lied to us about, was for both of us quite a sour grape to swallow. Tapes which were hidden in Mikey's office were taken by Frankie. A rendition of our husbands' day in the company of Michael Dooney and others was there for all to hear. It was Mikey's voice and then Charlies. Their introduction to Michael Dooney and his stories was very clear. –

"Hearing what in so many ways were heart-warming stories being shared by some members of the Dooney family, there was one in particular which made all of us reach for the Kleenex box. (Paper tissues). It's a true story and told by the mighty Michael Dooney who is a brother to Máiréad's father. Michael was well known throughout the pubs in Cork for his story telling. There is however a further story and it's the story of Charlie Regan and Mikey Rooney. Our request to Michael was that he would accompany us to an area of Cork which I was being drawn to. Michael would record the whole day leaving nothing out. We would then have that memory exactly of whatever happened as it happened. This is one to never be forgotten."

Myself and Frankie almost didn't want to let the tape continue to play, yet knew we had to hear it.

Michael had his audience captivated as he shared what he described as being a very special story. How it involved 2 men Mikey Rooney and Charlie Regan. They had been friends and business partners for a very long time. They live in Yorkshire in England. Having come to Ireland in the belief that as they have Irish surnames, they were in hope of perhaps finding their identity. Both men had been told that Michael Dooney (myself) would be their best chance of making that happen. I accompanied them both out to Castletownroche. An area of Cork where Mikey seemed to be drawn to. And so, the story begins.

It was a Tuesday mid-morning on a bright summer's day. Two men Mikey Rooney and Charlie Regan came cycling down Bridge street towards the bend. Having borrowed bikes from the local hire shop served their purpose for that day. Dazzling sunlight brightened up the road ahead of them. On the corner of Bridge street stood the old stone mill, which Mikey thought looked slightly familiar to him. Alongside him was his friend Charlie. Easing off the peddles Mikey watched his friend look around as they slowed down their speed. Dense woods lay on their right behind a rocky wall. Beautiful flowers of all shapes and colours clung to the ancient rock walls. Michael laughed as he shared how Mikey had told him, that the wall and woods were like a prison keeping the inmates at bay. On their left the river Awbeg flowed from beneath an old, five-arched humpbacked stone bridge. Mikey was curious.

"I wonder how many people have crossed this bridge Charlie?"
Mikey stopped his bike on the crest of the bridge and looked down upon the river as it flowed swiftly towards the mill. He had a curious tone in his voice.

"Wouldn't it be great now if these old stones could talk. Can you imagine the stories they would tell? Imagine all they've seen over the years."
Charlie felt his breath almost being taken away. He struggled to get his swords out.

"So, this is the beautiful Castletownroche. All the years I've known you Mikey, I don't think you've ever spoken about any other place as much as you have this one. Now your back in the place your obviously so fond of and why are you so fond of it?"
Mikey took a deep breath in ahead of sharing that he wasn't sure why the place meant so much to him.

"Maybe I was born here maybe I lived here. This bridge feels familiar so who knows. Frankie and Helen must never find out we've made this trip. They wouldn't understand our

need to discover our identity, if that ever becomes a possibility for us."
Pausing the tape, the women expressed their levels of shock. Hearing those words of lies and deceit from Mikey's mouth was painful beyond recognition for both women. Pressing play again they prepared themselves for whatever was to come next. Recording of Michael Dooney's voice was very clear as the story continued.
The men sat down a while taking in the beauty of their surroundings. Mikey then cleared his throat.

"You know Charlie, looking down at the little island in the middle of the river and how it divides the river in two, don't you think it's quite smart."
Charlie was impressed, telling his friend the river looks exactly as he had described it, after his visit there for their sons' weddings. Despite having been there himself Charlie had not remembered the bridge or the river at all.

Mikey went onto share how the purpose of that island was, so that water could be diverted to the mill to drive the wheel. A tear dropped from his eyes as he told Charlie

"I remember now. Now I know why this place felt special to me. It's all come back in a flash. I did live here in Ireland, here in county Cork. I used to sit there with my grandad fishing. It didn't matter if we caught anything or not. It was just him and me. The rest of the world didn't exist for those few hours."
Charlie encouraged his friend to continue.

"I'm sure it's feeling emotional for you Mikey but sounds like such an interesting story. I need to hear more."
Mikey's mind wandered back to those days before his grandad had a heart attack and his life changed for ever. He

shared with Charlie how the two of them would laze on the river bank, talking, laughing and just enjoying each other's company. He shared how they would meander over the old rustic bridge to the island in the river; put everything down and would lay everything out for the day. Mikey continued to reminisce and to share.

"I was only 5 yet I remember all of this so vividly. My grandad would have all his fishing rods and floats. He would get all the equipment ready and then start casting into the river. Grandad would explain all the techniques required to catch the trout. He would say how the Awbeg was the best trout river in the entire county of Cork"

Charlie wondered about and questioned the truth of that statement

"And is it the best Mikey?"
Mikey laughed.

"Do you ever believe a fisherman when he tells you about the size of his catch? I don't know if it has the best trout or not. It didn't matter to me Charlie. All that mattered was that I was with my grandad and nothing else mattered"

"Did your dad catch many fish then?"

"None at all Charlie. But it wasn't about the fishing really. It was special time for the two of us. After a couple of hours, we would get our lunch out. Grandad would have a bottle of beer and sing a song or two. He would ask me if I wanted a drop of the hard stuff?

Charlie's mouth dropped open in surprise. Mikey hastily added how his grandad always told him.

"Now don't go telling your grandma you've had some beer. Jesus, she would skin me alive if you told her that. I knew he was only joking. I would have a jar of cold tea and usually a sugar sandwich "

"A sugar sandwich."

Charlie was shocked.

"Yes, a sugar sandwich. Don't tell me you never ate a sugar sandwich as a kid!"

"No never not at all."

Mikey laughed

"I forgot that you were posh"

"We were not posh" Charlie said sadly as his best friend highlighted their differences.

"I'm joking Charlie But I can't believe that you never had sugar sandwiches. We had them often. I guess when money was short it was a cheap way to feed us all"

Charlie looked sad.

"So, did your grandad keep the fish he caught then?"

"No, he never did. This puzzled me about grandad. Whenever he caught a fish I always asked if he was going to kill it. I guess it was a kid's intrigue with death and wanting to see it. He would always unhook the fish then gently put it back into the river. On one occasion I asked him why does he go to all the bother of catching the fish and then just release it?"

Charlie even as an adult struggled with that concept too.

"What did he say Mikey?"

"What he said has always puzzled me."

Sharing how despite his (Mikey's) young age at the time that his grandad was sharing big boys' information, in a child friendly manner with the use of age appropriate words he remembered hearing, that Ireland had seen far too many needless deaths. That fish have the right to live just as any other living creature has the right to live and, hopefully, enjoy their lives. Who was he to play God and decide who lives and who dies.

"Wow, that was a very thought-provoking answer.

Sounds as though your grandad was a very caring man and at least for you now, you have something to work with in terms of finding your identity."
Mikey had a few tears and then.

"As an adult thinking back that response from him always made me wonder if my grandad was involved,"
Charlie was curious.

"What you on about...involved.... involved in what?"

"You know...1916 and all that stuff and what happened afterwards"

"Didn't you ever ask him?"

"No, I was too young to even think about that and he died when I was just turned 5"
Whilst making a terrible attempt at a Cork accent Charlie told his friend.

"Well your grandad was a Cork man and they are all rebels down here"
Mikey laughed

"That was the worst Cork accent I've ever heard. Your such an idiot."
Both men laughed. Charlie enquired?

"Your grandma doesn't come from Cork, does she?"

"No. grandma came from Dublin. A place on the south side, Rathfarnham. Grandad always teased her that Cork was the real capital of Ireland, not the Dubs."
Charlie was getting bored.

"Oh, come on now, there must be more to this village than the river"
Mikey looked thoughtful.

"Ah come on then" I wonder if grandad's favourite pub is still here"

"This is an Irish village, right? Then there must be a few pubs here.

"There were 6 here but grandad always liked just the one. It's up next to the national school."

Charlie laughed.

"That's convenient. Straight out of school and into the pub."

Laughing at Charlies comment the men left the bridge. They made their way up the hill towards the main part of the village and onwards to the pub. Charlie was grumbling.

"I wouldn't like to walk up this hill too often, but then again it would help to balance out the many hours we sit in the office back in Yorkshire."

Mikey was reflective in his thoughts.

"Imagine walking up here in the snow wearing hobnail boots. How did they ever do that? You know I'd never thought of that. We have it so easy compared to our parents and grandparents."

Agreeing with his friends' comments Charlie put in some reminders for both of them.

"Let's never forget that this trip has to be our secret. Frankie's parents being deceased and Helen genuinely not caring about any family she might have, they would never understand us coming here. Imagine how they would feel if they knew. How would they deal with it? How would they deal with us and all the promises we made regarding our pacts of honesty at all costs?"

As the hill levelled out the men passed the village garage on their left. It was complete with petrol pumps too. Mikey was loud as he observed a mechanic dealing with a car engine.

"Somebody has problems. I wouldn't know where to start with car engines. I would struggle to repair a puncture on this old bike."
Not getting a response Mikey had another go.
He shouted to an obviously worried customer at the garage thinking he was offering some good advice.
"Your car looks like a write off mate sell it for scrap"
The customer wasn't happy with Mikey's comments. He appeared to be agitated almost angry
"Get lost you little toe rag"
Charlie wasn't happy with his friends' comments either.
"For goodness sake Mikey. You're not in the kids home now! Keep your mouth shut. Diplomacy was never high on your achievements was it. Hoping you do better than that when abroad on business trips and hoping you do better than that in keeping this secret."

Mikey was apologetic saying his mind had wandered back to his time in the kids home and the behaviours he presented whilst there. He snapped himself back to reality and to the reason they were in Ireland. As they walked pushing their bikes the intended pub appeared right there in front of them.
Mikey was excited.
"There it is"
With a voice almost overcome with emotion he told his friend.
"You know Charlie I'm no drinker but this place means so much to me. Memories of me sitting outside with my grandad with a packet of crisps and a glass of red lemonade after a day's fishing."
Charlie was mesmerized. In a sort of a nervously joking manner he told Mikey.
"So, this is the holy of holy's...The bar you've spoken about so much. I never ever thought that one day after all

the years we have known each other, that I would be here with you. All the times you have told me about your trips here. Hairs on my neck are standing up."

Mikey smiled and that was his only response. Resting their bikes against the pub's wall they entered the pub. Going from bright sunshine into a typically dark Irish pub, it took a few seconds for their eyes to adjust to the change in brightness. The barman seemed friendly and sociable.

"What can I get you lads?"
"Usual Charlie?"
"Naturally"
"Two pints of Guinness please"
Barman looking for information or simply being friendly he enquired

"Are you just passing through lads. I can hear by the accent that you're from England?

"It's a pilgrimage laughed Charlie. We were both raised in kids' homes in Yorkshire. Met in a pub as young adults and the rest is history. We've been friends for more years than I care to remember. Mikey has always talked so much about Castletownroche and now here I am with him.

"Well you are both very welcome here. Do you have family here then?"

"No, well maybe I don't know for sure answered Mikey. Think I must have been born here though. As a child I used to come here fishing with my grandad. Sadly, we lost him some years ago I wanted to see the old place again and I'm searching for my roots for my identity, well we both are."

"Here's your drinks lads and good luck with the search."
The two friends lifted up their drinks from the bar and looked

with much affection towards the glass of cold Guinness.

"Cheers Mikey. Thank you for bringing me here with you"

"Cheers my friend"

As the glasses touched their lips the pub went dark. The small and narrow doorway was filled with the body of quite a tall man with a psychique to match his height. Shouting out to the barman as he pointed in our direction, we heard him accuse us of.

"These 2 are following me everywhere Michael."

That was new information for us. We then knew the barman was called Michael. He didn't want any trouble in his pub. He was quick to respond.

"What you talking about Richie?"

'I've met these 2 as they were walking past Frank's garage not 15 minutes ago and here they are now. I'm sure they'll be trying to make some more trouble."

Charlie was quick in his attempts to defuse any potentially unpleasant situation.

"Listen Richie I apologise for my friend. We are not here to upset people or cause trouble. Can I buy you a drink as a way of apologising for what Mikey said before?"

Charlie had learned the art of diplomacy and used it for what was perhaps the 1st time in his life.

"I apologise too mate. I was just having the craic you know. I didn't mean anything by it."

Richie was receptive thinking why not. A drink from 2 strangers would brighten up his day.

"Go on then lads a pint would be very welcome. Listen lads, I've had a rough day and you two were in the wrong place at the wrong time. I know you were only having a laugh. I apologise too for my accusations."

Michael was quick to present the pint to another grateful customer who began speaking in Gaelic.

"Here you go Richie"

"Go raibh maith agat lads. (Thank you lads) Slainte "
Mikey turned to Richie.

"You must be rich having a car."
Charlie wasn't amused.

"For feck sake Mikey. Can't you ever control your mouth and stop it from getting us into trouble."
Thinking the comment was humorous Richie laughed out loud.

"It's okay. But it would be very difficult to run a taxi firm without transport to do that - don't you reckon?"
Mikey looked humble and was so in his response

"I guess so"
Richie looked deep in thought for a moment.

"I had a good run booked today but this morning the car was playing up so I've Lost that fare. Frank's looking at it for me now.
Mikey couldn't resist his next question.

"Out of curiosity and I know it sounds crazy, your surname isn't Hunter by any chance?
Richie looked surprised

"It is. How the heck did you guess that?"

"Sometimes when I came here finishing with my grandad, if he was flush we would have a taxi down to killavullen train station. Even after all those years I remember the taxi company were Hunters. We would go home in style. More as a treat for me I guess as we were never well off."
Richie was curious.

"Do you have a photo of your grandad?"
    Charlie was thankful that the situation was now

friendlier. He was also hoping that his friend Mikey wouldn't mess things up again with the mouth he struggled to control. Taking his wallet from his trousers pocket he pulled out a photograph and showed it to Richie. Richie gasped as he looked at the old photo.

"Jesus Mary and Joseph...you're Jack's grandson."

Mikey smiled the widest smile anyone had seen from him in a long time.

"You remember him"

"I do indeed. I was very sad when I heard of his passing. My condolences. He was well known around these parts. How is your grandma? I hope she is still with us?"

"I have no idea but doubt it. She'd be very old now if she's still alive. We all lost contact when I was put in the kids home after the move over to England. Don t even know how I got to England, who brought me or why I was put in the kids home."

"Her names Nora isn't it"

"By God you have a good memory Richie"

"Well people like that deserve for people like us to remember them."

Mikey was confused

"What do you mean people like that"

Richie was quick with his compassionate response.

"I hope all those people who fought for Ireland in her hour of need will always be remembered."

Mikey was clear he had no idea what the man was talking about. Richie began to sing.

Mikey was intrigued.

"What's that song called? My grandad used to sing that when we went fishing."

Richie flipped his cap to the side of his head and told us.

"Young man we need to sit down over there. We having a lot of talking to do. Michael 3 more pints for myself and my friends."
So, the 3 men, 2 of whom were friends and Richie who had randomly been invited into their conversation, sat down together at a table over in the corner. Richie said he was sure they wouldn't be disturbed. He had been in that pub many times and never seen anyone sitting in that corner.

Richie started the new conversation. Turning to Mikey he suggested.

"Let's start with a very simple question. When you went fishing with your grandad, what was by you and how did you get to the riverbank."

"We walked across a little bridge."

"Any buildings near the river?"

"The Mill."

"Don't you know the song -The Old Rustic Bridge by The Mill?"

"I've heard of it but so what? What about it?"

The men heard how that song was written right there in Castletownroche, by a travelling entertainer from Dublin. Thomas P Keenan was his stage name. Mikey was encouraging.

"Wow-This sounds like an interesting story. Carry on."

Richie continued to share some sad news. He told the men how some years after writing the song, that the traveller's troop of entertainers came back to Cork to put on some shows. Might have been around 1927. Mikey and Charlie complimented the man's strong knowledge of local history. They then heard how whilst the music troops were in Cork that their travelling songwriter died. Money was very scarce. Funerals were expensive. An extra show was put on to cover cost of the traveller's funeral. They heard how he's buried there on the left-hand side as you enter the graveyard in Castletownroche. His song is almost an anthem in Cork.

Charlie enquired about the significance of Richie sharing that news with them. His own interest in the story had waned. Complaining fiercely and wanting to leave the pub, he was pacified with the promise of another pint of Guinness. Mikey was excited. He continued to show some interest in Richie's story.

"Wow. I never knew any of that. You said about my grandma and grandad and Ireland. What do you know? They never told me anything but then maybe they thought I was too young to be hearing stories."
Richie was clear.

"Okay you know your history. Yes?
Mikey thought for a minute.

"Well we learned some at school in Yorkshire"
Richie cleared his throat.

"Okay. Your grandad was very good at fixing up things. He went to Dublin hoping to get a job at Guinness. A Guinness man got paid very well. He would be a good catch for the local women. Jack got the job. Whilst in Dublin he got involved with the lads and with your grandma"
Richie laughed. Mikey was unsure what Richie had meant by the lads.

"The lads? The lads 1916 and all that? Hold on Richie. Your telling me that my grandad fought in the Irish battles of 1916?"
A smiling Richie replied

"Not just your grandad your grandma was in the

Cumann ma Mban."
Charlies ears had perked up.
"The what?"
"The Cumann ma Mban. Best way to describe them would be as a woman's army. Most were nurses like Nora was but many took up arms in support of The Rising."
Mikey was feeling a little stunned.
"So, are you telling me that my grandma took part in the 1916 Rising and my grandad fought in the GPO?
Richie wanted to give clear information.
"Your partially correct. Your correct about your grandma but your grandad did not fight in the GPO."
Mikey looked disappointed to hear that.
"Oh"
Richie hoped to console his new-found friend.
"You've nothing to be disappointed with. Although Jack didn't fight in the GPO he did fight at Boland's Mill. That was under the command of Eamon De Valera."
Mikey looked a little annoyed.
"For Jesus sake I knew none of this."
Richie had a very fast response
"Take it from me. Those who saw the most say the least. They wanted to forget."
"So, my grandad came back home in 1916"
Richie laughed
"Sort of via Wales"
"Richie, you're completely confusing me now. Why would he go from Dublin to Wales to Cork?"
"Your grandad didn't have a choice. Remember 15 of the leaders were shot and another was hanged. Those people who were not executed, but were considered of

interest were sent to Frongoch in Wales. Your grandad was sent there."

Charlie whom they had considered to be almost sleeping by now from after effects of the Guinness proved them wrong.

"Sorry to interrupt your story telling Richie but where and what is Frongoch?

"It was a prisoner of war camp Charlie. British authorities put all of what they considered to be trouble makers together. People who were held there got to know each other well, in the period leading up to their release in December of 1916."

Charlie thanked the man for his explanation. Mikey was asking for more.

"Something else which is very important Mikey. I'm sure your grandad met and got to know the famous Michael Collins."

Mikey looking towards his friend Charlie he exclaimed.

"He said my grandad met and knew Michael Collins"

Richie turned to Mikey. Smiling he told him how his grandad did more than meet Collins. How he was a Collins man.

"Jack worked for Collins throughout the black and Tan war. He joined a flying column in North Cork. At one point your grandads commanding officer was Tom Barry, who later went on to organize the ambush at KilMichael. So, your grandad met some important people in Ireland's fight for freedom.

Mikey was surprised by all which he had been told.

"Richie I never knew anything about any of this"

Richie smiling told him that well there's more. That people of a certain age will know more than they will ever say. That his grandad was awarded the Black and Tan medal for his

service against the Tans. He showed me his medal. Across the ribbon was the word COMRAC.
Once again Mikey was confused.

"What does it mean what does COMRAC stand for?"

Richie explained how people who had that word added to their ribbons had seen some action. How at some stage
or many stages Jack would have come under fire from the Black and Tans. Richie said smilingly

"Your grandad is a war hero Mikey you must be so proud."
Mikey again expressed his inability to comprehend all which he had heard about his grandparents. Frank Nash the motor mechanic from the garage came into the pub.

"Richie your car is fixed its ready to go."

"Thanks Frank I'll be down when I finish this pint."
Placing the empty glass back down on the table Richie stood up from his chair.

"Sorry lads but I need to go and earn money to pay Frank. It's been an honour meeting Jack's grandson. Be proud of your grandparents. Ireland may still be a poor country but at least 26 counties are under Irish rule. That's for the first time in 800 years because of brave people like Nora and Jack. I hope and pray that future generations will never forget them."

Richie still standing begins to leave the pub- the two men stood with him. Richie offered his hand to Mikey who immediately hugged the man and thanked him. Charlie shook Richie's hand at the same time offering his apologies once again for his previous behaviour. Richie laughed laugh as he told Charlie

"Without this little gobshite we might never have started talking and what a pity that would have been."
As Richie reaches the door he turns around and smiles.
"Come home again soon lads"

With tears in their eyes Mikey and Charlie said their final goodbyes to Michael the barman, before going to get their bikes. Whilst their secret from their wife's trip to Ireland, had been a very productive trip for Mikey Rooney, it hadn't brought any memories for Charlie. Their search for their identity would continue another time. Mikey would return back to cork in the future in the hope of discovering someone, who may have some information about his mam and dad. There would therefore be more lies and deceit for their wives. Both men feeling quiet emotional Mikey shared to his friend.

"What a day it's been Charlie we better go home."
"I think you are home my friend. You are home!"
Michael Dooney concluded the recording by expressing his disappointment in Mikey Rooney and Charlie Regan.

"You've both stressed to me the importance of not ever sharing information regarding this trip with any of the Dooney family. Always having respect for your request, you both have to know I don't condone it. Secrets in a marriage is always a door open for disaster. Goodbye my friends."

That was it. There was the evidence of the lies and deceit which our husbands had subjected us to. There was the evidence of them thinking how that was all right behaviour and how they would be going back for more. Well It wasn't all right behaviour and it never could be acceptable in any relationship where trust was supposed to be respected.

What to do and how to do it.

Mikey Rooney and Charlie Regan returned back to England the following day. Their wives having believed they were away in Holland on a business trip, that's exactly how the men wanted and still want things to remain. That's the story told in exact detail by the elderly Michael Dooney and exactly how the women read it in Mikey's emails. The trip having occurred quite a few weeks ahead of Frankie and myself making the discovery of their lies and deceit, lots has happened in that interim period, between the men, their wives and their families in general. Catherine Rooney had been admitted onto the labour ward for the 2nd time. On this occasion she was thirty-nine weeks pregnant. To everyone's delight Catherine gave birth to a beautiful baby girl and a handsome baby boy. Both babies being a good healthy weight, they were all discharged from hospital within 3 days of her delivery. Visiting our children and our grandchildren together with our husbands, was quite a challenge for myself and Frankie. It was nevertheless a challenge we faced head on. Having to get through our days at home with Charlie and Mikey wasn't the easiest either.

Frankie and myself had some deep discussion about our deceitful husbands. Both having the view that we could not understand, why the men would feel that we wouldn't understand their need to find their identity. Did they know us at all was a question going around in both of our heads? Did we know our husbands at all was the other question?

Discussing how we appreciated and held respect for Charlie and Mikey in so many ways, our thoughts always reverted back to their lies and deceit and how they considered it was perfectly okay to behave like that. Burning question for us both was, how many other times in our marriage, had our husbands been deceitful, dishonest and untruthful. There was no way we could secure a reliable answer for that question. We had no way of knowing the truth. Neither of us felt like we were able to move on from that dilemma nor did we think it would be the right thing to do. Knowing that our kids were grown and settled in life with partners was a huge positive for myself and Frankie in our decision making.

    Having decided that we would tell Mikey and Charlie about our future plans at the same time, would we hoped make the whole situation a bit less painful for us. Frankie booked a table at a restaurant in town. Frankie having the memory of so many good times at Gerry's as did we all as families, there was a desire from both of us not to spoil those memories. Hales for similar reasons wasn't the place we wanted to have our discussion either. Reminders were sent out to the men to be prompt. Meeting up inside of the restaurant at 7pm that evening, I could scarcely look Charlie in the eye. The same for Frankie. Our plan to order our food and then remind the men of our lives together, went like clockwork. Speaking about how much had been achieved in life between the 4 of us, how our children despite their life challenges were now settled. How all of their challenges had been resolved. We spoke about the many struggles we had endured and overcome, with our husbands partaking in all of the discussion. The whole conversation was executed to perfection.

      Both men began expressing some concern for our well-being. Reminding myself and Frankie, how it's totally out of character for either of us to reminisce that much about our lives, since we all met up so many years ago, we did agree with their statement. Frankie was delegated the role of telling our husbands what this was all about and how actions have consequences. She was considered between the 2 of us, to be the less likely to allow any diversion of conversation or any manipulation from either of the men. My job was simply to be there in the background. I would provide verbal support if required.

      The men heard how our plans for the kids home had changed. Frankie shared how we had on that day seen a bank manager, an accountant and the company solicitor. Our husbands were now officially removed from any further involvement, in every sense, in relation to the children's unit. How it would from here on in going forward, be the sole responsibility of myself and Frankie. Mikey and Charlie both sat looking aghast. Sharing their confusion about our decision making and our overall presentation of other information that evening, they politely asked for some sort of an explanation. Opposed to giving them an explanation we continued our plan, with Frankie once again doing the talking. She continued to uphold the strength in her voice. I was secretly praising her for that, with the wish she would be able to continue and not break down. She firmly and very clearly told our husbands.

    "Your both expressing confusion at and about our behaviour this evening and the information we have given to you. How about we look at some other facts."
Both men nodding in affirmation to her question yet they remained silent.

Frankie continued to share how deceit and lies are never at the best a pretty aptitude in any relationship. How at the worst they add up to an immense loss of trust? Where there's no trust there's nothing and I'm sure you'll both agree on that. Acknowledgements from the men, that she was correct in what she had said, had to make the next part easier for her to share with them.
They heard how Frankie had quite innocently gone into her husband's office and the discovery she had made. Frankie at that moment reached into her bag and pulled out the tape. In upper case letters in Mikey's hand writing the cover read.

"Frankie and Helen must never find out."

Both men took a very deep breath in as they gasped with an astonished look on their face. Placing the tape on the table in front of the men, myself and Frankie had also produced 2 more envelopes. 1 for each of the men. Inside was the written explanation that yes, we certainly would have understood their need to find their identity. That now they have both lost more in life than they will ever find. One month's notice was given to each man to find an alternative place to live. How there was, there never can be and never will be any excuse for their lies and deceit. How they're marriages were now broken beyond repair. Their husbands complained fiercely how the 'Rooney n Regan' business would collapse. How it couldn't go on and would become nothing without their wives being there in the background.
How they were all in this together with forgiveness being sought for their deceit.

Frankie and myself despite not having eaten our

meals and despite our husbands appeals for us to wait and don't go, we left the restaurant at that point. Discussions with the company solicitor had given us options. We could go forward with the plan to keep the house and open up the children's specialised unit, with no further involvement on any level from our husbands, or as the house was bought in our names only, we could insist the house be sold and keep all of the financial gain from it. Undecided which way to go we had conversations with all of our adult children. Each of them were left feeling devastated in the knowledge their parents had separated and were to be divorced. Hearing the facts of what the men had done, all of our children shared our view of the need for myself and Frankie to do exactly what we had done. Having our children's approval and their blessings meant a lot for both myself and Frankie.

    Mikey Rooney and Charlie Regan both being very distressed, duly moved out of our marital homes some 3 weeks after we had our discussions with them. Moving into their own rented flats. Frankie and I were very not devoid of emotion either. Huge chunks of our life's had been spent with those men whom we had trusted implicitly. Emotional pain was severe. Deciding to walk alone through the woods we had the hopes of our mind being cleared. It didn't work on that occasion for either of us. In the interim we offered for sale what was going to be the children's specialised unit. There was no solid plan of how to invest the money. Weeks down the line and me back on the mental health wards my phone rang out. It was Frankie. Remembering the last time, she called me at work then came to meet me, I couldn't help but wonder what might be wrong this time. Listening to her voice message I was very reassured. Informing me of some news regarding the kids home we were raised in, felt more than exciting. Meeting up that evening and yes back at Gerry's restaurant, we discussed what she had heard in meetings, as being the imminent closure of the kids home. Frankie was clear with her vision of possibility for us both.

"The homes closing in 2 months when the last 2 children become 18 and move in to independence. We know there's a need for a specialised unit for children with challenging behaviours. Wouldn't we with our professional and lifelong experiences, be the perfect answer after the closure. We have the finance to buy the home outright. We have the experience to run it bringing some more people on board too."

My attention having focused on every word which she had said, I was 100% in favour of the suggestion.

"Fabulous idea Frankie lets arrange a date to set up a meeting with the current owners."

The meeting having happened successfully and the clientele group ready and waiting, we made our move. The house in which we were reared had now been purchased by myself and Frankie. It would be called.

"Frankie and Helens."

Our new adventure with the children's home which the men had financed, was planned to be up and running within a 3 months period from the point of purchase. Keeping that as our focus was going to be a positive plan and the plan which would help get us through that awfully painful period in our lives. Once everything had calmed down somewhat, we did agree that maybe with the passage of time, we might see our husbands adventure to Ireland, more as an act of thoughtlessness and panic, as opposed to some deliberate act of lies and deceit. Reconciliation was not totally abandoned in our thoughts. The phrase Never say Never came to our minds. For now, we are saying goodbye to this chapter of our lives. With much enthusiasm we look forward to the next.

The end

About the Author

Beatrice Finn was born and raised in a small village called Derrinabroock, in the townland of Cloontia, in County Mayo West Ireland. That was a lifetime ago in the year 1949. She lived there for the first 14 years of her life. Living with her farming parents in rural Ireland and off the grid, gave her many experiences you would not find in the classroom.
Starting school at the age of 7 years, Beatrice had enjoyed a basic education.
Her broader education came from the experience of living on the farm, up to the point of emigration to England. That event occurred on September 6th 1963.
Beatrice has extended her education within her career as a support worker, for the National Health Service.
Beatrice has been working for her local authority for the past 24 years as a specialised foster carer. Fostering challenging teenagers is something which has enriched her life in many ways.
Continuing with her love of writing this story too has a very strong Irish theme in parts.
Beatrice has produced a further 14 novels all having an Irish theme.
All are available on
Amazon.com
Amazon.uk
Amazon.fr
Barnes and Noble online shops

Printed in Great Britain
by Amazon